The Treasure Within

A Parashah Companion

Jonathan Shooter

The Judaica Press, Inc.

First published 2004
Copyright © 2004 by Jonathan Shooter
ISBN 1-932443-126

The Judaica Press, Inc.
123 Ditmas Ave.
Brooklyn, NY 11218
Tel: 718-972-6200/800-972-6201
Fax: 718-972-6204
E-mail: info@judaicapress.com
Web: www.judaicapress.com

Printing plates, "Frank," Jerusalem

Printed in Israel

Talmudical College Institute
for Advanced Torah Studies
Rabbi Binyomin Moskovits
Rosh Yeshiva

Midrash Shmuel

ישיבה גדולה וכולל אברכים

הרב בנימין מושקוביץ שליט"א
ראש הישיבה

ח' מנ' אב תשס"ג

ידידי המחבר ר' יונתן שוטר נ"י, הלומד אצלנו ארבע שנים
בשקידה, הראה לי מקצת ספרו השני על פרשת השבוע. המחבר
מלקט ומסדר מאמרי חכמינו ז"ל ראשונים ואחרונים בעניני
יראת שמים לפי השקפה נכונה בטוב טעם ודעת וגורם להקוראים
להתעניין בדבריו. המחבר גם כולל משלים ומעשים של צדיקים,
בדרך שמושך את הלב.

ויה"ר שכשם שדברים אלו זכו להתפעלות כשיצאו לראשונה
בכל שבוע, כן יזכה ספר זה להיות מקובל אצל הקוראים.

וחפץ ה' בידו להצליח בלימודיו ויזכה להמשיך לשבת באהלה
של תורה מתוך נחת ויפוצו מעיינותיו חוצה לכבוד שמים
ולתועלת כלל ישראל.

הכו"ח לכבוד התורה ולומדי'

הרב בנימין מושקוביץ
ראש הישיבה

YESHIVAS BAIS YISROEL
Neve Yakov Mizrach

**Kollel Zichron Shlomo - Bais Yehudah Leib
Shlom Bonayich Graduate Institute, Inc.**

Horav Doniel Lehrfield
Rosh Hayeshiva

חרב דניאל לרפלד
ראש הישיבה

בס״ד

אור לי״ב כסלו תשס״ד

מוצש״ק פ' והנה סולם מוצב ארצה וראשו מגיע השמימה

לכבוד תלמידי נ״י היקר מפז איש מהיר במלאכתו מלאכת שמים
להלהיב לבבות של אחב״י לאבינו שבשמים ה״ה הרה״ג הצדיק
מוהר״ר יונתן שוטר שליט״א

ראיתי בספרך החדש שעומד לצאת לאור שבמעשהו בראשון כך
מעשהו בשני, זכית ע״י ספרך הק' באנגלית להלהיב לבבות ולהאיר
להם את הדרך אשר ילכו בו הדברים שנכתבו בטוהר לב וכשרון
גדול הוי דברים שיוצאים מהלב, ובודאי יכנסו ללב אחב״י,
וישתקומים בך, ודברי אשר שמתי בפיך לא ימושו מפיך ומפי זרעך
ומפי זרע זרעך עד עולם.

בברכת התורה והצלחה.

דניאל לרפלד

Americas Offices:
MRS. HILDA CHILL - 212-388-0795
268 A East Broadway N.Y. N.Y. 10002
Suite 301

7/9 Rechov Harav Zevin
Neve Yakov Mizrach
Jerusalem, Israel

Phone: 02-5711343 Rosh Yeshiva
6562000, 835481 Student Telephone
6561959 Office Telephone
6561724 Beis Medrash

הרב חיים היילפרין
רב ביהמ״ד דברי חיים
בעמח״ס שערי חיים
לונדון יצ״ו

בס״ד

ראש חודש אייר תשס״ב לפ״ק

באתי בשורות אלו להגיד שבחו של תלמידי היקר האבר״ך כמדרשו תי״ח ויר״ש
מו״ה יונתן שוטר נרו יאיר, היושב באהלה של תורה בהתמדה גדולה, והוא עובד
ה׳ באמת ובתמים, והיות שהוא מוכשר בחכמת הכתיבה וכעת עלתה בידו ללקט
דברי תורה על התורה ושאר עניינים שונים, וראיתי דבריו שנכתב ונלקט בטוב
טעם ודעת ובהשכל, לכן אף ידו תכון עמו שיפיץ מעיינותיו החוצה ויהנו רבים
מאור תורתו, וחפץ ה׳ בידו להצליח בלימודיו ויזכה לעלות מעלה מעלה על במתי
התורה והיראה מתוך בריות גופא ונהורא מעילא עמו״ש

כעתירת הכו״ח לכבוד התורה ולומדיה

חיים היילפרין

Rabbi Elimelech Kornfeld
Rav Of Kehillas HaOra
16/9 Nachal Rivivim
Ramat Beit Shemesh

הרב אלימלך קורנפלד שליט"א
רב דקהילת הארייא
נחל רביבים 16/9
רמת בית שמש
58-305-446-2 עמותה מס׳

The Ramban writes in his introduction to his *perush* on *Chumash* that the term "Torah" is from the root *horaah*. The Torah is our *moreh derech*, our guide, to our proper approach to life. Our *emunah* and *bitachon* are built on our understanding of the creation of the world that is described in *Bereishis* and appreciating the constant *hashgachah pratis* that we witness throughout the Torah. Our striving for perfection and *middos tovos* is based on our appreciation of Hashem's great *chassadim*, which arouses within us a strong desire to follow in Hashem's great ways and the ways of our forefathers.

Even though the Torah is meant to be the source of our spiritual growth, one cannot properly take advantage of it without the deep insights and interpretations that were transmitted to us from the *gedolim* of the previous generations. Their deep understanding of the Torah and its values help reveal the powerful messages that are hidden in the Torah.

Rav Yonason Shooter, who is a *talmid chacham* and *yerei Shamayim*, has compiled a wonderful work that exposes us to many of these great insights and opens up our eyes to a deeper understanding of the Torah and its messages that can have a profound effect on our lives. I am sure that those who read this *sefer* will both enjoy it and grow from its wealth of *divrei Torah*.

יהי רצון שספר זה יהיה לזיכוי הרבים ושהמחבר יזכה להמשך לשבת באהלה של
תורה מתוך נחת והרחבה ויפוצו מעיינותיו חוצה לתועלת כלל ישראל ולכבוד שמים.

הכו"ח בכה"ית ובברכה,

Dedication

Heinrich Rosenzweig
Chaim ben Aharon 1942

Paula Rosenzweig
Malka bas Alexander 1964

Oskar Rosenzweig
Meir ben Chaim 1964

Malwine Rosenzweig
Malka bas David Halevi 1993

David Feuerberg
David ben Eli Seinvel Halevi 1920

Klara Feuerberg
Chaya bas Shimshon 1942

by
Alexander Rosenzweig

Dedication

In loving memory of

Samuel Abraham Marrache, *z"l*

by
The Marrache family
Gibraltar

Dedicated
in loving memory of

Abraham and Millie Lebetkin

Mark and Esther Shooter

Samuel Shooter

Hubert Shooter

Henry (David) Ewig

Chaim Shimon and Elizabeth Ewig

Dedicated in memory of

my beloved grandparents
Edna Bonn, my mentor
Joseph Bonn
Rose and Goodman Mann,

by Melissa Shooter

Dedicated in loving memory of

שמחה בת שרה
Seemah Sadka

by the Benjamin family

לע״נ
ר׳ יעקב אהרן בן ר׳ חיים הלוי ע״ה לע״נ
מרת עלקא בת ר׳ אברהם שמואל הלוי ע״ה

נדבת בנם
יצחק בן-ציון עהרייך

In memory of	
Vivian Lawson	
אבגדור בן משה	
לעילוי נשמת	
רחל לאה בת הלל	
לעילוי נשמת	
משה יעקב	
בן הרב יחיאל מאיר רומר	
חנה בת נפתלי רומר	

לע״נ

אברהם בן אהרן יצחק

אלקסנדר בן דוד

פערל זיסל בת אברהם

לעילוי נשמת

נתן יהודה בן אלעזר
חיה יהודית בת דוד
ברוך יוסף בן יהושע לב
רחל בת אשר יהודה
מנחם מנדל בן אברהם הירש
אפרים בן שמואל אליהו

Dedicated by
Jonny and Henchy Kushner

לעילוי נשמת

רפאל ניסן בן יוסף • Nissan Shenny
יוסף בן ניסן • Joseph Shenny
נחמה פרומה בת פשע • Fay Shenny
אליהו חיים בן יעקב • Eli Jacob

Dedicated by
Miriam and Edward Saleh
and family

לעילוי נשמת

יואל בן מאיר לוביטש
חיה בת שלמה זלמן לוביטש
שמעון בן לוי רורקה
שרה בת אליעזר רורקה

Dedicated by the
Lovat family

לזכר נשמה

ר׳ מרדכי בן ר׳ שלמה ז״ל
אורמונד

פעל הרבה בצדקה וחסד
באמונה שלמה בבורא עולם

לרפואה שלמה
רבקה בת הראל רייזל

Dedicated in loving memory of
Maisie Ross
by her daughters
Sharon Faith and Alison Ross

Contents

DEVARIM

Acknowledgments

It is with great *simchah*, and with *hodaah* at the *siyatta diShamaya* at all that has occurred until now, that I present this second book on the weekly *parashah*.

I would like to thank my proofreader, Debbie Ismailoff, for her skill in bringing the manuscript up to scratch, and the staff at Judaica Press, in particular, Nachum Shapiro.

My profound appreciation goes to every one of the sponsors who contributed to this project. I have the utmost admiration for and gratitude towards them for their enthusiasm and recognition of the need to spread Torah and its commentaries. May they go from strength to strength and continue to merit supporting true Torah causes.

I would also like to thank those who continue to distribute the weekly *parashah* sheet — my father-in-law Henry Ehreich, my brother Simon Shooter, Edward Saleh, Julian Maurer and Jonny Kushner — for their efforts in helping to spread Torah to a wider audience.

Rav Binyomin Moskovits has created a unique *makom Torah*, Yeshivas Midrash Shmuel, where the drive for *emes* permeates all endeavors, from analyzing the Gemara to matters of *hashkafah.* There are tremendous opportunities for growth there, with many talented *bachurim* and *avreichim* with whom to discuss one's learning. I am grateful for Rav Moskovits's personal guidance in various matters, as well as for the *chessed* his family always extends to us.

The *mashgiach* of Midrash Shmuel, Rabbi Michael Jacobs, has provided me with his insights and advice on this project, and has given of his time to review certain parts of it, and for this I am most grateful.

I had the privilege to study as a *bachur* in Yeshivas Bais Yisroel. Rav Doniel Lehrfeld, together with the *mashgiach*, Rav Avigdor Brazil, helped lay many foundations in Torah and *hashkafah* that I have tried to build on, and I am grateful for their assistance over the years.

I want to thank my parents, Alan and Susan Shooter, for all their help and support in all matters, including the writing of both this *sefer* and the previous volume, *The Wisdom Within.* I feel fortunate to have been raised in such a special home, and no words can express the profound *hakaras hatov* that I have for the wonderful upbringing with which they have provided me over the years. I pray that they continue to get much Torah *nachas* from all of their children and grandchildren.

My profound appreciation goes to my brother Mark and his wife Melissa for their support and advice in all areas. Their expertise in many fields has been most helpful. May they have much *nachas* from Sam, Zack and David. I would also like to thank my brother Ben and his wife Katie for their intuition, help and advice, and may they see much *nachas* from Doron and Talia.

I am grateful to my Uncle, Alex Rosenzweig, whom I am fortunate to have had as a *chavrusa* for *bein hazemanim* for the last eight years. It is something I look forward to on any trip back to England. We should merit learning together for many more years. His support and encouragement in many aspects of life have been most valuable, and I am most appreciative for our relationship.

Acharonah acharonah chavivah, that which is dearest last: I thank my wife Shoshana. Her help, advice, encouragement and support is valued beyond words. Without her support and encouragement my learning and the publication of my *sefarim* would not have been possible. She also tirelessly and patiently edited the *parashah* sheets which formed the basis of this book. May we merit to have continued true Torah *nachas* and see our children, Yaakov Aaron, Ayala Malka and Shira Rivka, attain great heights in *yiras Shamayim* and *ahavas Torah*.

Introduction

When one thinks of treasure, various images come to mind. Chests full of silver and gold, diamonds, rubies, pirate ships — the list goes on. Yet we find in Scripture many verses which actually compare our Torah to treasure. How can it be that our holy Torah is compared to mere earthly commodities? The answer is that the verses are giving us images to which we can relate. When the verse says, "The Torah of Your mouth is better for me than thousands in gold and silver" (*Tehillim* 119:72), we have to imagine that shiny gold bullion stacked up, and say that Torah is worth more.

The Chafetz Chaim elaborates on this idea. Imagine the king were to open up his treasury for just one day and let you take whatever you wanted. You would arrive there as early as possible, stay until forced out, and you wouldn't let up the gathering for a moment. You know that with each second lost, another precious item is lost.

The verse says, "I rejoice over Your word, like one who finds abundant spoils" (*Tehillim* 119:162). When one finds treasure he rejoices over each item. So too with Torah, one must rejoice over his learning, as each word is equivalent to a new mitzvah of learning Torah, which in itself is equivalent to all the 613 mitzvos. We say every morning, "He gave us the Torah of truth and implanted eternal life within us." Torah is the primary means through which we can attain eternal life. This is something gold cannot buy.

There is another well-known verse mentioned in *Mishlei*: "If you seek it as silver, if you search for it as hidden treasures, then you will understand the fear of Hashem and discover the knowledge of God" (*Mishlei* 2:4–5). Here the Chafetz Chaim explains the comparison of Torah to precious items from a different perspective. He asks, Why is there a difference in the language used, that one "seeks" silver, yet "searches" for hidden treasures?

He answers with the following analogy. When one seeks to profit with his money, he goes to the market to find some profitable merchandise. If he sees that there is no business that day, he goes home and says, "Perhaps Hashem will make business come my way tomorrow." The next day he will go and try again. This is called "seeking" silver.

On the other hand, the search for treasure is different. To illustrate the difference, imagine the following. A father was worried about the instability in his region, so he hid by a certain mountain a treasure chest containing his wealth. He left instructions that after his death his children were to dig up the chest and divide it amongst themselves. Immediately following his death, his children went to that mountain and began digging, but to no avail. After a few hours would they just return home like the merchant, in the hope that on the next day they would be successful? Of course not. The merchant, on the one hand, has no guarantee that he will make a profit, so he just returns the next day to "seek" his fortune. The heirs to the wealth, however, know that they have a hidden treasure waiting for them, so they won't leave until they have found it. Thus, the search for hidden treasures is more intense than just seeking.

So too with Torah. Regarding Torah learning, *Chazal* say that if one says, "I toiled but didn't find," he is not to be believed. Everyone has a portion in the Torah that is his and that he has to attain; it is potential waiting to be realized. This is seen in what we say at the end of every *Shemoneh Esrei*: "and give us our share in Your Torah."

We can understand in another way the comparison of acquiring Torah to the search for treasure. Torah has many, many layers. There is always the surface level, the stories one was taught as a child, and then there are the secrets that are hidden within. In fact, every aspect of human endeavor and activity is expressed in the Torah, whether explicitly or implicitly. To attain heights in Torah, we must dig deep, searching it out like hidden treasure, and then we will "discover the knowledge of God."

It is hoped that this book will show that there is more than meets the eye in our weekly *parashah*. Our saintly commentators gave us these jewels, drawing out the underlying issues, messages and lessons for life that are a treasure lying beneath the surface.

The Gemara (*Sanhedrin* 98b) says that the students of Rebbi Eliezer asked him, "What can a man do to be spared the travails preceding the messianic era?" He replied, "Let him engage in Torah study and in acts of kindness." A prominent theme that I chose to focus on in this *sefer* is the importance of *chessed*. We are told that there is a requirement of "a love of kindness" (*Michah* 6:8). The Chafetz Chaim says that this means that with *chessed*, it is not enough to perform it. One has to actually love it, run after it, and cherish it. Just doing *chessed* by rote may have value, but that is not what is meant by having a love for it.

The Chafetz Chaim cites an example that will help us understand this. When one's child is getting married one will make sure all his needs are taken care of. Because of one's love for his child he will go to every length to benefit him. One will constantly be thinking about how he can help him, even when the child doesn't request it of him. So too, when one loves *chessed*, he constantly looks for ways to benefit others as well, and he will do it with a generous eye.

On Shavuos we read the Book of Ruth. Why is this book in particular read? The Midrash says that Rebbi Zeira once asked, Since the Book of Ruth contains no ritual laws whatsoever, what then was its purpose in being written? He answered, "To teach how great is the reward of those who do kindness (referring to Boaz, who did kindness and merited that the Davidic dynasty descended from him). While Shavuos commemorates the giving of the Torah, nevertheless, by reading the Book of Ruth, we learn that Torah and kindness go together. This is also seen in the penultimate blessing of the *shacharis Shemoneh Esrei*, "for with the light of Your countenance You gave us...the Torah of life and a love of kindness."

As mentioned, there is a certain protection afforded in the premessianic era for those who occupy themselves with Torah and *chessed*. Certainly the times that we live in are special ones. *Chazal* say that when we are in need of a *chessed*, Hashem sends an opportunity for him to do *chessed* for others. If we grab that opportunity, then we will receive it back.

Rav Elya Lopian said that in the prayer recited in *Selichos*, *machnisei rachamim*, we ask the angel to carry our supplication and place it before the throne of glory. How well the angel carries out this mission depends on how well we treat him. Rav Elya asked, "And who do you think that angel is?...He is the collector who was at your door last night. How well we treat him is how we will be treated."

Chessed has many forms. Every person we come into contact with is a potential recipient of our *chessed*, and let it be noted that *chessed* stretches beyond the financial side. Let us work to "engage in Torah study and in acts of kindness," that we may greet the *geulah sheleimah*, speedily and in our days.

Bereishis

Parashas Bereishis

A Bit of Give and Take

There is a famous question which all the commentators mention: What is the point of all the narrative that we find in *Sefer Bereishis*? Why didn't the Torah begin with the first mitzvah as mentioned in *Sefer Shemos*? While there are several answers, let us focus on one in particular. *Sefer Bereishis* is not just a history lesson; rather, it depicts the actions and deeds of our forefathers. We have a concept called *maaseh avos siman labanim*, that whatever happened to our forefathers is a sign of what would befall their descendants in the future. Another explanation of *maaseh avos siman labanim* is that we should learn how to behave from every action and word of our forefathers. For example, we learn from how Yaakov dealt with Esav about how a Jew should act in *galus*. Many laws of human behavior are derived from the events that took place in this *sefer*. In particular, we find many lessons about how man and wife should interrelate.

Who Is Perfect? Of Course...

Hashem said, "It is not good that man should be alone; I will make him a helper against him" (*Bereishis* 2:18). The well-known question is asked, How can a man have a helper who at the same time is against him? Rashi answers that if he is worthy, she will be a helper, and if he is unworthy, she will be against him.

This answer requires an explanation. The Dubno Maggid[1] cites a verse in *Mishlei* (21:2) that says, "For the way of all man is correct in his eyes." Everyone likes to think that he's correct. One cannot see his own faults and weaknesses. Instead of admitting he is wrong, one would rather cover up his wrongdoing or use some distorted logic to prove how he is in fact right. We see this in the *mishnah* (*Nega'im* 2:5) that says, "A man may examine every suspicion of an affliction (in anyone else), except for an affliction on himself." His own lack of objectivity will get in the way of a correct ruling.

It follows that since we can see the faults of others, and yet they cannot see their own, surely we must also have faults — after all, no one's perfect. The only problem is, if we want to discover our own faults, we cannot always trust another person, as he may not have our best interests at heart. Therefore, if one wants to grow and improve, how does one get around this dilemma? Who loves a person enough that he will have only his best interests at heart and yet have an objective opinion at the same time?

To solve this problem, Hashem created men and women with separate genders and established the institution of marriage. It is one's wife who can stand back objectively and say, "This is not right," or "This needs improving," yet she has only his best interests at heart. She is meant to be a mirror; through her, man will see his shortcomings. This is what the verse means by "a helper against him": if he is worthy, she will stand together with him through life, leading him in the right direction. On the other hand, for his faults, she must stand against him and lead him to improve.

Found or Find?

The Gemara (*Berachos* 8a) says that in Eretz Yisrael, when someone would marry a woman, they would ask him, "Have you found or did you find?" What is the meaning behind this mysterious question? The Vilna Gaon[2] says that the question is alluding to two conflicting verses regarding a woman. In *Mishlei* (18:22), it says, "One who has found a wife has found goodness," while in *Koheles* (7:26), it says, "I find more bitter than death a woman." The question they were asking, in subtle terms, was whether or not his wife was a good woman.

However, an additional question regarding this *gemara* needs to be resolved. Why is the term "found" used for a good woman, while "find" is used for a bad one? The Vilna Gaon answers that the nature of people is to take good things for granted. At first one will be grateful for his newly found wife and the goodness she brings, but over time, as he gets used to her, he will no longer appreciate the gift. That is why it is called "found," in the past tense; he appreciated her then but now takes her for granted. On the other hand, if one is having a bad experience with his newly found wife, he will be constantly "finding her" every moment, as he will be only too aware of his constant suffering and misfortune.

Blame It on Everyone Else

This human tendency to take things for granted manifests itself later on in the *parashah*. Chavah gave Adam the forbidden fruit to eat, and when Hashem asked him why he sinned, he replied, "The woman you gave to be with me, she gave me of the tree and I ate" (*Bereishis* 3:12). The Gemara (*Avodah Zarah* 5b) says that Adam denied the favor that was done to him; he was ungrateful for being given a helpmate. Rashi says there that he even went one step further and blamed Hashem for his sin, as if to say that he sinned only because Hashem had given him his wife, despite the fact that Hashem had made her only for man's good. The Gemara adds that many years later, in the desert, *bnei Yisrael* complained that they had had enough of the manna from Heaven, saying, "Our soul is disgusted by this insubstantial food" (*Bemidbar* 21:5). The Gemara says that Moshe called them "ungrateful people descended from ungrateful people." The behavior of the people in the desert was learned many years before from Adam, who had blamed his own shortcomings on Hashem's gift, denying the good done for him.

These two ideas — that of a woman being a "helper against him," and the importance of gratitude and not denying the good done to one — are seen in an essay by Rav Eliyahu Dessler.[3] He explains that every person has the ability to be either a giver or a taker. In fact, every act involving interaction between people involves either giving or taking. The ability to give is an inborn trait, as it says, "in the image of God He created him" (*Bereishis* 1:27). In other words, just as Hashem can have mercy and bestow good on others, a man can emulate His ways. On the other hand, the attribute of taking is the desire of a person to draw things towards himself as much as possible. Rav Dessler continues that everyone has the desire to give in varying degrees, some to a greater extent and some to a lesser extent. If it were not so, then the world would not function. There would be no interaction, and people wouldn't marry or have children.

An Obvious Question

Rav Dessler goes on to discuss how love develops between man and wife. If a person gives a gift to another, who has more intense feelings for whom? Many people would reply, of course, the receiver. He will be so grateful for the good done to him that his love for the giver is sure to be enhanced. However, the opposite is really the case. The more one gives to a person, the more his feelings and love for that person grow. For example, when one goes out to the store to buy someone a present, the time, energy and care spent to ensure the beneficiary will receive the most pleasure from the gift only increase one's love for the other.

What is the cause of this, and how does giving to another increase his love for that person? When one gives to another, he is giving a part of himself — his care and his energies — to that person. The receiver then becomes a part of the giver; this is because the giver literally gave of himself to the other. This is seen in the verse "you shall love your fellow as yourself" (*Vayikra* 19:18). By giving a part of yourself to your fellowman, he becomes like you. Therefore, you love him as yourself, because now he is like you. Even with someone you dislike, if you actually try and do something for him, anything, even the smallest of favors, your attitude towards him will change.

With all this said, Rav Dessler asks, why is it that often the love between a man and his wife doesn't last? He answers that at first there is a great burst of giving energy in the marriage, which increases their love. However, over time one's original nature sets in and one goes back to being more of a taker than a giver. Instead of working together, complementing each other, the couple reverts to making a series of demands on one another. Rav Dessler writes that he would say to young couples at the time of their marriages, "Be careful. Your desire should always be to bestow good and happiness on the other, the same way that it is your desire now. Know that the moment you seek only demands from the other, the tide will turn." He goes on to say that there are unfortunately people who even at the time of their marriage cannot separate from their natural desire only to take; they are never able to become givers. On the other hand, as long as both partners strive to give, then their love will know no bounds and will never cease. Their life will be filled with only happiness and serenity.

We can use this idea to learn about the role that gratitude plays in a marriage. The giver feels that he only wants to give; taking is hard for him unless he can pay back with something. If he is not able to do this, he will still want to do something to pay back the other giver. He can do this by expressing gratitude for what was done for him. In contrast, the taker constantly desires to draw as much as he can towards himself. He thinks that everything is his. Therefore, when someone does something for him, he doesn't feel that he has to offer any sincere gratitude in return. Even if one sees him giving thanks, his intention is only to encourage the giver to give more; he is still taking. We see that gratitude in marriage is characteristic of the giver, while ingratitude is characteristic of the taker.

Going back to Adam Harishon and his dialogue with Hashem about the forbidden fruit, it seems that certainly in this instance he is criticized in the Gemara for his speech, which demonstrates his ingratitude. Although this all-too-human failing goes back as far as Adam, we have seen through Rav Dessler how one can rectify one's inborn traits, and, in addition, how with the correct attitude and gratitude one will have a true "helper," and even the side "against him" will be used positively.

A New World Order

Following the flood, a new world order prevailed. Let us examine some of these changes and their effects as encountered by Noach. Upon exiting the ark, Hashem said to Noach and his sons, "The fear and dread of you shall be upon…everything that moves on earth and in all the fish of the sea" (*Bereishis* 9:2). The commentators explain that this refers to swarming creatures that crawl on the land and live in the sea.

Why is it that swarming creatures that fly are not mentioned here? Rebbi Avraham,[4] son of the Vilna Gaon, answers that originally, man ruled all creatures. As a result of the sins of the generation of the flood, man's dominion over them was revoked. However, when Noach left the ark, man regained authority. When something is uprooted and returned to its place, it is not the same as it was previously. For example, when you bend a coat hanger and try to return it to its original shape, it will never be as straight as it was originally. When Hashem returned man's sovereignty over all creatures, He left out flying, swarming insects. One can clearly see this. Usually, most animals live in fear of humans. Even the wild ones will not attack unless provoked. However, flies and mosquitoes pester man without fear.

Not a Good Investment

The verse says, "And Noach...debased himself and planted a vineyard" (*Bereishis* 9:20). Rashi says that he made himself profane because he should have engaged in a different sort of planting. Why was he given such criticism just for planting a vineyard? The question about Noach's demise is strengthened when we consider that he went from being called "a righteous man, perfect in his generations" (*Bereishis* 6:9) to a "man of the earth" (*Bereishis* 9:20), while Moshe went from being called an "Egyptian man" (*Shemos* 2:19) to "a man of the Lord" (*Devarim* 33:1).

The Dubno Maggid[5] answers this question with a telling parable. There was once a man who went to his Rebbe for a blessing that he have material success. The Rebbe told him that he should invest in the first venture he would find, and he would be successful. The man went home and opened the jar where he kept his last few coins and took them out, ready to do business. In walked his wife, and seeing him tampering with the few remaining coins they had, began screaming at and insulting him. The man got all wound up, and instead of explaining the situation to her, he argued back, increasing the temperature with insult after insult. He then stormed out into the marketplace and bought some merchandise. Unfortunately, his investment turned sour and he lost all his money. He returned to the sage and asked why this had happened. The Rebbe replied, "Do you remember what my words were to you, that your first venture would be successful? You chose to get involved in the argument with your wife, and since it was your first enterprise, it was very successful."

Similarly, following the flood there was a great outpouring of Divine mercy. The first efforts of Noach would certainly have been blessed. Things that would usually have taken longer to produce miraculously grew more quickly. This vineyard, for example, was planted, grew, and its fruit was picked all on the same day. Thus, Noach was criticized because he could have used this ko'ach for more productive enterprises, but instead his first endeavor was to plant a vineyard, which ultimately led to his downfall.

A second explanation as to why he was criticized for planting the vineyard is that it indicated that he failed to learn the lesson of the flood. The Midrash says that the root cause of the flood was that generation's unrestricted pursuit of pleasure, without regard for the consequences of their actions. Noach, upon exiting the ark, planted a vineyard, following the pursuit of pleasure, probably the most inappropriate thing to do immediately following the world's being wiped out for that very reason. How did Noach come to make such a mistake? One answer is that he saw the results of the behavior of that generation, but failed to see the causes of its destruction. This reflects a common problem, that people see the outcomes but fail to recognize the causes and take action.

A Changing World

The Midrash says that there were five individuals who witnessed a world entirely different from that which they were used to: Yosef, Moshe, Iyov, Mordechai and Noach. Yosef went down to Egypt in chains, and arose to become its ruler. Moshe fled for his life from Pharaoh and witnessed his drowning in the sea. Iyov had suffered the greatest of losses, and yet saw it returned to him twofold. Mordechai was destined to be hanged, yet he saw Haman hanged instead. And Noach saw the world destroyed, yet he emerged unscathed with his family.

The Ateres Mordechai[6] says that this *midrash* is telling us not only that they all saw a new world, but that we must realize the secret of their ability to see it. When Yosef came down to Egypt, he could have easily become depressed, feeling he was destined to spend the rest of his life as a slave. However, his faith, his belief that one day he would be freed and reunited with his father, kept him going. It is this faith that is the key to the ability to look beyond today and say there is hope for tomorrow.

In 1945 in Bergen Belsen there was a chassidishe lady whose father came to her in a dream and told her, "Don't give up hope. Have faith and you will survive." From then on, whenever someone was down, she would try and comfort that person with those words. One night she was walking in the camp and saw a man standing by the electric fence. As she approached him, she saw it was the Bluzhever Rebbe. She inquired as to what he was doing there, and he replied that he had taken as much as he could. He had seen his family and community killed, and it was too much for him. He knew it was forbidden to commit suicide, but he hoped one of the guards would shoot him. The woman said to him, "Rebbe, you are the son and grandson of people who brought life to generations. You can't do this. There will be a tomorrow and the world needs you."

The Rebbe stepped back from the fence and said, "Thank you." As this story illustrates, this belief in the future is the only way to survive in the darkest of moments.

A Time to Build

Rav Kahaneman, the Ponovezher Rav,[7] was another figure who lived through the darkest of times. He witnessed the destruction of Lithuanian Jewry firsthand, seeing entire Torah centers and communities uprooted. And yet, when it was all over, he spared no effort to rebuild Jewry. He helped clothe, feed and find shelter for the broken survivors. He built up the Ponovezh Yeshivah, around which the city of Bnei Brak grew.

At his funeral, Rav Shmuel Rozovsky compared the Ponovezher Rav's life to Noach's. As he explained, Hashem said to Noach, "Go out from the ark, you and your wife and your sons and your sons' wives with you" (*Bereishis* 8:16). The Midrash tells us that Noach reasoned: Just as I entered the ark only after I was told to do so, so too will I exit it only when I am told to do so. Had he not been so instructed to leave by Hashem he would have had to remain there indefinitely. Since Noach had been instructed to enter the ark, those instructions would remain in force unless he would receive instructions to the contrary.

Rav Shmuel then provided a further explanation. Before the flood, Hashem had to instruct Noach to enter the ark twice, first when He said, "But I will establish My covenant with you, and you shall enter the ark" (*Bereishis* 6:18), and then when Hashem said, "Come to the ark" (*Bereishis* 7:1). Why was this repetition necessary? He answered as follows. Because Noach could not bring himself to turn his back on the entire world that was about to perish, Hashem had to command him to enter the ark and leave the world to its fate. When the flood was over, Noach knew that a destroyed world was waiting for him outside, and he couldn't bring himself to step out into such a world. Only when Hashem directed Noach to leave the ark did he have the strength to face up to it. Rav Kahaneman knew firsthand of the great loss *klal Yisrael* had suffered and the destroyed world waiting outside. Perhaps what gave him strength was that as a survivor, he felt he had a mission, to rebuild Jewry and to rebuild Torah from the ruins. This enabled him to be active long into his very old age.

A Harsh Punishment

"Only (*ach*) Noach survived, and those with him in the ark"

(*Bereishis* 7:23). The Midrash derives from the extra word *ach*, that one day Noach was late in bringing food to the lion, and was subsequently mauled by the beast. Why was he deserving of punishment for being a few minutes late, especially when every other day he fed all the animals on time, carrying out his work with utter dedication?

Rav Avraham Kalmanovitz,[8] the *rosh yeshivah* of Mir, answered this question in a speech to the Vaad Hatzalah of America following the Second World War. Rav Kalmanovitz explained, "The animals in the ark were the only remnants of the world that was, and they deserved special attention. Noach was also of the remnant of the Old World and carried the burden of caring for the animals. Therefore, he was judged strictly, as his purpose was to sustain the whole world." Movingly, Rav Kalmanovitz continued. "So too with us, we were saved from the murderers. Just two from a village, one from an entire family remain. The burden lies on our shoulders to strengthen ourselves and save our brethren who are the remnant of *klal Yisrael*."

The Chafetz Chaim was a man of such faith in the imminent coming of Mashiach that he kept a bag packed, ready for his arrival. Once he asked rhetorically, How can people be so sure in their belief that tomorrow the sun will rise and it will be day again? He answered[9] that this is because it is promised in *parashas Noach*, "Continuously, all the days of the earth...day and night shall not cease" (*Bereishis* 8:22). Just as we have complete trust that tomorrow will be a new day, as is written explicitly in the Torah, we should also have complete *bitachon* that Mashiach will come, which is also written in the Torah, as it says, "But as I live, and the glory of Hashem shall fill the entire world" (*Bemidbar* 14:21).

Above the Stars

Hashem told Avraham that he and his descendants would be blessed: "And He took him outside and said, 'Look now towards the heavens, and count the stars if you are able to count them…so shall your offspring be' " (*Bereishis* 15:5). We can ask several questions on this *pasuk*. Firstly, what is the meaning of Hashem's taking Avraham "outside"? Secondly, why are stars an appropriate metaphor for his descendants? Thirdly, what did this blessing add, as earlier on, Hashem promised Avraham (*Bereishis* 13:16), "I will make your offspring as the dust of the earth."

Rashi says that when Hashem took Avraham outside, He took him out of his tent in order to see the stars better. The deeper meaning of this Rashi is that Hashem was telling him to go out from his astrological calculations. Avraham had seen in the stars that he was not destined to have children; however, Hashem was taking him outside the course of nature. At the time he was called Avram, and his wife was called Sarai. While he saw that the person called Avram was not destined to have children, it was not decreed that someone called Avraham could not father them. Similarly, while Sarai could not give birth, someone called Sarah could.

Rav Shimshon Raphael Hirsch[10] develops this idea. He says that there was great significance in the fact that Hashem told Avraham to count the stars. If a person is used to looking at our world only through *teva* spectacles — in other words, if he thinks that everything that happens is due to the laws of nature — then, he will reason, statistics say that some people will not have children, so who can complain? While this approach may hold for the nations of the world, it is contrary to the thinking of *klal Yisrael*. Thus, when Hashem told Avraham to go out and look at the stars, He was in fact telling him to look towards *Shamayim* and to realize that we are under the direct influence of Hashem, Who controls and directs every aspect of our lives. Avraham was at first looking at his life only in terms of *teva*, and so Hashem told him to look upwards at the stars and realize that his lot and that of his children were to be *lemaala min hateva* (above nature).

We have the ability to change the course of nature, in particular through *tefillah*. Rather than being left to the elements and astrological calculations, the Jewish people are under the Providence of Hashem. The survival of Avraham's descendants proves this point. While many mighty and powerful nations have ruled the world, they have vanished as quickly as they came onto the scene. Only the Jewish people have outlived them all, going against what nature would otherwise suggest.

You Must Be Joking!

Rav Meir Shapiro[11] provides a slight variation on this answer. If someone would tell us to go out and count the stars, unless one had a particular interest in this sort of thing, he would simply not bother. Obviously you can't count the stars in the sky. Yet we are told that Avraham actually started to count them! This is symbolic of another one of the characteristics that would be a feature of Avraham's descendants: when something looks impossible and beyond the reach of human beings, we should nevertheless try to do it anyway. We think that many of the challenges and trials with which we are faced are beyond us, yet once we put in our own effort we are given help from Heaven to complete the task. As we saw last week, how else could Rav Kahaneman have even begun trying to salvage the remnants of *klal Yisrael* after the Second World War if not for this attitude?

This idea is seen in the following story.[12] A certain blind Jew came to Rav Isser Zalman Meltzer and placed on the table two volumes of Torah insights he had written before he became blind. The elderly Jew told him to turn to a certain page and told the Rav that what he was looking at was the last insight he had written before he became blind. The Rav asked him what he meant by his "last insight." The man replied that he had been working on those volumes for years until he came to that insight and said to himself, "I've been working on these for too long. It's time for a break; I'm too old." Almost immediately he became blind. He went to the doctor, who told him, "The way your eyes are now, you should have been blind ten years ago. We can't understand how that didn't happen." While it baffled the doctor, it didn't baffle Rav Meir Shapiro. He understood that as long as the Jew wrote down those insights, he was given the gift of vision for another day. When he said, "Enough is enough," he lost this strength.

The fact that Avraham tried to count the stars is symbolic of this power that his descendants would have, to take the initiative even if the situation seems impossible. Perhaps this is what is seen in the haftarah when it says, "He gives strength to the weary, and for the powerless abundant might...but those whose hope is in Hashem will have renewed strength" (*Yeshayah* 40:29,31).

High or Low

We also see this idea in *Megillas Esther*. The tide began to turn when Haman was forced to take Mordechai around on a horse, to honor the very man he so despised. Haman came home and told his wife all that had happened, to which she replied, "If Mordechai, before whom you have begun to fall, is of Jewish descent, you will not prevail against him; you will undoubtedly fall before him" (*Esther* 6:13). What made Haman's wife so certain that the tables were about to turn? Rashi quotes the Gemara (*Megillah* 16a), which says that she knew that the Jewish nation is compared to both stars and dust, in that when they descend they descend to the level of dust, but when they rise they go up to the level of the stars.

Another explanation for the comparison of the Jewish people to stars and dust is that when the fortunes of the *bnei Yisrael* are high or on the rise, no one can cause them any harm. This is seen in the blessing Yitzchak gave Yaakov and Esav. First he blessed Yaakov that "Peoples will serve you" (*Bereishis* 27:29), indicating that he was on a higher level than Esav. Yitzchak then told Esav, "but your brother you shall serve," and he continued, "yet it shall be that when you will be aggrieved you may remove his yoke from upon your neck" (*Bereishis* 27:40). Rashi says on this verse that when Yisrael transgress the laws of the Torah, then Esav has a claim about the blessings which Yaakov took. Yaakov and Esav are like two people on a seesaw — when one side is up the other is down. As long as Yisrael do as they are supposed to do, then the hands of Esav have no power and they are like the stars. When Yisrael slip, then Esav is given a chance to let go and vent his frustrations. This is when *bnei Yisrael* are described as being on the level of the dust of the earth.

This is what Haman's wife was telling her husband. If the fortunes of *Klal Yisrael* are on the way up, they have done *teshuvah* and you will not be able to harm them. Indeed, she was never more correct.

There is another explanation of this *gemara*. When the Jews act appropriately, their actions are so good, involving Torah and acts of kindness, that they resemble the stars in the heavens. When they act inappropriately, their deeds make them like the dust of the earth. The following stories illustrate these ideas.

There was once a rabbi in a yeshivah who used to pay visits to his former students to see how they were doing. One particular former student was telling him about his business, which involved a certain operation that would undercut the tax liabilities of his company, as well as causing a certain loss from other companies. The laws of business practice are such that many halachic questions must often be addressed, and the rabbi quickly realized that there was much to discuss concerning this particular business operation. So the two men discussed things for a while, and in the end the rabbi had to tell his former student that what he was doing was forbidden by the Torah under no less than the prohibition against stealing. The rabbi tried his best to persuade the man to change his line of work, but he argued that it was very lucrative, and maybe it wasn't forbidden after all. Eventually, the rabbi had to give him his honest opinion: "If you want to continue doing this, you may as well not wear your *kippah* anymore — that's how bad it is."

The former student paused, and then said, "If that's so, then I won't wear it."

What this man was prepared to do for a quick buck, despite going against the Torah, is something that makes non-Jews look at Jews and say, "These people are like the dust of the earth."

Baseball Stars

The following story from Rav Pesach Krohn has a very different outcome from the previous one. There was once a boy called Shaya who was in a special school for children with learning disabilities. Once a week he would go to a yeshivah to study with the students there. One day his father was taking him to the yeshivah when they saw the boys outside playing baseball. Shaya turned to his father and asked if he thought they would let him play. While his son was not athletic, and neither team would really want him, the father thought that if the boys would let his son play it would give him a sense of belonging.

The father approached one of the players and asked him if his son could join in. The boy looked around at his teammates for a reaction, but it was not forthcoming, so he decided on his own accord. "We're six runs down in the eighth inning," he told the father. "He'll play on our team and we'll give him a bat." Shaya smiled as he took his position in the field.

Eventually Shaya's team batted, scoring another three runs, with four more runs needed for them to win the game. The bases were all loaded, and they now had a chance to win. The next player at bat was Shaya. Would the team risk forfeiting the game and let him bat?

The boys told Shaya to take the bat and to try and hit the ball. He couldn't even hold the bat properly, never mind hit a ball with it.

The pitcher stepped in a few paces and threw the ball slowly underarm to Shaya. Of course he missed it. This happened a second time, after which a teammate came in to help him. The pitch came in, they swung and made contact. The ball headed straight back to the pitcher, who could have easily thrown it to first base, which would have ended the game. Instead, the pitcher took the ball and threw it wildly way beyond the first baseman's reach. Everyone shouted, "Shaya, run to first," and he ran as fast as he could. By then, the right fielder had the ball, but instead of throwing it to second base, he threw it high into the outfield. The players screamed for Shaya to run, and he made it to second base. The player in the outfield, understanding his teammates' intentions, played along and made a similar overthrow. Eventually Shaya made it to third base, by which time both teams were screaming for him to run to home plate. As he stepped on the plate they lifted him onto their shoulders and made him into a hero who had just won the game for them.

Shaya's father later related that those boys, in the heat of their game, rather than worry about winning, turned their attention to making someone less privileged feel good about himself, and on that day they must have reached their level of perfection.

We see from this story that each and every Jew has the ability not only to try and be a star, but to rise up to the level of the stars.

Parashas Vayeira

Not the Last Laugh

The first event described in this *parashah* is the story of the three angels who came to visit Avraham after his bris. Sarah had been unable to have children for nearly a century when the angel informed Avraham, "I will surely return to you…behold, a son to Sarah your wife" (*Bereishis* 18:10). Sarah was listening in the tent behind them and laughed, since surely this could not happen, given how old she was. Hashem then rebuked Avraham, saying, "Is anything beyond Hashem?" (*Bereishis* 18:14).

Why was Sarah faulted for laughing? Firstly, she was indeed nearing the age of one hundred, so surely it wasn't unreasonable for her to be a little sceptical. Secondly, it wasn't a great prophet that told her the news; while they were in fact angels, they came dressed as mere idol-worshiping travelers. Why should she have believed them?

The approach of the Ramban to these questions is that despite these factors Sarah should not have considered their words to be implausible. She should have responded to their words with something to the effect of *"Amen,* may Hashem do so."

Rav Yehudah Ze'ev Segal[13] explains that this episode provides a crucial lesson in the sort of faith expected of us. We must not believe that Hashem operates the world with a hands-off approach. Rather, we have to believe what we say every morning: "in His goodness, renews daily forever the work of creation." Each and every moment, Hashem has to actively renew the existence of the world.

Another, related concept is a belief in *hashgachah pratis*, that Hashem is involved in all aspects of the world, including those aspects relating to one on an individual level. The centrality of this belief is evident in that the very first of the Thirteen Principles of Faith is "I believe with complete faith that the Creator…creates and guides all creatures, and that He alone made, makes and will make everything." It seems that Sarah was at fault in this incident. Despite nature dictating one thing, when Hashem decrees something else, it will be fulfilled.

Angels Don't Lie

As we mentioned above, the angel said that he would return to Avraham and that he would have a son. However, we never actually see that the angel returned. We cannot accuse an angel of lying, and the Torah would not mention this if it were insignificant, so when did the angel return?

The *Sefer Hapardes*[14] answers that in fact the angel returned at a much later time, when Avraham placed Yitzchak on the altar, ready to sacrifice him. He lifted up his knife, and then, according to the verse, "an angel of Hashem called to him from Heaven…And he said, "Do not send forth your hand at the lad" (*Bereishis* 22:11-12). The very same angel that was sent to inform Avraham that he would have a son, was the one who came and told him not to slaughter his son. This angel's entire purpose and reason for existence was to make sure there would be a Yitzchak. Therefore, having announced his birth, he was needed again to tell Avraham not to slaughter his son. This was the fulfillment of the original prophecy, "Behold, a son to Sarah your wife."

We see that Providence works in wondrous ways. Who would have thought that thirty-eight years after it first appeared to Avraham this angel would resurface? Yet Hashem is the Master over all events and runs things according to His plan, as can be seen in the following story.

There was once a rabbi who left Germany before the war and settled in England. With the outbreak of the war, all German nationals were sent to Canada and Australia. Before the rabbi set out for Canada, he sent a big suitcase full of *sefarim* to his destination, so he should have *sifrei kodesh* from which to learn. Unfortunately, the suitcase got lost in transit, but as it happened, shortly afterwards a *Shas* was printed in Montreal, so the rabbi did have access to *sefarim*. After the war, he met someone who had been sent from England to Australia when war broke out. He told the rabbi that the most amazing thing happened: as if from nowhere, a whole suitcase full of *sefarim* turned up, and these were the only ones available there. Hashem arranged that they would both have *sefarim* from which to learn.

Believing Is Not Seeing

The Chafetz Chaim[15] says that just as Sarah laughed to herself, we have inherited this trait in that we wonder about whether we will be redeemed imminently or not. We think to ourselves, "Can the world order really return to that system of the Beis Hamikdash, with sacrifices and all Jews living in Israel?" He says that the Torah's answer is in the words of Hashem's reply to Sarah: "Is any matter beyond Hashem?" (*Bereishis* 18:14). A similar expression is found in the prophet's words, where it says, "Is there anything too hard for Me?" (*Yirmeyahu* 32:27).

We learn from here that Hashem can cause any event to come about, even ones that are against the "laws" of nature. Not only this, but they can happen at the speed of a blink of the eye. So too, the redemption will eventually come about quickly.

The Chafetz Chaim goes on to ask why this passage dealing with the criticism of Sarah is dealt with in so much detail. He answers that it is a manifestation of *maaseh avos siman labanim*, that everything that happened to our forefathers is a sign of what would befall their descendants. This paragraph symbolizes what will occur during the *ikvesa de'meshicha* (the birth pangs of Mashiach's coming). As the time gets nearer, there will be *gedolei Yisrael* who will urge the people to have faith, to repent and to prepare themselves with Torah and good deeds. In our *parashah*, the Torah alludes to the other set of people, those of little faith who will not listen to the leaders of the generation, and it will be said to them, "Is any matter beyond Hashem?" He goes on to say that it is not that people will deny the coming of Mashiach; they'll simply doubt that he could come at any moment. And we have to believe that he will come at any moment, as the verse says, "Suddenly he will come" (*Malachi* 3:1). We also see in the Gemara that if one makes a declaration "I am a *Nazir* on the day Mashiach comes," he is forbidden to drink wine all his days in case Mashiach comes. This shows that one has to literally believe he could come on any day, at any time.

Business Advice

There is an interesting *gemara* in *Pesachim* (113a), where Rav gives over various pieces of business advice to Eivah, his son. One of them is "All items you may sell and have regrets over, except for wine, which you need not have regrets over." The Rashbam explains that when you hurry to sell an item and the price subsequently goes up, you may regret it. However, with wine, had you not sold it, it may have turned to vinegar in the meantime, so you need not have regrets. This *gemara* bothered me. What kind of advice is this? Here you have the great Rav, telling his son that if he makes a deal and could have made more money, he should walk around all day being miserable about this deal. What practical purpose is there in having regrets about such a transaction? There must have been some deeper piece of advice being offered here; after all, the statements of the Gemara all serve a positive, constructive purpose.

One answer I heard was that really Rav was telling his son that in business you have to be levelheaded. You have to know that despite your own initiative, Hashem also has a hand in the way things run and ultimately turn out. If you have trust and faith in Hashem, you can make a rational decision, taking all factors into account. However, if you lack faith you are likely to stumble. This is seen from the words of the Rashbam, when he says that you "hurry to sell." You are quick to make a decision without bringing Hashem into the equation. You may have regrets over such a transaction. The implication is that if, on the other hand, you made a well-thought-out decision, having trust in Hashem, if the deal were not to work out, you may not have regrets, because you will realize that the outcome was in Hashem's hands. Only when one goes ahead without putting his trust in the correct place can he have regrets.

We have seen the same idea with Sarah Imeinu. While she was perfectly righteous, in this one instance she is criticized. Perhaps the reason the Torah spells it out so clearly is so that we can learn from it and take the lesson to heart: "Is any matter beyond Hashem?"

Of Cats and Salesmen

This *parashah* begins with the account of the events that followed the death of our matriarch Sarah. Rashi notes that this section about her *petirah* follows that of the *akeidah*, to teach us that Sarah died when the Satan, in the guise of a human being, told her that her son had been bound and placed on an altar to be sacrificed. By the time she was told that Yitzchak had not been killed, it was too late.

The question is: How could the Satan have been given permission to do such a thing? Surely his only role is to lead a person to sin, not to cause people to die. Furthermore, if one looks at the text of this episode, one will notice that the letter *kaf*, in the word *velivkosa* (to bewail her), is written small. What is the reason for this?

The approach of the Kehillas Yitzchak to these questions is that we first have to understand that the Satan is the *yetzer hara* (the evil inclination). His sole purpose is to cause people to sin and prevent them from doing mitzvos. If he cannot succeed in preventing one from doing a mitzvah, he will do his utmost to cause the person to stumble by making him regret the good deeds he has already done. By doing this, the merit he would have gained from those mitzvos is canceled. We see this idea in the davening, where it says, "And remove the Satan from in front of us and from behind us." In other words, we pray that the Satan shall be removed not only when he is in front of us, trying to prevent us from doing mitzvos, but also when he is behind us, trying to make us regret those mitzvos which we have already done.

This is what the Satan attempted to do with Avraham. At first he tried to prevent him from succeeding in the test of the *akeidah* by placing all sorts of stumbling blocks in his way. When he could not achieve this, he tried to make Avraham think that it was the *akeidah* which caused his wife to die and that surely it wasn't worth it. However, Avraham stood up to this as well. In order to show that he didn't have regrets over the *akeidah*, he cried only a small amount over Sarah's death. We learn this from the fact that the letter *kaf* in the word *velivkosa* is written small. We also see this in the wording of the verse, which says that first Avraham eulogized Sarah and only afterward did he weep for her. This was a change in the usual practice in order to indicate that he didn't blame her death on the *akeidah*.

A Bad Job

There is another factor at play here. As we have said, the Satan is obviously not licensed to kill people. The fact is that Sarah was 127 years old and was destined to die that day anyway. The question is, how would people look at her death?

There is an old "joke" that Hashem was looking for someone to be the angel of death. Finally he found someone who was very reluctant to take the job. "I don't want to be the bad guy, with everyone blaming me for all the evil in this world," he argued.

Hashem replied, "Don't worry. No one will ever blame you. They'll blame the doctors, the nurses — you've got nothing to worry about."

So too, the test was to see if Avraham would blame the *akeidah* on his wife's death, or if he would demonstrate the same level of trust that he displayed at the *akeidah* itself and accept the decree with love.

The Father of All Salesmen

The next incident described in our *parashah* is Avraham's effort to purchase a burial place for Sarah. He meets the father of all salesmen, Efron, who initially offers him the field for free, and ends up asking for "four hundred silver shekalim; between me and you, what is it?" (*Bereishis* 23:15).

Regarding Efron's behavior, the Midrash says that the righteous say little and do much, as when Avraham said to his three passing guests, "I will fetch a morsel of bread" (*Bereishis* 18:4), and then he brought out cakes and other delicacies. On the other hand, the wicked say much and do little, as seen with Efron, who first offered Avraham the land for nothing, and then asked for four hundred silver shekalim. This amount even had to be paid in "negotiable currency" (*Bereishis* 23:16), a type of coinage which is valid everywhere.

Why did Avraham agree to pay such an exorbitant sum of money, an amount so large it allegedly could have bought the whole city? The Mesillas Yesharim tells us that a man's purpose is to benefit from the Divine radiance, something which takes place in the World to Come. In order to attain this one has to pass through this world and earn merit through learning Torah and fulfilling the mitzvos. The *sefer Hadra shel Torah* says that this fact is alluded to in the nature of the sale of the Cave of Machpeilah. By paying a price which was obviously too high,

Avraham alluded to the fact that man's stay in this world is only temporary, and one must invest in spiritual matters that will remain with him in the next world.

A Good Deal

There was once a man who came to a rabbi and told him of his financial woes, complaining that he had no money to marry off his daughter. The rabbi asked him, "Do you believe that Hashem can help you?" to which he replied that he did. The rabbi then continued, "If so, take a ruble and make the first business deal you can and you will make a thousand rubles."

The man went to the market and began dealing with a seller who scoffed at him and his one ruble. "I'll make only one deal with you: give me your one ruble and I'll give you my share in the World to Come." As this was his first chance at a deal, the man took it according to the rabbi's instructions and shook hands over it.

The seller went home and boasted to his wife about how he had made an easy ruble off a foolish peasant, promising the man his World to Come for a ruble. His wife, who had more faith than he, angrily declared, "I'm not prepared to remain with a man with no share in the World to Come. Annul the sale or give me a bill of divorce right now."

The seller then returned to the other Jew, who would only sell back his portion for a price of one thousand rubles. Faced with no other choice, he reluctantly paid it. The merchant subsequently took the Jew to a *din Torah*, claiming that something bought for a ruble could not be sold for a thousand rubles, to which the *beis din* told him, "There is no price or value on the World to Come which can possibly be paid by human beings. The sale is valid."[16]

Once a Cat, Always a Cat

The Alter of Kelm[17] asks, How it can be that Efron started out by saying, "And as for the cave that is in it, I have given it to you" (*Bereishis* 23:11), and ended up asking for four hundred shekels? How could he go to two opposite extremes so quickly? The Alter answers by citing a famous incident involving the Rambam. There was once a competition to see who could make a cat change its nature and do things like a person does and have all the good manners a human has. The Rambam said that it is impossible to change a cat's nature. One day some scholars announced that they had accomplished the feat. A great crowd gathered and they watched a cat set the table. Then a group of professors entered the room, and the cat took a bow and showed each one his place. Then it brought out wine on a tray. As it was approaching the table to give out the wineglasses, the Rambam, who was in the audience, opened a box and a mouse popped out. The cat jumped and chased the mouse, smashing the glasses and spilling the wine all over the table. The professors all agreed with the Rambam that one can't change the nature of a cat.

It was the same with Efron. As long as he didn't see the money in front of his eyes, he appeared as civilized as the cat in our story. As soon as Avraham took out the money and Efron heard the jingling of the coins, he turned into a different man.

Later on in the *parashah*, Eliezer, the servant of Avraham, sets out to find a wife for Yitzchak. The ideas we have already seen come into play once again. The Torah tells us that Eliezer "ruled over all that he had" (*Bereishis* 24:2). Simply speaking, the verse means that he was in charge of all of Avraham's property. On a deeper level, the Kli Yakar says that it means that he ruled over himself, meaning that he ruled over the money that he had; his money didn't rule over him. We then meet Rivkah, who like

Avraham, says little but does a lot, as first she said, "Drink, my lord" (*Bereishis* 24:18), but then offers to water the camels as well.

These traits, if internalized, can change one's whole attitude to life. Someone like Ephron is ruled by his money, and "One who loves money will not be satisfied with money" (*Koheles* 5:9). One who knows the real value of money will be like Avraham and Rivkah. They can give of their time and money because they know its real worth, and how it can be used in the right way.

Parashas Toldos

The Battle over Two Worlds

This *parashah* contains the origins of both the physical and the spiritual struggle between Yaakov and Esav. Let us examine the spiritual struggle and look at it in a particular light. Essentially, what it really boiled down to was a struggle over who would inherit this world and who would inherit the next. Even in the womb the battle had begun: "And the sons were jostling within her" (*Bereishis* 25:22). The Midrash says that when Rivkah would stand near a shul or *beis midrash*, Yaakov would struggle to emerge, but whenever she passed by a pagan temple, Esav would run to emerge.

Rav Zalman Sorotzkin[18] notes the choice of language used in the Midrash. Rivkah would "stand near" a shul, but would only "pass by" a pagan temple. She would try and pass by the pagan temple as quickly as possible but would linger by a shul or *beis midrash*. This explains why Esav would "run to emerge"; he had only a short time to emerge, while Yaakov merely "struggled," as his mother stayed near the *beis midrash* for longer.

How did the unborn sons actually know where they were passing? Rav Yerucham Levovitz says that just like we have material senses, we also have a spiritual sense. A compass always points to the north; in like manner, spiritual forces cause one to be attracted to that which one seeks most.

On a related note, later on, the verse states that when Yaakov approached his father in Esav's clothing to receive the blessing, Yitzchak "smelled the fragrance of his garments...and said, 'See, the fragrance of my son is like the fragrance of a field which Hashem has blessed' " (*Bereishis* 27:27). Rashi says that when Yaakov entered Yitzchak's room, the smell of Gan Eden entered with him.

These words need an explanation. After all, these were the garments of Esav. How could the smell of Gan Eden have attached itself to them? Rav Shneur Kotler[19] cites a Yerushalmi that explains the words "the choice garments of Esav" (*Bereishis* 27:15). These were the garments he would wear when he would serve and honor his father, to fulfill the mitzvah of *kibbud av ve'em*. The Nefesh Hachaim says that when one does a mitzvah, he surrounds himself in a special radiance that emanates from a higher source of holiness. This is only a part of what is reserved for him in Gan Eden. The garments of Esav, which were designated for this mitzvah, had this smell attached to them.

Like Mother, Like Son?

Returning to our topic, a question is asked on the above *midrash*: Even if the fetus could sense where it was, how could it even attempt to escape? Furthermore, what changed in the behavior of the fetuses? We all know that unborn babies kick, so maybe it was simply coincidental that these brothers kicked when Rivkah passed either shuls or houses of idolatry. What caused her to say, "If so, why am I thus?" and that "she went to inquire of Hashem"? (*Bereishis* 25:22).

The Yismach Yisrael[20] cites the Talmudic principle of *ubar yerech imo*, that a fetus is an intrinsic part of its mother. When the mother is hungry, so is the fetus; when she is sad, it is sad; and when she is happy, it is happy. Thus, when Rivkah stood by a shul and was happy, Yaakov was happy too and would jostle inside her. Because it was affected to some extent by the holiness of the place, the jostling of the fetus would appear to her as if it was trying to leave, but really it was just happy; it wouldn't attempt to leave before its time. When Rikvah would pass a house of idolatry she was sad, and therefore the fetus should have also been sad and stayed still. However, Esav was an exception; he was eager to escape to idol worship. Rivkah consequently asked herself why this was happening, that she was sad and the fetus was simultaneously rejoicing: "If so, why am I thus?" The verse then relates that "she went to inquire of Hashem." When she was told that "two nations are in your womb" (*Bereishis* 25:23), all was now resolved.

It is related that the Chasam Sofer[21] was very particular regarding whom his children were allowed to play with, so that they should be exposed to the right influences. He once explained why one must be so careful about whom children play with, and cited the above verse about how Yaakov and Esav jostled inside Rivkah. He then quoted the *midrash* about how each would try to emerge at their favorite locations. He then presented the following difficulty: We can understand Esav's need to emerge, but in Yaakov's case, surely he had an angel teaching him Torah in the womb. Why would he be so anxious to leave? He then answered that when one is together with an Esav, even learning from an angel won't help!

The following question was once asked of the Rav of Kishinev, who was six years old at the time. Why didn't Esav actually emerge? After all, he was in a position to come out first, and there was no one stopping him. He answered that really he did want to emerge, as indicated by the struggling. However, he was worried that if he would leave to go to the houses of idol worship, then Yaakov would be free to leave to go to the tents of Torah. He preferred to remain inside Rivkah rather than let this happen. This intention is something that would play itself out many times throughout future generations.

A Last Thought, Perhaps

The difference between Yaakov and Esav is articulated in the verse "Esav became one who knows hunting, a man of the field, but Yaakov was a wholesome man, abiding in tents" (*Bereishis* 25:27). Rabbeinu Bachaya comments that although they were twins, their actions were completely different. Esav was drawn after only the physical world, after that which is good today, "a man of the field." Yaakov, in contrast, was a man of the spirit. He was drawn after that which he perceived to be eternal. This idea played itself out when Esav came home hungry from a tough day's murdering (see Rashi) and said, "Look, I'm going to die, so of what use to me is this birthright?" (*Bereishis* 25:32). The Chafetz Chaim[22] comments here on the difference between the righteous and the wicked. With the righteous, a mere reminder of the day of death is enough to spur them to repentance and greater fear of Heaven. On the other hand, with someone like Esav, even staring the day of death in the face only made him more disparaging of the birthright, which represented spirituality and eternity.

The Hand That Feeds

It is interesting to note that the blessings given to Yaakov and Esav were different in one aspect, while similar in another. In the blessing given to Esav, it doesn't mention that the blessings come from Hashem. It is just "of the fatness of the earth" (*Bereishis* 27:39) with which he was blessed. Yaakov was blessed, "And may Hashem give you..." (*Bereishis* 27:28).

To explain the difference in the wording of these blessings, Rabbeinu Bachaya says that the materialism of Esav is based on the constellations; what the laws of nature will dictate is "written in the stars." There can be scarcity and plenty, and all are just "natural" occurrences determined through astrological factors. On the other hand, Yaakov's material needs are fulfilled directly through the hand of Hashem. If Yaakov is deserving, he will receive them, as it says, "It will be if you will listen to My commandments...then I shall provide rain" (Devarim 11:13).

Nevertheless, at first glance, the blessings that the brothers received seem similar. Yaakov was blessed with the "dew of the heavens and the fatness of the earth" (Bereishis 27:28), while Esav received "the fatness of the earth...and the dew of the heavens" (Bereishis 27:39). The Chafetz Chaim[23] comments on the fact that the order of the blessing is reversed. The "dew of the heavens" refers to spiritual blessings. Yaakov received that blessing first — after all, that is what he desired most. Esav, on the other hand, prefers the "fatness of the earth" — only materialism at its best. Rashi observes that Yaakov will receive materialistic wealth and blessings of the earth only if he is deserving of them. In contrast, Esav will always receive his material blessings, according to his constellations, whether or not he is deserving of them.

Anything, Just the Wrong Thing

Following Esav's discovery of how he was deceived, he pleaded with his father, "Have you but one blessing left, Father?" (Bereishis 27:38). This request is somewhat strange, as Yitzchak had already told Esav, "A lord have I made him [Yaakov] over you, and all his kin have I given him as servants" (Bereishis 27:37). What point was there then in Esav's request? Furthermore, how then did Yitzchak proceed to bless him, "of the fatness of the earth shall be your dwelling and of the dew of the heavens from above"? (*Bereishis* 27:39). If he had run out of blessings, from where did this one appear?

Rav Elya Lopian[24] explains that Yitzchak wanted to bless Esav with something purely spiritual. However, since Yaakov had already taken that, there was nothing left in that department. Esav replied by asking, "Is it only a spiritual blessing that you have? I want a physical blessing; it is only materialistic wealth that I seek." Yitzchak could then reply, "If that's the blessing you seek, then that I can give you."

We see these ideas later on in *parashas Vayishlach*. Yaakov sent messengers to tell Esav, "I lodged with Lavan and lingered until now" (*Bereishis* 32:5). Rashi says that Yaakov was telling Esav not to hate him for having taken the blessings; he had not become great through them. The Brisker Rav[25] asks on this verse, how could Yaakov belittle the blessings of his father, even if he only meant it to appease Esav? He answers that he was showing Esav that the blessings he received were only intended for the long run; in the short run they would be of no benefit at all. To Yaakov, this arrangement was fine, because he was thinking in terms of the next world for himself and his descendants. Esav wanted the here and now, so the spiritual blessings of Yitzchak were of no use to him anyway. That is why he was appeased by Yaakov's message.

A Higher Purpose

The *parashah* describes how "Yaakov worked seven years for Rachel and they seemed to him a few days because of his love for her" (*Bereishis* 29:20). How can this be? Conventional thinking suggests that when one desires something and longs for it, a few days seem to take forever. How then do we understand our forefather Yaakov, who had such a great love for Rachel, and yet an entire seven years seemed like only a few days to him? Surely the seven years should have felt like a lifetime.

The Dubno Maggid[26] answers that the love of Yaakov for Rachel was different. People are motivated by one of two factors: that which will bring them the greatest pleasure in the short run, the here and now, or that which is best in the long run. These concepts are known as *chefetz* — wanting something right now, and being motivated by desire — and *cheshek*, sensible planning with perspective, taking all things into account. These ideas are very applicable to love and marriage. One driven by *chefetz* has to reap the benefits now, without a moment's delay. One who believes time is on his side is guided by *cheshek*. He will think things over carefully in order to decide what will bring the best long-term results.

With Yaakov, these two factors worked in perfect harmony. On one hand, Rachel is described as being of "beautiful form and beautiful of appearance" (*Bereishis* 29:17). However, her beauty could not have been the sole factor motivating Yaakov. On the contrary, seven years were like only a few days to him. Yaakov knew that she was his Divinely chosen wife; indeed, she was to be the main wife of the four. Yaakov and Rachel had a specific role to play in history that could only be realized at the right time, and Yaakov understood this. That is why he was able to wait for her.

The Dubno Maggid adds that one motivated by *chefetz* is really only in love with himself. His interest is solely in how he can fulfill his own desires. If one likes sweets, does he eat them because he loves the candy? It is because he loves himself and wants to fulfill his desires. On the other hand, Yaakov was motivated by *cheshek*; it says, in fact, that the seven years seemed so short "because of his love for her" (*Bereishis* 29:20). It was not a love for himself and his own desires, but "for her." It was Rachel's spiritual qualities and what she would represent to *klal Yisrael* that caused this love.

The Seforno gives a different answer to the question of why the seven years seemed so short a time to Yaakov. Yaakov loved Rachel for her spiritual qualities and for her potential in building *klal Yisrael*. He thought that he would have to pay an even greater price for this. Therefore, to him, seven years seemed like a small price to pay for her.

The Maharil Diskin gives a different answer. The Mordechai (*Kesuvos* 2a) says that an engaged couple should avoid spending too much time together before the marriage. They may become too familiar with and begin to hate each other. If they spend only a short time together, their love will grow following the wedding. The Torah tells us that Yaakov spent seven years in Lavan's house, yet his love for Rachel was not diminished. This was because Rachel was pure and free of any faults, so that even over a long time his esteem for her would only grow. The seven years were like only a few days, a short time, as the Mordechai mentions, which would not lead to any bad feelings about the other.

Not Ready Yet

Rav Aharon Kotler[27] explains why Yaakov was willing to wait seven years to marry Rachel. He begins by quoting the *midrash* that says that Avraham was not able to build *Klal Yisrael* because Yishmael descended from him. Similarly, Yitzchak had Esav. It was only Yaakov whose offspring were perfect. Therefore, he established and was the father of the twelve tribes. Yaakov knew that he had to undergo an extensive purification process in order to father them. Perhaps this is because of the principle *maaseh avos siman labanim*: whatever happened to our forefathers is a sign of what would befall their descendants.

This also means that the traits of our forefathers were an indication of what their children would be. Yaakov didn't marry at the age of forty as his father Yitzchak did, because he felt that he was not on the spiritual level to father *bnei Yisrael* and imbue them with what they would need for the future. When he fled his home with the intention to marry, he stopped off in the yeshivah of Shem and Ever for fourteen years.

He reached the house of Lavan at the age of seventy-seven, and even then he didn't feel he was ready to marry. He needed to elevate himself even in the house of Lavan, in order to pave the way for his children to survive hostile elements, just as he would have to do. For this reason Yaakov readily agreed to serve Lavan for seven years. During this time he dwelled with the flocks of Lavan and was able to ready himself for the task of planting the spiritual seeds of what would shape his descendants for all time.

At the end of seven years he was ready and asked himself, "When am I going to father the twelve tribes?" The time had come, for he now felt he was on the level to imbue his children with the spiritual traits they would need for the future.

A Clash of Interests

Providence had it that Yaakov married Leah first. This was the way it was meant to be, that the twelve tribes would be descended from four mothers. Yaakov's intention, however, was to marry Rachel first. One reason given as to why Yaakov wanted to marry Rachel first is that she was to be the mainstay of the house, his main wife. (For an explanation of this see how the above quoted comment of Rav Aharon Kotler continues.) Rav Yonasan Eibeschutz[28] gives another reason why Yaakov wanted to marry Rachel first. At that time people were saying what a great *shidduch* could be made: Rivkah had two sons and Lavan had two daughters, so the elder should marry the elder and the younger the younger. Yaakov was worried that if he would marry Leah first, then Esav would marry Rachel. To prevent this he tried as hard as he could to marry Rachel first. If it was Leah who was left, Esav probably wouldn't have taken an interest in her, for she was described as having "weak eyes." Yaakov could then marry her as well. However, the plan went amiss, because despite Yaakov's precautions, Lavan still deceived him.

In the Correct Way

While on the subject of beauty, let us examine a fascinating idea of the Vilna Gaon.[29] On the one hand, the above verse describes Rachel's physical beauty, calling her "beautiful of appearance," but on the other hand, elsewhere it says, "Grace is false and beauty vain; a woman who fears Hashem, she should be praised" (*Mishlei* 31:30). How can it be that the Torah makes mention of Rachel's beauty and indeed the other matriarchs' beauty as well, and yet King Solomon speaks of beauty as vain? The Vilna Gaon answers that the verse in *Mishlei* refers only to a woman who does not possess fear of Hashem. For such a woman, her beauty is mere vanity. He describes it as a golden ring...in the nose of a pig. On the other hand, a woman that possesses fear of Hashem, "she should be praised" — even her beauty is praised.

The Vilna Gaon goes on to say that we find a similar idea in the prophets. "Let not the wise man glorify himself in his wisdom, and let not the strong man glorify himself in his strength, nor the rich man in his wealth. For only with this may one glorify oneself, contemplating and knowing Me" (*Yirmeyahu* 9:22-3). The explanation is that wisdom, strength and wealth are of value only when they are used in the service of Hashem. In all these areas one has to know how to use the tools he is given to enhance his Divine service, and not misappropriate them and let them take him away from that service.

What's in a Name?

This *parashah* describes how Yaakov struggled with an angel all night long. Rashi tells us that it was the guardian angel of Esav. When it was morning, it seemed that Yaakov had prevailed. The angel asked to be released, a request which Yaakov said he'd refuse until he received a blessing. The angel asked Yaakov his name, and informed him of the impending name change from Yaakov to Yisrael, a change which Hashem Himself would later confirm. Yaakov then asked the angel for his name, to which he replied, "Why do you ask my name?" (*Bereishis* 32:30).

Rav Leib Chasman[30] explains that the name one is given is highly significant, as it contains the definition of that person. The angel of Esav represented the *yetzer hara*. When Yaakov asked him his name, he didn't want to know merely for reasons of friendship. He was asking the angel what he was — what the *yetzer hara* is and what it represents. The angel's reply, "Why do you ask my name?" meant: "I can't tell you what I am because I have no reality. I am only part of a person's desires." It is like a shadow in the dark. When one sees it he is frightened, thinking it may be a robber or an enemy, but when he turns the light on

What's in a Name? 69

he sees it was his own shadow all along. That is what the *yetzer hara* is: part of a person's desire but without any objective existence. Therefore, when Yaakov asked its name, it gave no answer other than, "Why do you ask?"

Adding and Subtracting

In *parashas Toldos* we spoke about the spiritual struggle between Yaakov and Esav. *Parashas Vayishlach* continues this theme. The haftarah speaks about the future: "And the house of Yaakov will be a [spark of] fire and the house of Yosef will be a flame and the house of Esav will be as straw" (*Ovadiah* 1:18). Rashi says that Yaakov is only a spark, in that he is unable to deal with Esav on his own. Only when Yosef comes along can he be dealt with.

What is it about Yosef that only he can counter Esav? The Shem MiShmuel[31] answers by citing the significance of names. The name "Esav" comes from the word *asui*, which means "done" or "complete." Esav was born looking like a fully formed adult. Esav has this trait of considering himself as made, finished, with no room for further improvement, and he feels that he doesn't need to work on himself. This is the spiritual danger that Esav poses, that descendants of Yaakov learn from his example and see no need to improve themselves. On the other hand, there is Yosef. His name comes from the word *mosif* (to add on). He sees the need to constantly improve himself. Thus, the antidote to the attitude of Esav is a Yosef.

Chazal use the analogy of the ladder in Yaakov's dream to show that in matters of spirituality, one is only either rising or falling. Complacency is a subtle way of descending. The response to all this is Yosef — to constantly add more to ourselves spiritually.

We also find that Yaakov's name was changed to Yisrael. The

Gemara (*Berachos* 13a) says that whoever calls Avraham by his former name Avram has transgressed. However, if one calls Yaakov by that name, despite his subsequently being given the name Yisrael, he has not transgressed. We learn this from Scripture itself, which uses both names interchangeably. It seems that the name change to Yisrael did not require that he be called only that. Why then, was he given the name Yisrael if he was to be called Yaakov afterwards? Also, we could ask, if Yaakov was given another name and yet it was nonbinding, perhaps it should also be the case with Avraham as well?

Regarding this difficulty, the Vilna Gaon[32] points out that we have to look at the exact wording the Torah uses. When the Torah says *vehayah*, "but your name shall be" (*Bereishis* 17:5), regarding Avraham, it implies a change that takes effect immediately. On the other hand, when the verse states *"yiheyeh"* in the verse "but Yisrael shall be your name" (*Bereishis* 35:10), regarding Yaakov, it implies something in the future, referring to the fact that only later on will he be known as Yisrael. The Torah itself supports this idea, in that it subsequently still calls Yaakov by his first name, but from that point onwards refers to Avraham only by his new name.

For the Masses

The question remains, what does it matter whether one uses Yaakov or Yisrael? Yaakov is a private name, not suitable for the masses, while Yisrael denotes the multitudes. For that reason, the Jewish people are called *bnei Yisrael*. Therefore, when Yaakov defeated the angel, he was blessed that his name should not be the private Yaakov, but Yisrael, referring to a great and numerous nation. Perhaps one could also say that Yaakov was being subtly blessed that the defeat of the angel was a victory which should also manifest itself for the masses, and not just the individual.

The Devar Avraham[33] says that we also see this distinction with Eliyahu on Mount Carmel. The verse states, "Eliyahu took twelve stones, corresponding to the number of the tribes of the children of Yaakov, to whom the word of Hashem came, saying, "Your name shall be Yisrael" (I *Melachim* 18:31). The commentators ask, why is there this sudden change of name from Yaakov to Yisrael within the same verse? This can be answered with the above distinction. Eliyahu wanted to join the entire nation together according to their tribes, as seen by the taking of the twelve stones. Therefore, he utilized the contrast between the two names, starting with Yaakov, thereby alluding to them as individuals, and ending by mentioning the name Yisrael, thus demonstrating that they should unite in their service of Hashem.

Playing Tricks

Rav Yisrael Salanter[34] provides a different explanation regarding the change of name. The name Yaakov refers to trickery, as Esav said, "Is it because his name was Yaakov that he outwitted me these two times?" (*Bereishis* 27:36). The idea is that first one has to battle against the evil inclination, the Satan, the ruling angel of Esav, and the only way to do this is with trickery and clever schemes. The *yetzer hara* knows human nature only too well, and only something extraordinary can beat it. Even though in most cases trickery and deceit are bad traits, since the Satan uses it against us, convincing us that our sins are in fact mitzvos, we are allowed to use the same traits in the service of Hashem. In fact, if one exercises these traits in such a way, he will exhaust his drive for trickery and will not need to use it in other matters such as business. However, only once one is victorious over the Satan, rules over his spirit, and only good is in his nature, only then is he called by the name Yisrael.

We see in Yisrael the word *sar*, which means "rulership," as in the verse cited by Rashi, "he ruled (*vayasar*) over an angel and triumphed" (*Hoshea* 12:5). We also see the idea of the name Yisrael implying a higher level in *parashas Vayechi*, where it says, "Gather yourselves and listen, sons of Yaakov, and listen to Yisrael your father" (*Bereishis* 49:2). Again we see that the verse starts with the name Yaakov and ends with Yisrael. What is the reason for this? He was telling them, "You, the *bnei Yaakov*, in your present form are on the lower level, as indicated by the name Yaakov. Therefore, it is fitting for you to hear the *mussar* I am about to give you and you will end up on a higher plane, on the level of *Yisrael*.

Binyamin — the Son of the South

The verse says, "But his father called him (*kara lo*) Binyamin" (*Bereishis* 35:18). The *Sefer Aparion* by Rav Shlomo Ganzfried, the author of the *Kitzur Shulchan Aruch*, asks why the text contains the superfluous word *lo*. The Torah could have used one word, *kara'oh*. Rashi explains that he was called by this name to allude to the fact that he was the only one of Yaakov's sons to be born in Canaan.

The word "Binyamin" is made up of *bin yamin*, which means "the son of the south," a reference to Canaan, which is located south of the lands to the north of Eretz Yisrael. The Aparion says that in *Megillas Esther* (2:5), Mordechai is referred to as an *ish yemini*, from the tribe of Binyamin. Why are we not told simply that he was from Binyamin? Why was he called an *ish yemini*?

The Midrash explains that people asked Mordechai why he was transgressing the edict of the king by not bowing down to Haman. Mordechai replied that while the other tribes' ancestors were born outside of Israel, his ancestor was born in Israel. Similarly, Haman himself asked Mordechai why he did not bow to him, since surely his ancestors (the twelve tribes) had bowed down to his ancestor Esav (on Yaakov's return from the house of Lavan). To this Mordechai replied that Binyamin, his ancestor, had not yet been born. By calling Mordechai an *ish yemini*, the verse in *Megillas Esther* alludes to the fact that salvation came appropriately through Mordechai, as it was the merit of his ancestor's being born in Eretz Yisrael that helped them. This is seen in the superfluous word *lo*, which means "for him." In other words, he was called this name for his own benefit. The merit of the idea which the name contains would help him in the future.

The Aparion gives a second explanation for the name Binyamin. Usually, the mother does most of the raising of the children. In Binyamin's case, his mother died during childbirth. Therefore, it was his father who took on the task of raising him. Therefore, he called him Ben Yamin, "the son of my right hand," as the right hand is the main hand. Just as one controls what his right hand does, so too, Yaakov would have to pay more attention to this particular son.

The Aparion then adds another explanation for this name. The Ramban says that the forefathers kept the entire Torah only while in Eretz Yisrael. Thus, although Yaakov could remain married to two sisters while outside of Eretz Yisrael, once he entered the land he would be obligated to uphold the Torah prohibition against marrying two sisters. As Yaakov was entering the land, Rachel died. This rectified the situation, in that he entered Eretz Yisrael married to only one sister. Rachel called her son Ben Oni, "the son of my affliction," but his father called him Binyamin, "the son of the south," to indicate that it was their entering Eretz Yisrael that caused this tragedy.

The Butler, the Baker, the UN and Napoleon

Yosef was cast into jail for a crime he didn't commit and was placed in charge of all the prisoners. There he met two of Pharaoh's servants who had fallen out of favor with the king. One night each dreamt a dream. The butler dreamt that he was squeezing grapes into Pharaoh's cup, while the baker dreamt that he was standing with baskets of bread on his head when some birds swooped down and grabbed the bread. Troubled by the dreams, they described them to Yosef, who interpreted them to mean that the butler would be reinstated, while the baker would be hanged. Many commentators deal with the question of how Yosef was able to interpret the dreams of the butler and the baker. What clues gave them away?

One approach is based on the following riddle. Two people drew paintings on a wall. One drew a child holding a bunch of grapes and the other drew a window covered by a curtain. The pictures were so real that a person who entered the room tried to close the curtain. Then a bird flying by tried to eat one of the grapes. The question is, which artist was the better of the two? Obviously it is the one who drew the curtain, as he was able to fool a human, while the other artist only managed to fool a bird. Also, the fact that a bird tried to take a grape shows that the picture could not have been very realistic, since no bird in its right mind would try to take a grape from a human. Using similar logic Yosef was able to interpret the baker's dream. The fact that a bird tried to take bread from the basket on the baker's head suggests it must have been that he was doomed; otherwise, a bird wouldn't dare take bread from a living human. This indicated to Yosef the fate of the baker.

Rav Elchanan Wasserman[35] gives a slightly different answer. Yosef saw the fate of the baker by looking at the role he played in the dream. The baker was completely passive while the birds flew in and took the bread from the baskets on his head. Since he was standing there doing nothing, he was like one who was dead, and that must have been what was in store for him. On the other hand, the butler played a very active role in his dream. He was constantly doing things, as it says, "and I took the grapes...I gave the cup into Pharaoh's hand" (*Bereishis* 40:11). From this we can see that he must have been destined to live.

We can also understand the difference between the fate of the butler and that of the baker in the way Yosef's answers are reported. Regarding the butler, it says, "and Yosef said," while regarding the baker, it says, "and Yosef answered." Rav Moshe Landinsky explains with a parable. When a doctor examining a patient sees there is hope he will advise the patient to take the medicine without delay. However, if he sees that the patient is suffering for the worse, he will voice his opinion only when asked by the family. The same applied with Yosef. He knew the butler would live, so he volunteered his opinion: "and Yosef said." With the baker, he knew his fortune was not good, and so he offered his opinion only after the baker pressed him for it. That is why it says, "and Yosef answered."

Napoleon and Yosef

The French armies were conquering eastern Europe when a nobleman of Kovno held a banquet in honor of Napoleon. The ecclesiastical authorities from all faiths were invited to come and make a speech in Napoleon's honor, with one exception — the Jews. Napoleon sat at the banquet as each speaker droned on, one after the other, singing his praises. The guest of honor was getting bored, so he asked his host, "Why is there no representative of the Jews to meet me?" The host searched for the nearest rabbi, who was brought to the hall trembling with fear at meeting the great emperor.

When the rabbi's turn to speak came, he began, "Your Honor, I'm not qualified to sing your praises. I'm merely a small-town rabbi, used to speaking only words of Torah."

"That's fine. I've heard enough praises from these people," the emperor replied. "I want to hear what your Torah has to say on the wars and campaigns we are conducting."

The rabbi was encouraged by the emperor's words and began to speak. "You may have heard about how Yosef was in jail and interpreted the dreams of the butler to mean that he would be reinstated to his position. Yosef subsequently asked the butler to put in a good word for him to Pharaoh so that he would be released. Yosef said, 'Because you should remember me when he will be good to you' (*Bereishis* 40:14).

"Why did the request begin with the word 'because'?" the rabbi asked. "Apparently, Yosef was also giving an explanation for his interpretation of the dream. In every government there are officials of different rank. If suspicion falls on a minor official, he will be arrested immediately and left in a prison cell for as long as the investigation lasts. If he is found innocent he may even return to his former office. A minister, on the other hand, is treated in a far different manner. If he is suspected of wrongdoing, the investigation will take place first. If he is found guilty, he may be asked to take early retirement, allowing the scandal to die out. If the offense is too serious, he will stand trial. Therefore, the chances of his returning to his previous position are virtually nil. The investigation would have already done the damage.

"This was also the case in Pharaoh's court. The butler was a high-ranking official. Under normal circumstances he would not have had a chance of returning to his previous position. When Yosef informed him that he would return, he was astonished, for this was not the normal practice. Yosef then explained to him that the decision to imprison him was taken before any investigation was carried out. Therefore he could return to his position.

"But why were events as such? Yosef answered, 'Because you should remember me when he will be good to you.' In the normal way of things, the arrest of the butler was unusual, but Providence sent him to jail before trial so that he would meet Yosef there. The only reason for the imprisonment of the butler was 'Because you should remember me,' so that two years after his release, when Pharaoh's dreams also needed interpreting, the butler would recommend Yosef to the king."

The rabbi continued, "Your Majesty, I can't help but wonder what brings you to the cold lands of eastern Europe. Everything you want is in the West. Also, how can we account for your remarkable victories over every nation? It must be that you have been sent by Heaven to see how the descendants of Yosef are imprisoned and suffering, how they face laws and decrees like no other. Heaven has made you victorious so that you should be sent here and see, 'because you should remember.' You must release the Jewish people from their suffering and persecution and improve their lot. Thank you."

Napoleon shook the rabbi's hand and thanked him for his wise words.[36]

The verse says, "Within another three days...and restore you to your post. And you shall place the cup in Pharaoh's hand like you did previously. Because you should remember me when he will be good to you" (*Bereishis* 40:13-14). The question is, Why, after Yosef told the butler he would be restored to his post, did he have to tell him that he would place the cup as he did originally? In addition, how could Yosef put all his trust in the butler? Surely one who trusts in man and not Hashem is not looked upon favorably.

Rebbi Akiva Eiger[37] says it is normal for a person who is sitting in jail to lament his crimes and take it upon himself never to repeat them. Once he is released he will be extremely careful not to stumble again. The butler also made such resolutions, vowing to be more careful in the future so that no more flies would enter the cup of Pharaoh. When Yosef informed him of his release, Yosef added that he need not worry about the future. This was because his imprisonment was only "Because you should remember me." Everything was orchestrated by Heaven so that the butler would meet Yosef, who in turn would set about his release. Therefore, Yosef added that his serving Pharaoh would be "like you did previously"; he would have the same tranquility and sense of job security that he had previously. Now we can also understand that, according to Rebbi Akiva Eiger, Yosef was not demonstrating a lack of faith, but on the contrary, was giving the butler a lesson in the workings of Divine Providence.

Don't Tell the UN

In my opinion, from the last two ideas, it is relevant to mention an idea spoken about by Rav Elchanan Wasserman.[38] He asks, how we are to determine where Hashem is guiding the world, especially in light of daily events? He first quotes a verse from *parashas Haazinu*: "When the Supreme One gave the nations their inheritance...He set the borders of peoples according to the number of *bnei Yisrael*. For Hashem's portion is His people" (*Devarim* 32:8-9). He explains that while all of Hashem's creations were created according to His will, the main creation and nation is Yisrael. We see from the above verses that even the boundaries of the lands of the nations were set according to the needs of the Jewish people. It follows that all events that take place in the world happen only for the purpose of how they affect Yisrael. This is seen in the prophet, where it says, "I have cut off nations, their pinnacles are desolate; I have made their streets waste so that none passes by, their cities are destroyed...surely they will fear Me, you will accept rebuke" (*Tzefaniah* 3:6-7). Rav Elchanan says that we also see this idea in the *gemara* that says, "Punishments come into the world only for the purpose of Yisrael" (*Yevamos* 63a). The Jewish people should see what goes on and take the lessons to heart.

Rav Elchanan was writing during the post-World War I years, in the dark times leading up to the Second World War. He continues that from the above verses in *Devarim*, we learn that while we think the borders set after the war originated in Warsaw, in fact, they were given the approval of the Heavenly Court above for the purpose of the Jewish people.

Whether for the good, the bad, or to give warning, all events that happen in the world must be seen in the context of their effect on, or what message they are to convey to, the Jewish people. The verses in *Devarim* support this idea, as the passage first talks about how the borders are set according to the needs of His people, and the reason for this is, "For Hashem's portion is His people."

Rav Elchanan goes on to explain that while we may not understand why any particular state acted as it did, if one puts things in perspective, looking at events over the entire course of history, we see how even remote, seemingly unrelated events had an effect on the Jewish people. An example of this is found in the Gemara, which mentions one who built a great palace, and its only purpose was that many years later a Jew would benefit from it. The same point was made when Yosef told the butler that his imprisonment was only "Because you should remember me."

Parashas Mikeitz

Teaching Pharaoh a Lesson

The subject of dreams continues into this week's *parashah*. This time it is Pharaoh's turn. Pharaoh's dream involved cows and sheaves, while last week we read that Yosef's dreams were about sheaves and stars. The Kol Yehudah[39] explains why each dreamt as he did. Yosef started by dreaming of the sheaves, a lower entity, and then dreamt about the stars, which are symbolic of things on a higher plane. Pharaoh started by dreaming of cows, which contain life, and ended up dreaming about sheaves, mere lifeless vegetation. Yosef's dream symbolizes the stature of Yisrael, who have to strive to grow and increase their level of holiness, as if to try and reach the level of the stars. On the other hand, Pharaoh represented the nations of the world, who only diminish in stature.

We see this idea with tefillin, which we first place on the arm, which represents physicality, and then place on the head, which contains the brain and has the ability to learn Torah. Similarly, on Chanukah, we rule like Beis Hillel, that we add a light each night, symbolizing the fact that we seek to grow upwards and continue to reach new spiritual heights.

Unsolicited Advice?

Yosef provided Pharaoh with an interpretation of his dream and concluded by saying, "And now let Pharaoh appoint a wise and understanding man and place him over the land of Egypt" (*Bereishis* 41:33). The question is asked, Why is it that Yosef offered this piece of advice? Surely he was consulted only to interpret the dream. Wasn't he overstepping the mark slightly?

The Techeles Mordechai[40] cites the *gemara* in *Rosh Hashanah* (10b), which says that on Rosh Hashanah Yosef was released from prison. It follows that Pharaoh's dream, which led to Yosef's release, also occurred on Rosh Hashanah. One could ask, surely it made more sense for this dream to be dreamt on Pesach, as the Mishnah in *Rosh Hashanah* (1:1) says that on Pesach the world is judged for produce, while on Rosh Hashanah people are judged. Yosef realized this and told Pharaoh that this dream was in fact appropriate for Rosh Hashanah, as it must contain a message for people as well, namely, that someone would be raised up and put in a position of authority over Egypt. His advice was all a part of the interpretation of the dream.

Another answer is provided by the Ari Hakadosh,[41] who cites the *gemara* (*Berachos* 55a) that says that there are three things Hashem Himself announces: famine, plenty and a provider. This is seen in what Yosef told Pharaoh: "That which Hashem is doing He has shown to Pharaoh" — in other words, the years of plenty and famine are being announced by Hashem through Pharaoh's dream. Since of the three events — famine, plenty and a provider — the first two are being announced through the dream, it must be that the remaining one, the appointment of a provider, is also being announced, which is why Yosef felt it fitting to tell Pharaoh, "And now let Pharaoh appoint a wise and understanding man...."

Supporting the Winning Team

The verse says, "And Pharaoh said to Yosef, 'Since Hashem has shown you this, there is none so understanding and wise as you' " (*Bereishis* 41:39). We see that the ruler in Yosef's time, despite being an idolater, believed in the interpretation of Yosef. In contrast, the Pharaoh in the time of Moshe said, "Who is Hashem that I should listen to His voice?" (*Shemos* 5:2). All the miracles and wonders failed to win him over. What is the reason for this difference?

Rav Yaakov Neimann[42] explains that the Pharaoh in Yosef's time heard great news — the stocks of Egypt were on their way up, and Egypt would be the only country to survive the global recession. It was very much to his advantage to believe in Hashem concerning these tidings. On the other hand, the later Pharaoh was set to lose his main source of labor. He was being threatened with the loss of all the cheap foreign workers, which would do great damage to his economy, and so, upon hearing such news, he did not want to believe in God.

These two divergent responses reflect the fact that there is a fundamental difference between a Jew and a gentile. A Jew, even in times of great distress, maintains his faith in Hashem. We all know of stories of great Jews defiantly keeping their faith in the face of their enemies, despite the bitterest pain, even until their last moments. On the other hand, a gentile retains his faith only when it is useful to do so. This is seen in the *chazal* on the verse "Behold, he was standing over the river" (*Bereishis* 41:1). *Chazal* explain that the Egyptians would worship the river Nile, and from the verse we see that they would "stand by" their gods. It's not that they would stand by them through thick and thin, but as long as they fooled themselves into thinking they were gaining, they would follow them. Once the benefits stopped, they would search for some other deity. On the other hand, Jews endure whatever it takes to sanctify and publicize Hashem's Name in the world. Whether one's lot is of plenty or scarcity, he always has to use his blessings in the service of Hashem and grow, rising spiritually from the level of sheaves to the stars.

Meeting Its Match

Regarding Chanukah, which falls when we read *parashas Mikeitz*, Rav Yaakov Kamenetsky[43] says that there are two types of lights we are commanded to kindle: Shabbos lights and Chanukah lights. Shabbos lights are solely for benefit and use, while it is forbidden to benefit from Chanukah lights. Another difference is that Shabbos candles are for *shalom bayis* (peace in the home), while Chanukah lights represent the lights from the Beis Hamikdash and testify to the fact that the Divine Presence rests upon Yisrael.

The Gemara (*Shabbos* 23b) discusses which lights are more important and concludes that it is the Shabbos lights. Why is it like this? The Chanukah lights publicize the Name of Hashem; what can be greater than that? We can answer this question by looking on a deeper level at what the Shabbos lights represent. The Shabbos candles represent *shalom bayis*. Simply speaking, this means the ability of the husband and wife to live together in harmony. On a deeper level, it symbolizes the unity of the physical world and the spiritual. The Shabbos meals are described as *me'ein olam haba* (a taste of the World to Come). How can it be that something purely spiritual can manifest itself in something physical? Rav Kamenetsky answers that the two worlds are somehow intertwined with each other, and we are therefore able to experience a taste of the World to Come even in this life.

Rav Kamenetsky continues that it is the way of our ancestors to connect matters of Heaven with everything in their lives. We see this with Yosef, who was having a conversation with Pharaoh and was asked, "I heard it said about you that you comprehend a dream to interpret" (*Bereishis* 41:15), to which he replied, "That is beyond me; it is Hashem Who will respond with Pharaoh's welfare" (ibid., 16), bringing Hashem's Name into the discussion. Following his interpretation, Yosef said, "That which Hashem is doing He is showing Pharaoh." This sort of talk continued until Pharaoh, who was a great nonbeliever, was forced to testify to his ministers and courtiers, "Can a man like this be found, a man in whom there is the spirit of God?" (*Bereishis* 41:37). This is an example of where the physical and the spiritual meet and combine in total harmony.

We are often confounded by events. One bumps into someone he hasn't met for years and says, "Wow! What luck!" The chance meeting then leads to a renewal of friendship or business contact for the future. Often we attribute such occurrences to the stars, calling it chance or luck. Or is it that Providence made you miss that bus in order to meet this person? Everyone has experiences where he feels something extraordinary made something happen. The question is, do we look at it as chance, or as part of Hashem's plan for the world? Although we do not have a Yosef to interpret everything for us, certainly we have to try to see how the hand of Hashem enters our lives. That is the lesson Yosef taught Pharaoh: in all incidents in life, it is Hashem Who is behind the scenes, orchestrating events in His infinite wisdom.

Parashas Vayigash

In a Meeting

In this week's *parashah*, Yosef revealed his identity to his brothers. After an emotional encounter, the brothers returned to their father Yaakov to bring him down to Egypt to be reunited with his beloved son. Let us examine some of the events surrounding this encounter.

"And they repeated to him [Yaakov] all Yosef's words that he had spoken to them, and he saw the wagons that Yosef had sent to carry him, and the spirit of their father Yaakov was revived" (*Bereishis* 45:27). The Hebrew word for "wagon," *agalah*, can also mean "heifer," or "calf." Rashi says that Yosef was sending Yaakov a sign, since the last portion they had studied together before their separation was that of the *eglah arufah* (the beheaded heifer). The *agalah* would remind Yaakov of what they last learned together.

Why was Yaakov's spirit revived only after he "saw the wagons," and not when they told him "Yosef's words"? One answer is that while Yaakov may have had doubts at the back of his mind that it was really Yosef, when he saw the wagons, which represented the last portion they had learned together, he knew with certainty that it was him. Only Yosef would have sent back a sign involving matters of spirituality. It showed Yaakov that Yosef had remained righteous despite being away for so long, and had remembered the Torah they learned together.

There was once a woman whose husband went on a trip and didn't return. Years passed, and she gave up hope of seeing him again, but she was tragically left as an *agunah*, a chained woman unable to remarry. One day, a man appeared claiming to be her husband. He did look somewhat similar to her husband, and was able to provide various bits of personal information only a husband would know, like what she ate for breakfast and where she did the shopping. However, while everything seemed to make sense, she still had some doubts within her, and so the matter was taken to the Vilna Gaon. He took the man to the local shul and asked him to point out where his seat was. The man became discomfited and admitted to being a fraud, sent by the husband to exploit the poor woman.

People were amazed at the wisdom of the Vilna Gaon, and he explained what led him to pose this question. "I always suspected the husband would fill the imposter in with all the mundane details about his wife. However, he would never have thought of matters of spirituality when trying to commit such a sin. He wouldn't think to tell him where he sat in the shul, or what he was learning."

Similarly, Yosef sent a sign to Yaakov involving what they had been learning. Any other information would have provided inconclusive evidence that it was in fact Yosef; it could have been someone else who had some details of Yosef's life. What was important to Yosef was what they had been learning before they parted, and with that Yaakov was able to recognize the wagons as coming from his long lost son.

No Time but the Present

The verse says, "and he wept continuously on his neck" (*Bereishis* 46:29). Rashi says that while Yosef wept on Yaakov's neck, Yaakov neither kissed nor hugged his son. Instead, he was reciting the Shema! Why did he have to say Shema at this particular moment? Surely he could have done it any other time. After all, he had waited twenty-two years for this moment. Also, if it were the correct time to say Shema, then Yosef should have said it as well.

The Maharal[44] explains that it wasn't the normal time for saying Shema, yet Yaakov was so joyous at being reunited with his son that he wanted to show his love for Hashem by reciting the Shema. Yosef, on the other hand, was involved in the mitzvah of *kibbud av ve'em*. Since that was an obligatory mitzvah he could not interrupt it with the nonobligatory mitzvah of expressing his joy to Hashem.

Rav Chaim Soloveitchik[45] gives a different answer. He says that really the correct time for reciting the Shema had arrived. Yosef had already recited it prior to the meeting. Yaakov, however, was involved in another mitzvah: he was busy fulfilling Hashem's commandment to go down to Egypt. A principle in halachah is that one who is involved in a mitzvah is exempt from fulfilling another mitzvah. Once Yaakov had arrived, however, he had fulfilled the mitzvah of going down to Egypt and was consequently free to recite the Shema.

Following their reunification, Yaakov said, "Now I can die after having seen your face, because you are still alive" (*Bereishis* 46:30). How could Yaakov make such a declaration? Surely it is forbidden to place an evil eye over oneself. The Maharil Diskin says that, as we have mentioned, Yaakov was saying Shema at that time. The halachah is that when we say the words "And you shall love Hashem...with all your soul," one has to be prepared to give up his life for Hashem. Yaakov knew that he was meant to have twelve tribes descend from him, and since one was missing he was suffering such anguish that he couldn't say this declaration with the proper intentions. Also, Yaakov had been informed that if all his children would outlive him, then it was a sign he would inherit the World to Come. As long as Yosef was missing he feared for his own sake as well. Now that he saw that Yosef was alive, he could truly declare his willingness to give up his life for the sake of Heaven. Therefore, as soon as he finished the Shema he said, "Now I can die," meaning that now he could truly die for the sake of Heaven, because he saw Yosef alive and was freed of his anguish.

How Old?

The communal leaders of Metz came to visit the Shaagas Aryeh[46] to offer him the post of rav of their town. They were surprised at his aged appearance, and they began to wonder whether perhaps appointing a younger man would be wiser. The Shaagas Aryeh sensed their feelings and began to reassure them. He related that Yaakov was taken to meet Pharaoh, and was asked, "How many are the days of your life?" to which he replied, "A hundred and thirty years. Few and miserable have been the years of my life" (Bereishis 47:8-9). The Shaagas Aryeh posed two questions on this exchange. Firstly, why did Pharaoh ask such a question? Is this usually a conversation starter? Secondly, how could Yaakov answer "few and miserable"? Surely he wasn't asked for such information.

The Shaagas Aryeh answered that when Yaakov would walk towards the river Nile, the river would rise to his feet and water the land. Pharaoh was particularly happy with Yaakov's arrival, for he understood that because of Yaakov's presence there, the famine would end and the land would be watered. Therefore, when Pharaoh saw that Yaakov was old and weary, he was worried that he would soon die, which would cause Pharaoh to lose this blessing. Therefore, Pharaoh wanted to know how old he was. Yaakov then answered that it wasn't because he was so old that he appeared so weak, but because of his suffering. The worry and the tragedies that had befallen him made him appear old. He then continued, "They have not reached the days of my forefathers in the days of their sojourns" (*Bereishis* 47:9). Yaakov was telling Pharaoh that his forefathers also suffered much and yet they still lived to old age; therefore, there was also hope that he would live long as well. The Shaagas Aryeh then said, "It is the same with me. If I look old it is because I have had a difficult life, but I assure you I will be your rabbi for no less than thirty years," which he was.

Parashas Vayechi

Israel and US

Yaakov's final days were drawing near, so he requested from Yosef that he be buried "in my grave which I have dug (*karisi*) for myself in the land of Canaan" (*Bereishis* 50:5). Rashi cites a *midrash* that says Yaakov took all the gold and silver which he had earned in the house of Lavan and made a heap (a *keri*) from them. The word *keri* is a play on the word *karisi*, and the *midrash* uses this to show that he made a heap and offered this entire treasure to Esav in return for his share in the Cave of Machpeilah.

The question is, What kind of business technique is this? Standard business practice says that he should offer him a slightly lower price, Esav would reject it and demand something higher, Yaakov would say "no way" until finally they would agree on a price, each one feeling that he got the better deal. Yet here Yaakov is literally throwing his money away.

Rav Yissachar Frand answers this question, citing the verse "And Yaakov feared greatly and was troubled" (*Bereishis* 32:8). The simple meaning of the verse is that he was scared of big brother Esav and the physical damage he would do to him. *Chazal* say that in fact he was fearful of the two extra merits Esav had that Yaakov didn't. Esav had honored his parents during the twenty-two years that Yaakov was in the house of Lavan, and Esav had also been living in Eretz Yisrael all that time. By offering Esav all of the money he had made outside the land, he was trying to negate these two extra merits Esav had. Yaakov was showing that he wanted to be buried next to his fathers, and that he wanted to be buried in Eretz Yisrael. On the other hand, by accepting Yaakov's offer, Esav showed how insignificant living in Eretz Yisrael was to him, and how little he really cared about his fathers.

Borders and Bedouins

With that said let me share one or two thoughts I heard from a guest speaker in yeshivah. In *Sefer Bereishis*, where we find the family trees of both Yishmael and Esav, there is a great difference in the endings of the two descriptions. At the end of *parashas Vayishlach* it gives Esav's genealogy, ending with the words "These are the chiefs of Edom by their dwelling places in the land of their possession" (*Bereishis* 36:43). In *parashas Chayei Sarah* it says, "These are the names of Yishmael...by their courtyards and by their strongholds...over all his brothers he lay" (*Bereishis* 25:16,18). In addition, Yishmael's rulers are called "chiefs," while the rulers of Edom are called "kings."

Rav Yitzchak Hutner explains the apparent differences. While Esav had land, Yishmael did not inherit any. Esav has the land which was called Har Seir, which was Divinely given to him. On the other hand, regarding Yishmael, Sarah said to Avraham, "The son of that slave woman shall not inherit with my son" (*Bereishis* 21:10). Sarah was alluding to the fact that Yishamel would not inherit any land. This also explains why Esav's leaders were called "kings," since they ruled over their specific lands, while Yishmael's leaders were chiefs, for without land they were more tribal in nature. Rav Hutner explained that because Esav has land of his own, he has no interest in Eretz Yisrael. On the other hand, Yishmael has no land and therefore has his eyes on Eretz Yisrael.

Yearnings

The guest speaker continued with a profound idea. "People are always buying new houses, renovating their old ones or buying a car. Does anyone in *chutz la'aretz* ever say to himself after making such a purchase, "Oy, oy! I wish this house would be in Eretz Yisrael. I wish I could have this car in Eretz Yisrael." He went on to say that these ideas weren't meant to be taken as political views, but as what a Torah Jew should feel. The point is that we have to want and desire Eretz Yisrael. If we don't want or desire it, then Yishmael certainly does, since Yishmael is upset with us because we got the land.

The truth is that three times a day in the *Amidah* we express our longing for Yerushalayim to be rebuilt: "And to Yerushalayim Your city may You return." We then pray for the restoration of the Davidic reign, then again we say, "and restore the service to the Holy of Holies," and then we pray, "May our eyes behold Your return to Zion." Out of nineteen blessings, no less than three have this theme. In *bentching*, both the second and third blessings contain these themes. From here we see that praying for Yerushalayim is a tenet of Judaism, to desire a return to the land under the Davidic reign.

On Tishah B'Av, one of the *kinos* we read describes the destruction of the community of Worms. The Sma wrote about why that community suffered more from the Crusaders than others did. The community was founded by exiles from the First Temple. Seventy years after the destruction of the First Temple the Jews were able to return to Eretz Yisrael and while they came from many places, none returned from the city of Worms. The community in Jerusalem wrote to the community of Worms, asking them to join them in Eretz Yisrael, and they wrote back, "You stay where you are in the great Jerusalem, and we will stay where we are in the little Jerusalem." It seems that a thousand years later retribution came for this sin. In our time as well one can see the warnings of the Meshech Chochmah, who described around the beginning of the twentieth century what the fate would be of those who called Berlin, Jerusalem.

Holy Land

The land also has specific warnings attached to it. The Jewish people were severely punished for the sin of the spies, which was caused by speaking badly about the land. Once a Rebbe came to visit Eretz Yisrael and went on a trip with his chassidim on a particularly hot day. When one of the Rebbe's followers approached him and asked, "Would the Rebbe mind if I took off my *bekeshe*? It's so hot out here for me," the Rebbe replied, "I don't care if you take off your trousers as well. Just don't say anything bad about Eretz Yisrael."

It is related[47] that when the Gerrer Rebbe reached Eretz Yisrael before the Second World War, he sent a letter back to his followers and mentioned "the holy city of Tel Aviv." His followers were taken aback. They could understand the holy city of Jerusalem, Tzefat or Chevron, but Tel Aviv? They wrote back to the Rebbe for clarification and he replied that while all the other cities contain mosques and churches, in Tel Aviv the only houses of prayer are shuls. One sees what you want to see in Eretz Yisrael. One can look for imperfections, or one can lift up his eyes and see its spiritual, as well as its physical beauty.

Shortly after the lecture I heard, I was in a taxi heading across town, when I got into a discussion with the driver. There's a famous joke that all the people who seem to know how to run the country drive taxis! His story was that he went to America at the age of twenty-one, got married and lived there for over twenty years. He had made it. He owned a store, and then bought a business or two, followed by a gas station. He lived in Boca Raton, Florida, and, he assured me, his house was absolutely gigantic. And yet he sold his business and moved back to Israel with his wife and two kids. He told me that he would love to move his house over here! I said to him, "Wow. You're like Avraham Avinu, uprooting yourself and coming to Israel."

He assured me with a look of satisfaction that he really was like Avraham Avinu. Yet I was still curious as to why he moved back, and when I asked him he replied, "I moved back because I wanted my kids to marry Jewish. It's terrible over there!" Before I could say anything he added, "But you know I want to move back!"

Life here in Israel had clearly been harder for him, and materialistically speaking, however nice his house was here, it probably didn't compare to what he had over there. I asked him what was stopping him from moving back, to which he replied, "My kids don't want to leave."

Whether we're living in Yerushalayim or New York now is really beside the point. What all of us must do is to desire the land more than Yishmael does, and pray with intent when we say the blessings in our davening, that we should be brought to the land for the final redemption, speedily in our days.

Shemos

Great and Small

People usually think that the sign of whether a person is great or not is how many headline-grabbing accomplishments he has to his name. While some of these acts may be great, the Torah shows us that in fact, real signs of greatness are determined by the small things one does.

In this week's *parashah* we are told how Shifra and Puah, otherwise known as Yocheved and Miriam, saved the newborn Jewish baby boys by defying the evil decrees of Pharaoh and refusing to throw them into the river. Rashi tells us that Yocheved was called Shifra because she would help form the baby (*meshaperes es havlad*), while Miriam was called Puah because she would help the mothers calm (*poah*) the babies. Everyone in Egypt knew of their heroic actions. They were famous, yet they were given these special names because of the seemingly small things they did, how they treated the babies they had just saved. There lay their true greatness, in the small things they did that didn't grab the headlines.

Rav Shmuel Rozovsky[1] says that in addition to their greatness in saving lives, the midwives were also prophetesses. Yet they were given credit (as seen in their names) mainly for the great self-sacrifice they demonstrated in dealing with the babies after birth. Their other achievements were of course admirable and involved unbelievable courage and strength, yet Rashi explicitly praises the way they cared for the children after they were born. Although these women did great things, what Rashi points out is that raising and caring for children after birth is no small matter.

Measure for Measure

The Torah describes how the midwives were rewarded for their deeds: "and He made for them houses" (*Shemos* 1:21). Rashi says that the houses of *kohanim*, *levi'im* and the kingship would descend from them. From Yocheved came the *kohanim* and *levi'im*, and from Miriam came the house of David.

Why were they given these rewards in particular? The Brisker Rav[2] says that Pharaoh's decrees were against only the males and not the females. Since Jewish lineage goes after the mother, this decree never threatened the existence of the Jewish people per se. However, the priesthood and kingship both go after the father, and these were being threatened. By saving these lives, they were rewarded measure for measure: their descendants would have the priesthood and the kingship.

The verse describes why they saved the baby boys: "And it was because the midwives feared Hashem" (*Shemos* 1:21). Rav Yaakov Kamenetsky[3] explains that despite the fact that they performed these great acts, and that they even cared for the children after the birth, which involved great risk and self-sacrifice, the verse here seems to praise them mainly for their great fear of Heaven. He continues that the Torah has already informed us about this, as it says, "But the midwives feared Hashem" (ibid., 18). By stating this at the beginning of the description of how they reacted to Pharaoh's decree, we see that their self-sacrifice in saving lives was only a result of their fear of Heaven. If not for this fear, which was deeply ingrained in them, they would never have put themselves in such danger.

Rav Yaakov Kamenetsky finishes by saying "and this is of the fundamental powers of a person which only Hashem knows." Only Hashem could give Yocheved and Miriam the real accolade that they deserved, which stemmed from their self-sacrifice. This shows us that it is often what other people don't know about a person at all which is his greatest praise.

Nothing Better to Do?

It is related[4] that one *erev Yom Kippur*, Rav Yisrael Salanter was seen in shul extracting nails that were sticking out of benches in the women's section. This is unbelievable. It was the day before Yom Kippur, the holiest day of the year. Rav Yisrael could have been learning, or saying *Tehillim*, yet all he had on his mind was that the women would be distressed at damaging their *yom tov* outfits. He felt their suffering and had to act. He knew that even at such a time, that was the will of Hashem, now and without a moment's delay.

One *erev Yom Kippur* in Pressburg the Chasam Sofer summoned his daughter for a mission. She was to go to the home of a particular orphan boy and tell him that after the fast the Chasam Sofer was going to propose a *shidduch* between him and an orphan girl, also from Pressburg. She was then to go to the other side of town and tell the girl the good news. His daughter was happy to carry out the mission, but before she left, she asked her father, "Can it not wait till after the fast?"

The Chasam Sofer replied, "My daughter, I must take this mitzvah with me to shul. It cannot wait."

Defying and Giving

This idea, that it is the seemingly small acts which matter most, is seen in a *gemara* (*Avodah Zarah* 18a) that says that Rav Yosi ben Kisma publicly taught Torah at a time when it was forbidden to do so by the Roman government. Rav Chananyah ben Teradyon came to visit him and said, "Don't you know this nation [Rome] was given dominion from Heaven? How dare you flaunt them?" Rav Yosi replied that he was hoping he would be shown mercy from Heaven. He then asked Rav Chananyah whether he would merit the World to Come, and Rav Chananyah asked him if he had ever done anything outstanding in his life. Rav Yosi replied that once he unintentionally mixed up some of his own money with *tzedakah* money, so he gave it all to *tzedakah* to remove the doubt. Rav Chananyah replied, "If so, may my portion be as great as yours."

This *gemara* shows us an amazing fact: Rav Yosi risked his life to teach Torah to the masses, yet only when Rav Chananyah heard about some "small" incident involving *tzedakah* money was he impressed. The highest form of greatness was not what he did in front of the masses, but what he did privately when confronted with a monetary question.

We find the same thing in Egypt. Everyone knew that Shifra and Puah saved the babies, yet they were given even greater credit for having cooed to them and comforted them to stop them crying after having saved them.

Another *midrash* conveys this idea. It says that Hashem doesn't elevate a person to greatness until He has tested him with some minor matter first. In Moshe's case, he was tested with caring for sheep. This is quite difficult to understand. It is said that when Moshe was born the whole house was filled with light, since he would later speak "face-to-face" with Hashem. Here we have the most holy of people, yet he is tested with mere sheep. What was so special about sheep that he had to be tested through them?

The answer is that while a leader of the Jewish people must fulfill many requirements, such as being a *talmid chacham* and a saintly man, a major factor in determining his leadership abilities is how he relates to the common problems people have. While a leader would love to be questioned only about matters of spirituality, he is just as likely to hear about problems of *shalom bayis*, business disputes, and the like. How he relates to the common man will determine his success as a leader.

Although it was already known — even from his birth — that Moshe was extraordinary, Hashem needed to test his ability to relate to the common man. Moshe was thus tested through his having to look after flocks of sheep. When Hashem saw that he cared for each one of them — how he carried the thirsty one on his shoulders, for example — then Hashem knew that he was ready to lead His flock.

Hold On

Another example[5] of Moshe's leadership qualities is seen when Moshe requested permission from his father-in-law Yisro to return to Egypt to "see if they are still alive" (*Shemos* 4:18). Rashi comments that Moshe was seeking permission from Yisro to go. The Midrash says that Moshe said to Hashem, "I can't do it. Yisro welcomed me and opened his door to me and treated me well. I can't go without his permission."

This *midrash* is unbelievable. The Jewish people are suffering daily, yearning for an end to their anguish. Moshe has a G-d-given command to go and redeem the Jewish people, yet he says, "Sorry, Hashem. I have to ask my father-in-law first." And this is despite the fact that Yisro received more from Moshe than Moshe received from him. Moshe rescued Yisro's daughters from the hostile shepherds. Also, the Torah says that when

Moshe agreed to marry Yisro's daughter, he also agreed to reside with Yisro. That he had to agree to it meant that Yisro had more to gain. (See the Midrash for more details on how Yisro treated Moshe at first.) Nevertheless, we see how far the obligation of gratitude goes, that Moshe even excused himself from Hashem, telling Him he had to gain permission from Yisro first before going to Egypt.

There is a *gemara* (*Bava Basra* 10a) that relates that the son of Rav Yehoshua ben Levi was desperately ill and fell into a deep coma. When he awoke, his father asked him what he had seen in his unconscious state. The son replied that he saw a world where everything was upside down. People who were on top in this world were on the bottom in the other world, while those who were humble in this world were right up there in the next world. His father said to him, "My son, the world you saw was not upside down; it was perfectly in order."

Some people are not so famous down here. Their names are not known the world over, nor are they particularly wealthy. Yet those who are quietly righteous are the ones who will be the stars of the World to Come. Again, this is seen with Moshe, Yocheved, Miriam, Rav Yosi ben Kisma, the son of Rav Yehoshua ben Levi, the Chasam Sofer and Rav Yisrael Salanter. Although it is easy to look at the headline-grabbing deeds people do and then to think, "Wow! That is amazing!" Heaven looks at our actions "upside down." Sometimes it is the small things that really count.

Whose Problem Is It?

The verse says, "Moshe grew up and went out to his brethren and saw their burdens" (*Shemos* 2:11). Rav Shach[6] comments that the verse is praising how Moshe would bear the burden of suffering with his fellow Jews. Despite his belonging to the tribe of Levi, who were not involved in the servitude, he was motivated to go out and see how they were suffering, to try and share some of their troubles. Rav Shach says that this was the foundation stone of Moshe's greatness, which made him suitable to be the leader of Israel. In every generation, its leaders are praised for this attribute, taking on the responsibility not only for the community as a whole, but for the individual as well.

I was once discussing something with a rav. In the middle of our discussion, we were interrupted, so he told me to call him later that night. I could call back only at an extremely late hour, so I asked if it would be all right to call then. He replied, "Whatever time you're up, I'll still be up." From incidents such as this one, we learn that the burden of the community's problems and the effort a leader puts into them is not always known to his congregants, yet we see it as the trademark of any great leader.

Focus on It

Rashi says on the above verse that "he (Moshe) focused his eyes and heart to be distressed over them." What is this telling us that we didn't know before? Surely if one goes out to see other people's troubles his heart and mind will be focused on them.

One answer is that there are two types of people who see someone's suffering. One type sees others in pain but life continues as normal. Let's face it. The daily news is only about the difficulties and suffering in the world. Often a five-minute news summary is a collection of the most terrible tragedies and misery perpetrated by human beings on their fellowman. After daily doses of this, if one ever felt bad to start with, he certainly won't feel too bad after a while.

Moshe Rabbeinu was of the second type. He actually focused his heart on others' pain to try and feel some of the burden with them. We see that this trait actually requires active participation, to try to visualize and feel another's suffering. The Midrash says that Moshe actually took off his princely garments and went into the field to help his brothers in their tasks. Hashem then said, "You left your comforts to participate in the pain of Yisrael. I'll leave My lofty place to speak with you."

The Alter of Kelm[7] says that we learn an unbelievable and crucial lesson from this statement. In this event, it was as if Hashem followed the lead of Moshe and began the redemption process. In other words, if we feel the burden of our brethren, if we pray for their recovery from sickness, if we daven that their wives should give birth safely, and so on, then a response will come from on High. If Hashem sees that the suffering of others is of consequence to us, then He will in turn respond.

What Is Important?

Sharing the burden of the suffering of others is actually one of the forty-eight ways in which Torah is acquired. One may ask, What has this got to do with Torah study? Surely factors such as diligence, concentration and perseverance are more important than this?

The Mishnah describes these forty-eight ways in which Torah is "acquired," meaning how it remains everlasting in a person. Without these traits one can still study Torah, but only with these special features will it remain within him. This is because Torah is not just another form of wisdom, something to undertake as a course; rather, it is our *horaah*, our instructions in life. One who does not try to attain these traits may be able to lecture on Talmudic analysis, and he may even be good at it, but he will never be a living example of what the Torah wants from a person. Sharing one's burden is one of those traits. Moshe, who excelled in this aspect (as well as others which are beyond the scope of this discussion), could go on to become the leader of *bnei Yisrael*.

At this point we have to mention the words of the Shela Hakadosh. The verses list the descendants of Reuven and Shimon, stating, "the sons of Reuven...the sons of Shimon...," yet only with Levi's descendants does it say, "These are the names of the sons of Levi" (*Shemos* 6:14–16), adding the words "the names of." What is the reason for this difference?

As we have mentioned, the tribe of Levi was not involved in the servitude as their brothers were, and yet they wanted to join in their suffering and feel their pain. Levi, in fact, named his children after the suffering of his brothers. The eldest was called Gershon because *bnei Yisrael* were strangers (*geirim*) in a land not theirs. The second was called Kehas, since their teeth were darkened (*kehas*) because of the affliction. The third was called Merari because "and they embittered (*vayemarraru*) their lives" (*Shemos* 1:14).

We have said (in *parashas Vayishlach*) that the name of a

person is highly significant, as it represents the essence of that person. Thus, we learn from what Levi did that a person should always join in the pain of the community, even if it is not directly applicable to him.

The Shela continues, saying that we saw the expression of this idea earlier, when Hashem revealed His Name to Moshe as "I shall be what I shall be" (*Shemos* 3:14). Rashi says that with the repetition of the words, it is as if Hashem was saying, "Just as I am with them during this trouble, so too I shall be with them during their subjugation by other kingdoms." After this Hashem told Moshe to reveal His Name with only one expression of "I shall be." The reason for this was that Hashem wanted to reveal this aspect — that He is with them during their current exile as He will be with them in subsequent ones — only to Moshe. He did not want *bnei Yisrael* to be informed of future exiles and therefore be further distressed at the thought that in later times they would again be in exile. Through concealing this information from *bnei Yisrael*, Hashem Himself was thus teaching Moshe that one has to be involved in another's suffering.

Where Is He?

It is related[8] that once during the First World War, the Chafetz Chaim's wife woke up in the middle of the night to find that her husband was not home. After going out to search for him, she found him sleeping on a bench. When she asked him why he was doing this, he replied, "The Jewish people are in the middle of a war. There are people who have lost their houses and been displaced from their communities. There are Jews out there tonight who don't have beds. How can I sleep comfortably in my bed when this is going on?"

We see this trait elsewhere, at the incident of the burning bush, where it says, "Hashem saw that he [Moshe] turned aside to see and Hashem called out to him from inside the bush" (*Shemos* 3:4). The Midrash says that it was precisely because Moshe came over to look that Hashem called out to him. The Midrash also says that when Moshe saw the bush burning, he said to himself, "This is a situation where there is fire and destruction, yet the bush is not being destroyed. If so, there is hope for the Jewish people. Although there is destruction they will not be destroyed.

One explanation[9] of this *midrash* is that Hashem was particularly impressed with Moshe for this. Moshe had been away from his brothers for forty years. One would have thought he would have lost contact with their suffering. Yet by having these thoughts about the Jewish people, it showed that they were at the forefront of his mind. He had never forgotten about their suffering. That is why it was then that Hashem revealed to Moshe that he was the chosen leader.

Another example[10] of Moshe's feeling the suffering of his brethren is found in *parashas Beshalach*, when *bnei Yisrael* were battling Amalek. Moshe sat in a position overlooking the battlefield, and when he would raise his hands above his head the Jewish people would be the stronger force. The verse says, "Moshe's hands felt heavy, so they took a stone and placed it under him and he sat on it" (*Shemos* 17:12).

The Gemara (*Taanis* 11a) asks on this verse, Didn't Moshe have something more comfortable to sit on, like a chair or a cushion? But Moshe decided that since the Jewish people were suffering, he would suffer along with them. Along these lines, the Gemara says that when the community is suffering, one shouldn't go to one's house and behave as if all is fine, eating and drinking as usual. Rather, he should feel the suffering along with his brethren. In addition, the Gemara informs us that whoever suffers along with the community will see its salvation. Similarly, the verse says about Jerusalem, "Be glad with Jerusalem and rejoice in her, all you who love her...all you who mourned with her" (*Yeshayah* 66:10). We see that those who truly feel the suffering of Jerusalem and its people and mourn for its loss will merit to see it rebuilt. May it be speedily in our days.

Borrowing for Free

This week's *parashah* describes how *bnei Yisrael* departed from Egypt. An unusual request was made of them when Hashem instructed Moshe, "Please speak in the ears of the people, 'Let each man request of his fellow and each woman of her fellow silver vessels and gold vessels' " (*Shemos* 11:2). They were to "borrow" from their Egyptian hosts precious items and they would then leave the country. Let us examine some of the issues and reasons behind this request, and look at four different approaches to understanding this episode.

The Gemara (*Berachos* 9a) says that Hashem instructed *bnei Yisrael* with the word "please." This word was added so that Avraham would not say, "Hashem fulfilled His promise of 'They will enslave them and they will afflict them,' but He did not fulfill 'And afterwards they will leave with great possessions' (*Bereishis* 15:14)." Hashem was, so to speak, worried that if *bnei Yisrael* wouldn't leave with great wealth, then Avraham would have claims against Him. The Gemara continues that upon hearing that they should "borrow" this wealth *bnei Yisrael* said, "If only we could leave now (even without the wealth)."

The Gemara then cites the following parable in relation to

this incident. Once a prisoner was languishing in jail, when he was informed that the next day he would be taken out and given a great fortune, to which he replied, "Just take me out of here now, even without the fortune."

Three Questions

The Vilna Gaon[11] asks several questions on this perplexing *gemara*. Firstly, even if Hashem did make a promise to Avraham, why did it have to be fulfilled by what looks like trickery? Surely Hashem has other ways of ensuring that His will is carried out. Why was this "borrowing" method used? Secondly, why did Hashem refer to the promise He made to Avraham specifically? It's self-evident that despite the fact that He said it to Avraham, Hashem would have fulfilled His word. Thirdly, the parable is problematic. If you say to a person that he will be free and receive treasures now, he would not spurn any of what is coming to him. *Bnei Yisrael* were also being freed right away and had the opportunity for wealth at that moment. This is different from the parable, which says that the prisoner had the chance to leave with the wealth only the next day, enduring another day of suffering.

The Vilna Gaon answers all his questions with the following idea. The full redemption from Egypt was in fact only complete at the Sea of Reeds when the Egyptians were drowned, measure for measure for what they tried to do to the Jewish baby boys. Since this was a part of their suffering, full redemption came with the miracle at the sea. This is seen from the verse "And also that nation [Egypt] I will judge" (*Bereishis* 15:14). This is because although the Jews were going to be in exile anyway, the Egyptians took the liberty of treating them worse than they should have done, so they received retribution in kind. For this reason *bnei Yisrael* were told to borrow silver and gold, only to satisfy the promise made to Avraham. Since Avraham considered the end of his children's slavery — before the drowning of the Egyptians in the Sea of Reeds — as the time of redemption, it was then that they had to receive their silver and gold. The real redemption, however, as determined by Hashem, was when justice was done with the Egyptians at the sea. Therefore, that is when they were really meant to receive all the treasures.

Now we can understand the parable as well. *Bnei Yisrael* would have said, "Leaving now even without the money is enough," just like the prisoner in the parable, because anyway they would receive even greater spoils at the sea. In fact they wanted the full redemption to be immediately, without having the worry of Pharaoh chasing after them, for they knew that the treasures would anyway come later.

Enticing Them to the Sea

Rabbeinu Bachaya and others say that while the borrowing and then keeping of the precious items may initially be viewed as somewhat of a trick, in fact it was nothing less than what *bnei Yisrael* were owed. The work they had done for the previous 210 years was worth far more than what they took.

The Ran, as cited in *Talalei Oros*, looks at this episode in a different light. He asks, Even though the Jews were owed their wages for these years, why did they have to go about getting it through this roundabout way, which could be viewed as trickery? The question becomes stronger when we consider that *bnei Yisrael* now had the upper hand vis-à-vis the Egyptians. The Gemara (*Bava Kamma* 27b) says that if someone has an item of yours, you are not allowed to take it back from him by sneaking in quietly; rather, you must enter making as much noise as possible and take what is yours. What then is the meaning behind this incident?

The Ran answers that in fact this whole plan was Hashem's way of avenging Himself against His enemies and of delivering them into the hands of *bnei Yisrael.* Hashem wanted to punish the Egyptians measure for measure — that they would bring themselves into the sea and be drowned, as they had done to the Jewish baby boys. Had Moshe told Pharaoh that the time of the Jews' servitude in Egypt was over, Pharaoh would have let them go, and certainly he would not have then chased after them. But Moshe asked only for permission to go and sacrifice in the desert for three days. When Pharaoh would be told the people had escaped, he would think that Moshe was just a liar and not a prophet after all, and it was time to give chase. Therefore, Hashem told Moshe that they should be commanded to "borrow" the precious objects, using this form of trickery, even though they really had every right to the money, as explained by Rabbeinu Bachaya. Then the Egyptians would be induced to follow them into the sea, and suffer their fate.

Since *bnei Yisrael* may not have wanted to use this form of coercion, Hashem said to Moshe, "Please speak...." In other words, they should fulfill this request even if they didn't want to. Pharaoh would interpret their borrowing and subsequent escape as proof of dishonesty and would pursue them. This plan was not known to the people and perhaps not even to Moshe, so they may have been somewhat skeptical about what they were instructed to do. Yet we are told following the sea crashing down on the Egyptians, "And Yisrael saw the great hand...and they believed in Hashem and in Moshe His servant" (*Shemos* 14:31). They now understood Hashem's whole plan in their borrowing, that the Egptians would chase after them and receive the punishment they deserved.

Please, Please Take It

Let us examine this incident from a slightly different perspective.[12] How can it be that the people would turn down money that was being offered to them? Usually one jumps at the chance, yet here Hashem had to implore them, "Please take the money." The answer is that by taking the riches, *bnei Yisrael* would be faced with the test of wealth, to see whether despite their riches they would still adhere to Hashem's Torah. Knowing that the test of wealth is harder than the test of poverty, the Jewish people didn't want to put themselves in that situation. Therefore, in order to fulfill the promise He made to Avraham, Hashem had to ask them to take the riches.

Avraham had actually faced both challenges. He left home lacking everything, and yet later on became exceedingly wealthy. Since he passed both tests, he implanted in his children the ability to pass them also. Therefore, despite their fears, *bnei Yisrael* could be asked to "borrow" their neighbors' wealth, as they could also pass this test.

This explains why they were instructed only to "borrow." They were being taught that it is better to view one's possessions in this world as only borrowed — after all, whatever one possesses ultimately comes from Hashem. Furthermore, the borrowing would also help *bnei Yisrael* after the sin of the golden calf. After that incident, Moshe prayed for forgiveness and said, "and if not, erase me please (*nah*) from the book you have written" (*Shemos* 32:32). It is as if Moshe was telling Hashem that if they would not be forgiven, He should erase the *nah* from the verse "Please (*nah*) speak in the ears of the people..." Although the people had sinned, it was with the wealth that Hashem had asked them to take.

The Ultimate Wealth

The Dubno Maggid,[13] who was a contemporary of the Vilna Gaon, comments that in fact the "great possessions" that were promised in Hashem's vision to Avraham was in fact the Torah which *bnei Yisrael* would receive forty-nine days after they left Egypt. Why then were they commanded to borrow material wealth if they were to receive the greatest prize of all at a later date?

The Dubno Maggid answers with a parable. Once there was a boy who hired himself out to a merchant for a number of years, for which he would receive a bag of silver coins in compensation for his work. When payment time came, the master felt the agreed-upon sum was too small a reward, so instead he wrote out a check for a far greater amount. He gave it to the lad, whose face dropped as he sadly put the piece of paper in his pocket and headed home. The next day the boy's father called on the merchant and said, "Thank you for the way you treated my son and for paying him more than you promised, but he's too young to understand what's behind a check, so could you at least give him some of his earnings in silver coins?"

So too, Avraham said to Hashem that the Torah is indeed the greatest form of wealth, but the nation emerging from Egypt would not be able to understand its value. They would ask, "What about the great possessions?" Therefore, they were commanded to take with them some tangible wealth which they could appreciate at the time. Fortunately, as our nation matured, it learned that wealth comes and goes, but the ultimate wealth of the Torah is here to stay.

Falling from the Sky

This week's *parashah* contains the landmark event of the splitting of the sea. On this episode, the Ibn Ezra asks, When the Jews left Egypt, why were they told not to wage war with the Egyptians at the sea — they were instructed to "stand and see the salvation of Hashem" (*Shemos* 14:13) — while at the end of the *parashah* they were involved directly in the battle with Amalek?

Rav Yaakov Neimann[14] answers that Hashem didn't want them to do battle with the Egyptians, because, should they emerge victorious, they would think in terms of "the strength and might of my hands," that it was their power and military prowess which caused the victory. Instead they had to be taught "Hashem is Master of war" (*Shemos* 15:3). Hashem wanted to sow trust in their hearts, so that they should realize where victory comes from.

In this respect, this battle was the "mother of all wars." It showed the Jewish people at the outset that although they would emerge victorious in their future battles, it is only because of the will of Hashem. Therefore, Moshe said to them, "Hashem will do battle for you and you remain silent" (*Shemos* 14:14).

And after the Egyptians were drowned, *bnei Yisrael* attained the highest level of *emunah* (faith and belief in Hashem), as it says, "And the people revered Hashem and they had faith in Hashem and in Moshe His servant" (*Shemos* 14:30). *Chazal* say that even the simplest maidservant merited Divine revelation that surpassed even that of the prophets. Now that the people had acquired the proper outlook after having seen the hand of Hashem, that it is He Who controls wars and decides who the winners and losers are, they could subsequently be involved in the war with Amalek.

Teaching at the Outset

Other aspects of our *parashah* also deal with issues of trust and faith in Hashem, in particular the portion dealing with the manna, the food from Heaven that *bnei Yisrael* ate all forty years in the wilderness. Rav Aharon Kotler[15] explains that this is in fact the fundamental source from where we learn the idea of having *bitachon* (trust in Hashem). Just like the "battle" at the sea was a hallmark for the lesson of belief, manna would teach all generations about trust. This is seen in the verse "And He afflicted you and suffered you to hunger and fed you the manna...that you should know that man does not live by bread alone, but by that which comes from the mouth of Hashem" (*Devarim* 8:3).

Rav Aharon says that all the wonders and miracles performed during the Exodus were performed only to teach future generations that there would be events which seem natural and perfectly in keeping with cause and effect, yet we have to realize that they are all really orchestrated by Hashem. For this reason, the Jews were commanded to take a single measure of manna and place it in a jar "to be kept for your generations" (*Shemos* 16:32). The manna in the Mishkan would serve as a living testimony to the way Hashem runs the world in a supernatural way.

Along similar lines, Reb Chaim Shmulevitz[16] says that the manna taught us about not only the nature of miracles, but also *bitachon*. Here was a whole nation in a dry, barren desert. They were allowed to take only enough food for that day, and no more. Any extra that was taken would spoil. They literally had no choice but to focus their attention Heavenwards and hope that more food would come. Every day, Hashem would provide exactly the amount for all their needs, "everyone according to what he eats had they gathered" (*Shemos* 16:18), and each person was satisfied with what he had collected. This would serve as a lesson for all generations that the sustenance they receive would be only "that which comes from the mouth of Hashem."

You Can't Be Serious!

The manna that *bnei Yisrael* were told to keep in a jar would later serve as testimony to how they lived in the desert. In the days of Yirmeyahu, the Jewish people were living under the threat of exile, and the Beis Hamikdash was under siege. Yirmeyahu came and said to the masses something along the lines of "Look, we're in trouble. Why aren't you learning Torah, which could save us?"

The people said to him, "With all due respect, Yirmeyahu, if we close down our businesses to learn Torah, from where will we be sustained? Who will provide for us?"

On hearing this he ran into the Beis Hamikdash and took out the jar of manna to show the people. He said to them, "You, see the word of Hashem" (*Yirmeyahu* 2:31). The verse doesn't say that they merely heard the matter, but that they actually *see* the matter of Hashem, in the present tense. He then said, "Hashem has many messengers and ways of sending sustenance to those who fear Him."

We see from this incident that manna wasn't a one-time

event, something for the history books. It served as a sign for all future generations, that what one receives cannot be put down to "the strength of my hands," but rather, "that which comes from the mouth of Hashem."

Sefer Yirmeyahu in fact contains certain other references to these ideas. "Blessed is the man who trusts in Hashem" (17:7) is said of those who put their faith in the right direction. Similarly, the whole of the last paragraph of *Birkas Hamazon* (which contains this verse) is a collection of verses relating to the theme of Hashem being the Source of all sustenance and blessing. It is as if this were the final message the Sages wished to impress upon us at the end of every meal, so that before we go about our mundane affairs, we realize that all our efforts bear fruit only if they are blessed by Hashem. On the other hand, regarding one who believes that all that he achieves is entirely of his own doing, it says, "Cursed is the man who trusts in man, and makes flesh his arm, and whose heart departs from Hashem" (*Yirmeyahu* 17:5).

A Matter of Interest

Rav Shmulevitz quotes the Kli Yakar, who says that the main reason for the prohibition of lending on interest is because it removes one from trusting in Hashem. One who operates a business looks Heavenwards in the hope that he will be sent customers and that his business will thrive. On the other hand, one who lends on interest has a known and fixed income, and even if the borrower is risky, he relies on the pledge or collateral that he holds. (This is all regarding lending to a Jew; as to the reason why one can lend with interest to a non-Jew, see the continuation of the Kli Yakar.)

Rav Shmulevitz says that it seems that because of the severity of not having one's trust in the proper place, *Chazal* say that one who violates this and lends on interest will not arise when *techiyas hameisim* (the revival of the dead) occurs. He concludes that *bitachon* isn't just a desirable trait one should try and possess, but it is what gives blessing and life to a man. It is fundamental to our whole perspective as Torah-observant Jews.

Along these lines, the Gemara (*Berachos* 4a) says that whoever recites the *Ashrei* prayer with the proper intentions is destined for the World to Come. There is also a halachah stating that when reciting the *Ashrei* prayer, if one lacks concentration when reciting the verse beginning with the word *pose'ach*, he has to go back and repeat what he has said from that line on.

Why is this prayer treated in such a special way? In addition, why does the verse beginning with *pose'ach* contain such a stringent law, the likes of which are found only in prayers such as the first line of the Shema?

The Gemara says that one who recites *Ashrei* with concentration is destined for the World to Come precisely because it contains this line: *Pose'ach es yadecha umasbia lechol chai ratzon*, "You open Your hand and satisfy the want of every living thing." We see that having *bitachon*, trust that everything comes from Hashem, is so fundamental that if one hasn't absorbed its meaning properly, he needs to return to that place in order to understand this lesson. With this we can also understand why one who recites this prayer with proper intentions is destined for the World to Come: because he lives his life accordingly, trusting that Hashem is the Source of everything.

I recently heard a *shiur* from a certain speaker who said that in the United States, originally they put the words "In G-d we trust" on coins only, and it was only later that they began to write the phrase on bills as well. What was the reason behind this change? Surely it couldn't be that the government became more religious. He answered jokingly that originally they thought that only one who was mainly using coins needed to trust in G-d. Later on the attitude changed and they realized that dollar bills are the god, so they wrote it on the bills as well. While he said it as a joke, there is definitely some truth in it. Let us take the lesson of the manna, that it is G-d Who sends the money, and not money that is the god.

Idol Worship

L ast week we spoke about faith and trust in Hashem. This week let us examine how those ideas manifest themselves in the Ten Commandments. The fourth commandment instructs us to "Remember the Shabbos day" (*Shemos* 20:8). Rav Yosef Chaim Sonnenfeld[17] was very involved in bringing others to Shabbos observance, and on Fridays he would go around trying to persuade business owners to shut their doors for Shabbos.

One Friday night Rav Yosef Chaim's rebbetzin became desperately ill, and so he went to call on a certain doctor. He knocked on the door of the doctor's home, and when the doctor answered Rav Yosef Chaim immediately noticed a lantern in the doctor's hand. He was very sad at seeing the Shabbos desecrated in such an unnecessary and casual manner, but he felt it was not the time to start a discussion about religion. They went to the Rav's house, where the doctor gave the Rebbetzin medication which improved her condition.

Afterwards, when Rav Yosef Chaim went out to accompany the doctor home, he asked him, "You are a doctor, so tell me, what proportion of the whole body does the head take up?"

The doctor, who was somewhat surprised at the Rav's interest in these matters, replied, "About one-seventh."

The Rav replied, "Wow, only a seventh. What would happen if one day all the limbs, sinews and organs decided they had had enough? 'It's not fair! We do all the work — the hands write, the feet walk, every part of us is important, yet when it comes time to eat the head takes all the food. When it's time to speak, again the head steps in. It's not fair. We want democracy!' The head would then reply, 'Indeed, that's how it seems, yet we can't have democracy, as the one with the brain must be in charge. This is only right, since I direct and orchestrate all the organs of the body and their functioning. If not for me they would all be worthless pieces of flesh.' "

The doctor seemed to be enjoying the story, so Rav Yosef Chaim continued. "One in seven is the same ratio Hashem used when He divided up the week between weekdays and Shabbos. On the Shabbos one refreshes his spiritual side. Also, from this one day, blessing spreads to the other days of the week, as we say in "Lecha Dodi": "For it is the source of all blessing." Just as the head has control of the entire body, so too, Shabbos gives the rest of the days meaning. Without the Shabbos one would become a servant to his passions and monetary aspirations and his spiritual side would be subdued. We see that it is the Shabbos which gives the rest of the week purpose. That is why it is such a fundamental aspect of being a Torah Jew, and we have to make every effort to preserve it, just like it preserves us."

The doctor was so impressed by the Rav's words that he vowed to begin observing Shabbos.

Banished Once and for All?

The second of the Ten Commandments is the prohibition against idolatry. The Torah in fact gives us many other warnings against idol worship, but the whole idea of idol worship is something we have great difficulty understanding. Why would one bow to a golden calf? Why would one send his children through fire? Did they really believe all those fairy tales about those wooden statues?

Fortunately, these forms of idol worship are somewhat rare these days, but once upon a time these practices were extremely prevalent amongst our people. If one looks through *Tanach* one will see countless examples of Jews involved in idolatry. Exactly why there was such temptation is beyond the scope of this essay, but suffice it to say that there existed a great *yetzer hara* for idol worship, one that we can hardly imagine, yet that would drag people towards it. Nowadays we are by and large untroubled by this phenomenon. This is because the Men of the Great Assembly saw the effects of the desire for idol worship and prayed for its banishment. This relegated idols to the history books, once and for all.

If this is the case, what meaning do the Torah's warnings against idolatry have for us? One answer is that today, we have to heed the verse "You shall not make...gods of silver and gods of gold" (*Shemos* 20:20). This means that one shouldn't make a god out of his silver, gold and money. This is a test which is perhaps no less difficult than the original drive for idolatry.

I would suggest that this answer applies in two areas. Firstly, it is very tempting to rest assured that the money one has will last him through thick and thin. Fixed income, "safe" institutions are words which make people feel at ease. As we saw last week in the Kli Yakar, we must not be tempted into ways of thinking that make us believe that we don't need to trust in Hashem; we must not feel too trusting of our own resources and initiatives. We must recognize that ultimately, Hashem is in charge. We must really mean "In G-d we trust." Secondly, we must realize that we are "working to live" and not the opposite. Unfortunately, one can get carried away and become a workaholic. While one may have started with good intentions, when one's work takes over his whole life, leaving precious little time for spiritual pursuits, a reassessment of one's priorities may be in order.

Big or Small Idols?

There is another example of how idolatry is applicable even in our times.[18] The Gemara (*Shabbos* 105b) says that for anyone who becomes angry, it is as if he worshiped idols. How can anger possibly be compared to idolatry?

The Gemara cites the verse "There shall not be a foreign god in your midst" (*Tehillim* 81:10). The Radziner Rebbe asks, "What is an example of a foreign god that's in one's midst? He answers that one's ego is compared to a foreign god. When someone gets angry, let's say because he feels someone is ignoring him, it is only his ego that is causing him to be upset. "Who is he to ignore me? Who does he think he is?" he thinks to himself.

Part of the reason a person gets angry is because things are not going his way. His will has been thwarted, and he can't carry out his plans. In fact, the underlying cause of his anger is that his vision of himself is too great. There is only one Entity for Whom everything goes His way, and that is Hashem. If we realized this we would understand our limitations and would not be brought to anger.

Therefore, when one becomes angry, the Gemara says, it is as if he is worshiping foreign gods, and which one in particular? Himself. The Radziner Rebbe advises us that before one becomes angry he should remember that this is a subtle form of idol worship, and that if he passes the test and doesn't get angry, he has successfully avoided idol worship.

Making It Worse

We likewise learn a lesson about the destructive force of anger from the plague of frogs. The verse describes how Aharon stretched out his hand over the waters and "the frog ascended" (*Shemos* 8:2). The plague involved millions of frogs. How can the verse then say that only one frog ascended?

The Midrash says that indeed at first only one frog emerged. The Egyptians grabbed their sticks and took a swipe at the frog, but instead of being killed, more frogs emerged from it. The Egyptians were determined to kill these new frogs, yet they couldn't; only more and more emerged until they covered the entire land.

Shouldn't the Egyptians have stopped striking the frogs and taken a look at what they were doing? With each frog they hit, more and more would emerge, so just by stopping they would have contained the plague somewhat. Why didn't they think of this?

The answer is that they became angry. Their will was not being fulfilled; their egos were being hurt. Once they were lost in their anger there was no turning back.

We see from this how damaging anger is. One loses his rationality and forgets about logic. Someone who becomes angry risks saying things and behaving in a way he will only come to regret later. In one moment of madness he could destroy friendships and trust that have taken years to achieve.

The Gemara (*Nedarim* 22a) says that for one who is constantly angry, all forms of Gehinnom rule over him. One meaning of this *gemara* is that he will receive a harsh judgment and be subjected to punishment. Another meaning is that he will also live a form of Gehinnom even in this world through his constant feelings of anger and where they will lead him.

In light of all the above teachings, we can better understand the evil of idol worship, whether those idols are of stone, silver and gold, or our own egos. Let us work to keep all forms of idols at bay.

Lots of Stories This Week

The following story will probably be appreciated by at least 51 percent of its readers. The Alter of Slobodka[19] once asked a young married student whether he helped his wife with the Shabbos preparations. The student said, "Of course. The Gemara (*Shabbos* 119a) says that we should do something to honor the Shabbos. I know my obligations."

The Alter replied, "That's very *frum* of you. Is the only reason you help your wife because of what the Sages said? You're so concerned for the honor of Shabbos? But the reason for helping one's wife is based on nothing less than a positive commandment of the Torah: 'You shall surely help him along' (*Shemos* 23:5). Certainly if you have a commandment to help a stranger, you must help your wife, to whom you have a greater obligation. This applies all the more so on a Friday when she is working hard to get everything ready in time for Shabbos. Is there a greater opportunity to fulfill the mitzvah of showing kindness?"

Some Torah As Well

The whole of *parashas Mishpatim* is dedicated to the laws regarding how man should treat his fellow. It is therefore somewhat surprising that this *parashah* opens with a lengthy section about how we are to treat a Hebrew slave. A slave is a man who was sold to pay off his theft. Had we been writing the Torah, we would have put people of greater repute at the top of the bill, such as those who lend for free, or unpaid guardians — but the common crook?

To answer this question, Rav Yaakov Neimann[20] cites the Alter of Kelm, who says that the Torah was given by Hashem, and we are His children, and if the Father has a child who is stealing, all of His worry and attention will be focused on correcting this. Therefore, the Torah begins the *parashah* with this section.

Rav Neimann goes on to explain that for this reason, the thief is sold, as opposed to being thrown in jail. In jail he would meet all types of common prisoners. This atmosphere is a great place for a criminal to hone his skills. He will tell his fellow inmates how he was caught, and they will be able to offer counsel on how to improve his activity in the future. Following his release from prison, he will have no means by which to support his wife and children, and more than likely he will return to stealing.

Therefore, the Torah provides a different solution. We sell him to someone who will be able to act as a good example for him. In six years he will learn to improve his character and gain proper *derech eretz*. His children will remain with him, so they will be influenced (for the better) by the master's children. This is because apparently, when people steal, it is only out of want of food. Now all his needs are provided for, so he can work on improving himself.

The former thief will also see how well he is being treated, since there are many laws regarding a slave that a master must follow. For example, if there is only one pillow in the house, the slave gets it. The slave will reason to himself, If they honor me so much, how can I ever be a robber again? Furthermore, the Torah worries about his future. The Torah instructs us that after six years he must be sent away with great gifts and sufficient money so that he can begin to provide for himself.

Who Cares for the Thief?

We can also understand the rule that if one steals an ox, then slaughters and sells it, he is required to pay five times its value, while if he stole a lamb, he pays only fourfold. *Chazal* explain that he pays less with the lamb because he has already suffered the humiliation of carrying it on his shoulders, while with the ox he only leads it away. Only our Heavenly Father could be sensitive to the embarrassment of a son even when he is stealing. This level of sensitivity would not be possible from a human, who would just say, "Well, who told him to steal in the first place?"

We see from here how the Torah cares for even the lowly slave and thief. Therefore, how much more important is it that we are given instructions on how to treat those who are more worthy. Let us take one particular example, that of the widow and the orphan.

Who Cares for the Widow?

The verse says, "You shall not persecute any widow or orphan. If you will persecute him (*aneh se'aneh*), if he will cry out to Me (*za'ok yitzak*), I shall surely hear (*shamoa eshma*) his cry. My anger will burn and I shall kill you by the sword" (*Shemos* 22:21-23).

The Midrash asks on these verses, Why does Hashem love orphans and widows so much? It answers: Because their eyes look only towards Hashem. They have no one else to rely on, so when something is troubling them they can only cry out to Hashem. This is seen in the verse "the Father of orphans and the

Judge of widows" (*Tehillim* 68:6). The Midrash continues and says that it follows from here that if one steals from a widow or orphan, it is as if he is stealing from Hashem. Therefore, he is dealt with in the way the above verse in *Shemos* describes.

The whole of the above verse uses double expressions. The Kotzker Rebbe[21] says that the reason for this double language is because when one hurts a widow or orphan, he is really hurting the person twice. Firstly, there is the usual pain that someone feels when one hurts him. Then there is a second type of pain they feel, since they are reminded of their state. They will think, "If only my husband were alive, I wouldn't be treated this way," or "If I had a father he would protect me." Because of this double dose of pain, the tormentor is promised to be dealt with in such a harsh way.

The following story illustrates this point. In the Chafetz Chaim's time there lived a widow who rented a small house from a very tough landlord. Times were hard, and because she was unable to make ends meet, the landlord threatened to turn her out on the street with everything she had. The townspeople tried to persuade him to have mercy on her, but their pleas fell on deaf ears. One freezing winter's morning she returned from the market to find the few possessions she owned lying in the street. Despite many pleas and protests, the landlord could not be moved to change his mind.

Time went by, and the Chafetz Chaim wondered how it could be that the landlord hadn't suffered for his actions. It wasn't that the sage was a vengeful person; it was just that he had total belief in the verse describing what happens to those who mistreat a widow or orphan: "I shall surely hear his cry. My anger will burn and I shall kill you by the sword, and your wives will be widowed and your children orphaned." In time, the punishment described in the verse in fact came about: ten years after the event, the man was bitten by a wild dog and died.

Avoiding the Army

In Russia,[22] soldiers would serve in the army not just for three or four years; rather, army service was a life sentence of a full thirty years. People would dread the czar's officers, who would come to the villages and take children with them. In desperation, many people would look for other children for the officers to seize, and unfortunately, orphans were often taken to fill the quota, as there was no one who would offer a bribe on their behalf.

At that time, there was a wealthy butcher whose son was due to be drafted. He bribed an officer to take an orphan instead of his son. When the Chafetz Chaim heard this story, he said, "Wait and see what will happen to this man." Thirty years later the man's own son was afflicted with cholera and died. The burial society refused to touch him because of his contagious disease, and the butcher had to dig the grave and bury his son with his own hands. It wasn't that the Chafetz Chaim was out for revenge. He was just a believer in the Torah's promise, "I shall surely hear his cry. My anger will burn...."

We can see how seriously our leaders take this Torah prohibition against afflicting orphans and widows in the following story. It was 19 Elul, less than two weeks before the *Yamim Nora'im*, when the chazan of the shul of Rav Yosef Chaim Sonnenfeld died suddenly. Following the burial, the *gabba'im* of the shul were extremely worried about who would lead them in prayer that year. The Rav assured them that everything would be fine and they should not worry. It was a few days before Rosh Hashanah, and still no one had heard of who the replacement for the deceased chazan would be. People again approached the Rav, who told them a chazan would be found. They went away thinking that the Rav himself would lead them.

On the morning of Rosh Hashanah, the Rav approached the

son of the deceased chazan and told him that he should lead the congregation in prayer. The congregation was flabbergasted; surely the Rav knew the ruling that a mourner should not lead the services on Shabbos or *yom tov*.

After the service, Rav Yosef Chaim explained to them what was behind his decision. The reason for the ruling that a mourner may not lead them was only because of *kevod hatzibbur* (that it may be slightly disrespectful for the congregation should a mourner lead them on this holy day). In this case, however, they were faced with a different situation. The chazan's widow was no doubt feeling broken at the sudden loss, and hearing someone else davening would only increase her anguish. Since it is a Torah prohibition to do anything that could trouble her, Rav Sonnenfeld ruled that it was extremely important for the son to lead the prayers and try and comfort the widow, and this would certainly override the prohibition against a mourner leading the prayers.

Fashionable?

On the last Chanukah before he died, Dayan Yechezkel Abramsky[23] was sitting in his chair when a widow came in to visit his rebbetzin. He got up and greeted the widow with a "*gut Shabbos.*" He then went over to the hall cupboard and took out his coat. He took it to the widow and said, "They brought me this coat this week. What do you think? Do you like it?"

What is going on here? An elderly man is asking whether his coat looks nice, whether it is fashionable? From here we can glimpse Dayan Abramsky's greatness. He was overlooking the honor due to him; all he wanted was to make the widow feel important because the Rav wanted her opinion. This is the theme underlying all the mitzvos in this *parashah*, that we should learn from these examples and increase our sensitivity to others.

Call 1-800-MISHKAN

This week's *parashah* begins with Hashem instructing Moshe to gather donations from *bnei Yisrael* for the purpose of building the Mishkan. In the first three verses of the *parashah*, the word *terumah* (a portion) appears three times. Rashi says that this alludes to three different collections. The first collection was for the sockets, which would support the boards of the Mishkan, the second was for the offerings that would go upon the altar, and the third was for the building fund.

We can understand why we need a collection for the running of the altar, and of course for the building, but why do we need one especially for the sockets? The sockets were not one of the larger items associated with the Mishkan. While many would relish the chance to donate the funds for the holy ark or the menorah, it is unlikely that there were many who would make a donation particularly for the sockets. Therefore a separate fund was needed for it.

The Beis Av[24] says that a special message is being conveyed to us here which emphasizes the importance of solid foundations. Building the Mishkan had to be done with the highest of motives and intentions. This is where Hashem would rest His Presence, and from the outset it had to be established with purity. The sockets were the foundation of the entire structure, and even if one builds the most magnificent structure, if the foundations are weak it is in trouble. The Torah is telling us that even though the sockets weren't the most desirable items to contribute towards, nevertheless, they also had to be made in holiness and purity because they formed the Mishkan's foundations. Therefore, they had their own special fund. So too regarding all our endeavors, if we lay their foundations with purity, they will be more likely to succeed.

Start Right

The verse says, "Take for Me a portion" (*Shemos* 25:2). Rashi comments on the words "for Me," that the donations must be taken with the requirement of *lishmah*, specifically for the sake of Heaven. We have a teaching that one should do mitzvos even for ulterior motives, because from doing them for impure reasons, one will eventually come to do them for the right reasons. Why then was there a specific requirement of *lishmah* here?

Rav Yaakov Neimann[25] says that there is reward for one's doing a mitzvah, even when it is not done *lishmah*, yet what he does will not cause a resting place for the Divine Presence. When it comes to building a Mishkan, all the efforts that go into it must be able to cause a fitting resting place for the Shechinah. Everything from the sockets to the holy ark had to be made with the utmost purity and devotion. Only if the giving is done for the sake of Heaven will it bear fruit.

The Dubno Maggid[26] says that Hashem wanted His building to be made of silver and gold, not because He loves or needs those materials, but rather because they are precious in the eyes of man. Hashem wanted man to give of what *man* loves most.

When someone gives of his most precious objects, some of his love will come with it. For Hashem's part, the Jewish people are loved and called "a treasured people." When the love of the people is forthcoming, then it is an opportune time to build a house for the Shechinah. Therefore, Hashem commanded that everyone give a part of his love for Hashem to construct the Mishkan.

The question is, How can one give of one's love, something which is purely metaphysical, hidden in the recesses of one's heart? Therefore, Hashem commanded that *bnei Yisrael* give of a material item. By donating silver and gold, something which man loves, he will be giving a part of that love which is hidden in his heart. The silver and gold acts as the receptacle for his love.

Sanctifying Everything

Rav Neimann then gives his own answer as to why *bnei Yisrael* brought physical donations of silver and gold when in essence the Mishkan was really a spiritual place. The whole purpose of the Mishkan was to enable the Divine Presence to dwell not only there, but also among the people. This is seen in the verse "And make for Me a Mishkan and I will dwell amongst you." It does not say dwell "amongst it" but "amongst you."

The purpose of the Mishkan was to bring holiness to all aspects of life. Nowadays, in our own lives, we must continue to behave with this same purpose in mind. The kitchen in a home, for example, has to be a mini-Beis Hamikdash, in that only kosher food emanates from there. One's table has to be a receptacle for holiness through the poor who eat there and the Torah one learns there. One can sanctify all physical matters, even when involved in the mundane. Therefore, the Mishkan was to be built of silver and gold, demonstrating that the physical must be sanctified, that our physical lives must be only holy, free of *tumah* and dishonesty.

Chazal say that each of the items the *kohen gadol* wore would atone for a particular sin, again showing us how the spiritual must manifest itself through the material. One must not learn and daven and then return to living a secular lifestyle; rather, holiness must permeate one's entire existence, even the more mundane matters, as symbolized by the Mishkan.

No Rush

Of all the items that were donated to the Mishkan, the precious stones — the two *shoham* and twelve *miluim* stones, which were donated by the princes of each tribe — were listed last. Why were items of such high value relegated to last place?

The Ohr Hachaim answers that it was because of the manner in which they were given. The princes saw all the people rushing to donate items, so they said, "Let them bring what they bring, and whatever is needed at the end we will donate."

One may have thought that this is the proper attitude. The princes were offering to give the entire remainder from whatever would be lacking. Yet we see that Hashem was not pleased with this approach, and their donation was listed last, as if it was the least significant. This is despite the fact that their intentions were for the sake of Heaven.

In fact, the desirable way of giving is when you offer generously at the outset, when you feel uplifted to give, and not just to finish the job off at the end. This idea is quite unbelievable. One would have thought that, on the contrary, the princes made a great offer. Surely any fund-raiser would be only too pleased to hear someone say, "You raise what you can and whatever you still need I'll donate." Yet the princes were taken to task for this. This is because for the Mishkan, the donations were to be "from every man whose heart uplifts him." The Mishkan wasn't going to struggle to be built. If Hashem desired it, it would come about. The only question was who would be privileged to donate. The princes missed the boat by not jumping in at the outset and contributing right away. They were somewhat negligent regarding the *midrash* that says, "More than the wealthy person does for the poor person, the poor does for the wealthy."

Similarly, it is related that someone once came to the Chafetz Chaim and offered to underwrite the entire cost of running the yeshivah. Yet what did the Chafetz Chaim do? He refused to accept. He didn't want to remove the merit of supporting the yeshivah from the rest of the people.

Stories This Week As Well

When Rav Leizer Gordon got married, his father-in-law offered to support him in learning. In those days that meant living in his father-in-law's house and being sheltered and fed so that he could learn. Rav Leizer's reputation was good, and he was approached by one community after another to become a community rav. Each time he would ask his father-in-law for permission to take a position, he would be denied permission; he was told that he had to sit and learn. Finally, after many years, his mother-in-law said, "It's time for him to move on. We can't support him forever."

His father-in-law replied, "We never know who is supporting who," and pushed it off again. Eventually Rav Leizer went and took up a position as a rav. The day after he left his father-in-law's house, his father-in-law died.

The Ohr Hachaim gives another reason for the precious stones being listed last. *Chazal* say that the clouds would bring the stones to the princes. Therefore, what they gave, despite its high value, was done without any effort or monetary sacrifice on their part. This was unlike the rest of the people, who had to carry heavy skins and wood all the way from Egypt.

What a person has toiled for and acquired with his own effort is far more precious to him than what comes to him for free, as seen in the Gemara (*Bava Metzia* 38a): "A man prefers a *kav* of his own to nine of his fellow's." Therefore, the common folk, who would give bronze of their own, were more meritorious than the ones who gave precious stones. This was because their offerings came of their own efforts. Their giving had far greater significance to them, as it was from what they had toiled for.

The Urim Vetumim: Past and Present

Parashas Tetzaveh describes the priestly garments worn by the *kohanim*. The *kohen gadol* would wear the full eight garments, while the regular *kohanim* would wear only four. Following the description of the breastplate, worn by the *kohen gadol*, the Torah says, "Into the breastplate of judgment shall you place the *Urim Vetumim*" (*Shemos* 28:30). What were the *Urim Vetumim*, what did they do, why were they given that name, and why have we never heard of them until now? Let us follow the path of the Ramban to understand this fascinating item.

The breastplate of the *kohen gadol* was folded in half so that there was a pouchlike pocket inside. The side facing out contained the twelve stones representing the twelve tribes. These were the stones which were brought by the princes (see last week for more details on this). The *Urim Vetumim* consisted of a piece of parchment which contained Hashem's holy Name. According to some opinions it contained several of Hashem's Names. This parchment was placed inside the pouch.

Why are we not commanded to "make" the *Urim Vetumim*,

but are only told to "place" them into the breastplate? The answer is that the *Urim Vetumim* were different from the other utensils of the *kohen gadol*. They served a purely spiritual function, more so than any other item in the Mishkan, so they could not be made by ordinary people. They were written solely by Moshe himself, who was on the highest level, deemed worthy to speak to Hashem and receive the Torah. Only he could make them, as they were a way of communicating Divine messages from above. They were mainly used to seek answers as to whether or not to go to war, or as to who would be the first to lead *bnei Yisrael*. That is why we don't find them listed among the items brought for the Mishkan.

Light and Analysis

Let us examine the meaning of the words *urim* and *tumim* in order to gain some insight into what their function was. The word *urim* means "light," signifying that when a person would pose a question to the *Urim Vetumim*, certain letters on the breastplate would light up. The word *tumim* means "completeness." The *kohen gadol* would see the lit-up letters and would hopefully know how to unscramble the hidden code. He had to be on the level to arrange the letters in the correct way in order to understand their true interpretation. If he were not on this level there could be misinterpretations and the consequences could prove costly. If read correctly he would get a complete and true picture of how to proceed.

Rabbeinu Bachaya describes the procedure for inquiring of the *Urim Vetumim*. Only the king or another representative of the community was permitted to ask. The *kohen gadol*, wrapped in the splendor of his priestly garments, would stand facing the holy ark. The inquirer would stand behind the *kohen gadol*. He wouldn't raise his voice and shout out the question, neither would he silently think about his question. Rather, he would speak like someone praying, with his words quietly leaving his mouth. The *kohen gadol* would immediately become enveloped in *ruach hakodesh* and would look at the *Urim Vetumim* to see which letters lit up.

One example of when the *Urim Vetumim* were consulted was when *bnei Yisrael* first crossed into Eretz Yisrael and had to decide which tribe would lead them in the war against the Canaanites. When Pinchas, the *kohen gadol*, inquired of the *Urim Vetumim,* the name Yehudah lit up, along with the letters spelling the word *yaaleh* (to go up). While the letters had other permutations and combinations, the *kohen gadol* had the wisdom to understand what they alluded to.

Not So Smart

On the other hand, the letters could also be misunderstood. The Vilna Gaon[27] cites an incident at the beginning of the First Book of Shemuel. Chana was a barren woman who went to the Mishkan to pour out her heart to Hashem and implore Him to give her children. Eli, the *kohen gadol*, saw her unusual intensity and accused her of being drunk: "How long will you act drunkenly? Remove the wine from yourself" (I *Shemuel* 1:14). Chana then answered him "No, my lord, I am a woman of aggrieved spirit. I have drunk neither wine nor aged wine, and I have poured my soul before Hashem" (ibid., 15). The Vilna Gaon says that Eli knew that Chana was a righteous woman; therefore, he couldn't understand why she was acting this way. He consulted the *Urim Vetumim* and the letters that came up spelled the word *kesheirah*, indicating that she was kosher and he should not suspect her. However, he misinterpreted the letters and saw that they also spelled *shikorah* (a drunkard). The Gemara tells us that when she said "No, my lord..." she continued and said, "You are not a master in this matter; there is not sufficient holy spirit within you that you know how to interpret correctly the *Urim Vetumim*."

In the last years of the First Temple era, King Yoshiah, seeing that the land would be conquered, hid away some of the most holy items, lest they fall into the wrong hands. He hid the holy ark and the anointing oil, as well as the *Urim Vetumim*. These items were not recovered for use in the Second Temple and are most likely still hidden beneath the Temple Mount.

Now that we are without the physical *Urim Vetumim*, what is left of their spiritual power? I saw an unbelievable idea cited by Rav Yissachar Frand, who quotes the *sefer Beis Av*. He says that certain people are blessed, even nowadays, with *Urim*, which as mentioned, means "light." It is well known that light is often a metaphor for Torah. Thus, people blessed with *Urim* have great abilities, knowledge and depth in Torah. However, not everyone who has the *Urim* has the *Tumim*. What then is the *Tumim* power of nowadays that they lack? This is a much rarer commodity and is possessed by even fewer still: it is the power to interpret what the Torah is saying and apply it to one's decisions and the questions one is asked. It refers to having true *daas Torah*.

Wipe Out...Almost

An example of this is in the haftarah of *parashas Zachor*. The prophet Shemuel told King Shaul to go out and obliterate Amalek. He was commanded to kill men, women and children, and even the animals, all as the will of Hashem. He indeed killed almost all of them, but left the king and all the animals alive. Hashem was angry with Shaul and told Shemuel to take the monarchy from him, yet when Shaul came back from the battlefield he said to Shemuel, "I have fulfilled the word of Hashem" (I *Shemuel* 15:13).

What was going on here? How could Shaul claim to have carried out Hashem's mission when he had not? The answer is that Shaul truly believed that what he was doing was the will of Hashem. He thought that by saving the animals and offering them as sacrifices, he would be doing a *kiddush Hashem*. This was an example of having the *Urim*, but not the *Tumim*. For whatever reason, Shaul was blinded into misinterpreting the word of Hashem. And so the story continued with the reemergence of Amalek and the problems it causes us to this very day.

Another example of having the *Urim* without the *Tumim* appears at the end of *Sefer Shofetim*. The story of the concubine in Givah is one of the most tragic incidents in the history of the Jewish people. The tribes gathered against Binyamin and fought a war, with thousands upon thousands being killed on both sides. The war seemed justified, for an outrageous deed was done and the tribes wanted to avenge it. However, after the event we are told that they had second thoughts about having waged war against Binyamin. They sat down and cried, did *teshuvah* and tried to come up with ways of preserving the tribe of Binyamin.

If their intentions at the outset were so noble, how then did the tribes get so carried away on the road to disaster? The last verse of *Sefer Shoftim* gives us the answer: "In those days there was no king in Israel; each man did as he saw fit in his own eyes." This reflects the idea above. One may be well versed in Torah, act for the sake of Heaven with good intentions, have the light of the *Urim* in full force. Yet if one does not have access to one who possesses the *Tumim*, he will not be able to interpret the *Urim* correctly.

With this we can understand the importance to us of the *roshei yeshivah* and *gedolei Yisrael*, who literally act as eyes for the generation. Here in Eretz Yisrael we see people come from all over the world to seek their advice and counsel on difficult questions, on the best way to run a particular institution, how a specific person can find the right *shidduch*, how to gain mercy from Heaven for a sick person, and so on. The opinions of those who hold the *Tumim* are highly valued, because of their ability to understand the will of Hashem.

The Chafetz Chaim was known as the *Tumim* of his generation, a man connected with Torah in a way that is beyond our comprehension. In more recent times we have seen the Chazon Ish, the Steipler Gaon and Rav Shach, amongst a few others. While a number of eyes are open to *Urim*, only a select few possess the ability of *Tumim* as well.

When Half Is Better
Than Whole

This week's *parashah* contains the mitzvah of *machatzis hashekel*, the commandment that each male above the age of twenty give a half-shekel to the communal funds. One of the purposes of this mitzvah was to serve as a census of the adult male population.

There is a rather unusual instruction regarding the donation of the half-shekel: "The wealthy shall not increase and the poor shall not decrease from half of the shekel" (*Shemos* 30:15). Surely, a command to give a half-shekel means one should give only a half-shekel. Why does the Torah have to explicitly warn us against giving more or giving less? If you were to say that giving more would ruin the head count, why not have everyone give a note? Some would give one dollar and others a hundred, and they would just count the pieces of paper. What is the reason for the Torah's insistence on the half-shekel donation? We can understand that when you ask for a minimum everyone comes up with excuses, but why should people be prevented from giving more?

Rav Yerucham Levovitz[28] says that this mitzvah has an important underlying message. There is often a desire for the wealthy man to want to give more than his neighbor. He may see it as beneath his dignity to give the same amount as the common man. This attitude has to be countered, and that is what the giving of the half-shekel did.

To cite a modern-day example, when you walk onto a British Airways plane you step on at the front and see the first-class seats that people pay thousands for to ensure that they have a good night's sleep. As you move further back you see the business class with their wide seats and ample legroom. Immediately upon being seated these passengers will be offered a glass of wine. As you move even further back there is a small section called economy class where you pay normal prices to get from A to B. This is what's known as price and product differentiation. On the other hand, if you fly charter or with a budget airline you are treated to a different experience. First class doesn't exist, because many seats are packed in, sardinelike, in order to economize as much as possible. On some airlines there is not even any seat allocation; the first ones on board get the window (or aisle) seats. Yet everyone will reach their destination. Even if one wanted to pay extra for a more comfortable ride, such facilities do not exist on these carriers.

And so it is with the half-shekel. It acts as an equalizer. The message is that the rich shouldn't get too haughty just because they have more luggage. Rather, everyone is viewed as equal regardless of economic status.

When Go Merged with Easyjet

The airline metaphor is even more apt when we consider that the Torah says that the half-shekel be given "to atone for your souls" (*Shemos* 30:15). The Me'am Loez says that when it comes to atoning and saving oneself from death, there is no difference between the rich and the poor. If the rich were allowed to give more, then people would say, "It's not fair. The rich are more worthy before Hashem. They were given more and they can give more, so they have a better chance of being saved." On the other hand, had the Torah allowed people to give a lesser amount, then the poor would be embarrassed. Therefore, Hashem commanded that everyone give an amount which even the poor could afford. This system would convey the message that before Hashem all are equal. There is no first class when it comes to atonement.

As mentioned, since the half-shekel was given as an atonement, rich and poor alike gave equally, to show that in these matters, their souls are equal. This was unlike the contributions for the Mishkan, where varying amounts were collected. Rav Aryeh Leib Nathanson[29] (the father of the Shoel Umeishiv) says that it cannot be that Hashem gave this mitzvah because of the external amount that would be collected, for the Jewish people are the smallest of all nations and could gather only a relatively small amount of wealth. Rather, the Jewish people's value lies in their inner souls and in the perfection that they strive for. In this feature they excel above all the nations. The Torah's requirement of a half-shekel demonstrates that a person's worth is measured by his inner self, not his earthly possessions.

With this we can understand a statement in the Gemara (*Megillah* 13b) that says, "It was revealed before Hashem that in the future, Haman would weigh out shekels for the privilege of killing the Jews. Therefore, Hashem preceded Haman's shekels with their shekels." Haman argued before Achashveirosh that the Jewish people are small and scattered amongst the people, and therefore if the king got rid of them he wouldn't stand to lose much revenue. Haman's shekels were viewed on a superficial level, in terms of what the king would lose in tax revenues should the Jews not be around. Hashem countered this by giving *bnei Yisrael* the mitzvah of the half-shekel, which demonstrates that a person's true value stems from his inner worth before Hashem.

The Full Shekels amongst Us

There is another message in the fact that the commandment was to give only a half-shekel and not a whole shekel. Each person's giving only a half — in other words, something incomplete — shows us that an individual is also incomplete. Only when he joins with others is he viewed as complete. This counters the views of those who think that they are above the *tzibbur*, since in fact the ideal position of a Jew is to be part of a community. This is seen in the requirement of a minyan for prayer. Only when one is part of the wider community are his prayers best received. (See Rav Dessler, who writes regarding Rosh Hashanah that one's prospects of a favorable judgment are greatly improved if he davens as part of a community.)

Rav Yosef Chaim Sonnenfeld[30] employs this idea to give us a unique insight into the first *mishnah* of *Shekalim*: "On the first of the month an announcement is made regarding the donation of shekalim and *kilayim* (forbidden mixtures of crops)." What is the connection between these two seemingly unrelated matters?

Rav Sonnenfeld explains using the idea of how essential social interaction is. If one leads a totally self-centered life he is considered an incomplete person. On the other hand, when mixing with people one must be careful to choose friends of a caliber that will bring him closer to Torah and mitzvos. Just as certain crops are forbidden to be mixed, so too, associating with people of questionable character is unwise.

We also see this idea in the Mishnah (*Avos* 2:13), where they asked Rabbi Yehoshua what is the proper way that a man should cling to, and he answered, a good friend. They then asked him what one should avoid most, and he answered, a wicked friend. Just as social interaction is important to one's essence as a Jew, the other side of the coin is that he should ensure he is around only the right sort of people. This is the connection between the half-shekel and *kilayim*: when interacting socially one should pursue some relationships and avoid others.

Unity in Building

Rav Chaim Shmulevitz[31] explains that there is another lesson to be derived from the fact that everyone gives equally. There was a second half-shekel that was given specifically for the collection of the sockets used to support the pillars of the Mishkan, while donations for other items in the Mishkan were not limited to a specific amount; each person could give as he wished.

As we mentioned two weeks ago, the sockets represented the foundations of the structure; therefore, at the outset the Mishkan had to be seen as being from everyone. The foundation of the Mishkan could be built only through the *tzibbur* joining together and not by individuals. If all give equally, then the foundation is given from the *tzibbur*, but if one gives more and others give less, then it is considered as coming from individuals.

The purpose of the Mishkan was to be a resting place for the Shechinah on earth, and the only way this can come about is when everyone is united. Perhaps now we can also understand the *chazal* that says that the Second Beis Hamikdash was destroyed because of *sinas chinam* (baseless hatred). From the beginning, the Mishkan had to be built with unity and togetherness. When that ended, it was destroyed.

The Torah says that the half-shekel had to be given by "everyone who passes through the census" (*Shemos* 30:13). The

Yerushalmi (*Shekalim* 81) says that the "passing through" refers to those who crossed the sea. The question is, what has the giving of the half-shekel got to do with the crossing of the sea?

Rav Moshe Shternbuch[32] cites the *midrash* that says that at the time of the crossing of the sea there was an accusation in Heaven: "Surely these [the Egyptians] are idolaters, and You're going to kill them, but *bnei Yisrael* are also idolaters!" The Meshech Chochmah relates that this accusation was made specifically here at the sea because at that point *bnei Yisrael* were no longer united. They were split into four groups, each with its own plan of action. Once they were fragmented, then an accusation against them could be heard. The remedy for this disunity is the half-shekel, where everyone gives the same amount, and then the half-shekels all unite. One of the uses of this money was for the community offerings, and the merit of the community stands by all individuals. History has shown that indeed, when Jews are united they have been able to withstand many trials and tribulations.

Parashas Vayakhel

Putting Money on the Horses

Reb Chaim of Volozhin would personally go collecting for his yeshivah until eventually he became too old for the long trips and appointed a fund-raiser on his behalf. The fund-raiser would write down in his records how much each donor had given and would present the list to Reb Chaim to bless the donors.

One time the collector came up with a business idea: "Each time I go out collecting I have to spend much time on the roads, traveling slowly from village to village," he said. "In the winter it's freezing and in the summer it's hot. If we got our own horse and cart, I could travel much faster, visit more people and collect more money." Reb Chaim accepted his request.

And so it was. The fund-raiser set out the next time and collected the money, traveling via his horse and cart. When he returned Reb Chaim perused the list of donors and noted that the name of his biggest benefactor was absent from the list. "What happened? Is there no money in his house?" asked Reb Chaim.

The collector replied, "Indeed, there was, but he opened the door, saw the new horse and cart and said, 'I give to Torah and not for horses' before slamming the door in my face." Reb

Chaim replied that he would personally travel with the collector next time he visited this man.

Of course, the next time, when the donor saw the great sage at the door, he welcomed them in. The Rav explained to him an insight gleaned from our *parashah*. "The Torah lists the praises of Betzalel, 'to weave designs, to work with gold, silver' (*Shemos* 35:32). There is another meaning of what those designs were. The Mishkan was commanded to be given from all those of 'generous heart,' and the giving was dependent on the level of purity of heart and willingness to give. Each person in Yisrael gave with different intentions. Part of Betzalel's job in 'weaving designs' was to discern each donor's intentions when he gave. The gold that was donated with the purest intentions would be used in the cover on the ark. That which was given with less pure intentions would go towards more peripheral items. All was according to the intentions of the giver."

Reb Chaim then explained why he had cited this episode: "Nowadays we don't have the Mishkan; neither do we have a Betzalel who can discern thoughts and intentions. Yet Hashem Himself oversees this. *Chazal* say that the yeshivos and *battei medrash* are equivalent to a minature Beis Hamikdash and it is there that Hashem rests His presence. Those who learn Torah are the equivalent of the golden ark. Hashem also guides where each donor's money goes. If one gives with a pure heart, then the money will go to the food and drink, the equivalent of the sacrifices and libation offerings, that will sustain the students and enable them to diligently learn Hashem's Torah, as symbolized by the golden ark itself. If one gives with a less pure heart, indeed, his money will go to horses and carts." Reb Chaim concluded, "I have no doubt that your pure heart in giving will mean that your money will go straight towards strengthening the Torah itself."

The Wrong Cause? Let Them Waste It

On a related note, at the beginning of *parashas Pekudei* Moshe gave an accounting of all the materials used in the Mishkan and what they were used for. Why did Moshe have to give an account of the materials used? Hashem must have trusted him, since Moshe is described as "trusted in My whole house" (*Bemidbar* 12:7).

The Midrash answers this question. It says that the scoffers of that time were murmuring about Moshe, saying, "Someone in charge of so much silver and gold, of course he became rich." When Moshe heard this he said, "I swear by your lives that when the work of the Mishkan is complete I will give you a full accounting." Indeed, as soon as it was finished he began with, "These are the accounts of the Mishkan" (*Shemos* 38:21).

Rav Zalman Sorotzkin[33] observes that there was a stark contrast between these grumblings, and what took place during the sin of the golden calf. There no one protested, no one batted an eye about where the gold was going. Despite the fact that much gold was thrown into the fire, only a single calf emerged. No one stood up and said, "Hey, where did all my gold go?" Yet with the Mishkan there was this murmuring that could only be stilled by a full audit!

Rav Sorotzkin continues that this tendency has lasted even until this day. Those who bring merit to the multitudes are subject to intense scrutiny. People ask them, "Where did my money go to? Why did they use that postage stamp when they could have dropped off the letter themselves? and so forth. On the other hand, those who collect for the golden calves of our day are never questioned.

Why is it like this? Perhaps one could answer that deep down, every Jew wants to fulfill the word of Hashem by doing mitzvos and avoiding sin. When one gives money to the right sort of charity he is very pedantic that it go to the right address in order that he get full reward for his money. On the other hand, if one gives to the wrong causes he subconsciously experiences an inner guilt, and therefore he won't be too upset if it is used in the wrong way.

No Second Thoughts

The verse says, "Every man and woman who had the generosity of heart to contribute to all the work that Hashem had commanded to be done through Moshe, *bnei Yisrael* brought their offerings to Hashem" (*Shemos* 35:29). What is the relevance of the seemingly superfluous phrase "*bnei Yisrael* brought their offerings to Hashem"? It is obvious and has been mentioned before.

The Chida[34] says that sometimes one is inspired and makes a donation to a cause, but once the moment of inspiration passes he has second thoughts. He asks himself, "Should I have done it? Perhaps I can't afford it." The will behind his gift becomes flawed. Likewise, when *bnei Yisrael* made their pledges to the Mishkan, one would have thought that of the large number of people who offered them, surely some of them would have had second thoughts. The Torah therefore comes to tell us that in fact the inspiration behind their pledges stayed with them for the entire duration until the delivery. "*Bnei Yisrael* brought their offerings to Hashem"; not one of them had any second thoughts from beginning to end.

Rav Yonasan Eibeschutz[35] offers a different explanation. As we know, when *bnei Yisrael* left Egypt, a mixed multitude came with them. Some of them also wanted to contribute to the Mishkan, yet the Jews did not want to accept their offer, since they were not worthy of donating to such a lofty cause. But because of their own piety and zeal, *bnei Yisrael* had no choice but to cover the deficit from their own pockets. That is why first the verse says, "Every man and woman," telling us that everyone — the mixed multitude included — pledged, yet *"bnei Yisrael* brought their offerings"; only they were the ones who actually contributed.

A Good Name

The verse says, "See, Hashem has called by name Betzalel..." (*Shemos* 35:30). The Chasam Sofer[36] says that there are three names a man is given: that which his mother and father call him, that which other people call him, and that which he acquires for himself. So too with Betzalel, because he had a good name, he merited to perform the work of the Mishkan.

Let us elaborate on this idea. One who goes in the way of Torah and mitzvos only so as not to aggrieve his parents will separate from Torah and mitzvos as soon as they are no longer around. So too, one who serves Hashem only because he is in good surroundings will distance himself from the ways of Hashem as soon as he parts company with the people in that environment. These two types of people are symbolized by the two names that are the least important, that which his parents call him, and that which other people call him. On the other hand, the name that a person acquires through his actions and good deeds is the most significant and is everlasting. This is what King Solomon meant when he said, "A good name is better than good oil." This idea is seen in the above verse: "See, Hashem has called by name." Hashem chose Betzalel because of the good name that he acquired for himself.

The Chafetz Chaim[37] says that Hashem would give the necessary skills to whoever desired to do work in the Mishkan. This is seen in the verse "for every wise-hearted man whom Hashem had put wisdom within his heart, everyone whose heart inspired him to approach the work to do it" (*Shemos* 36:2). Hashem had to help *bnei Yisrael* in this way, as the Jews in Egypt were more accustomed to building pyramids, shlepping bricks around and making straw. Where were they meant to learn these finer crafts? Therefore, Hashem put the knowledge in their hearts and the skills within their hands.

The Chafetz Chaim continues that the same holds true for all matters of a spiritual nature. If one desires to master a particular Talmudic tractate, for example, and if he is willing to put in the effort, then Hashem will bestow on him a blessing from Heaven, and he will have all the skills he needs to acquire it. All it takes is the desire and will on our part, and then we can reach all our spiritual goals.

Parashas Pekudei

Essentials and Luxuries

The *parashah* begins, "These are the accountings of the Mishkan, the Mishkan of the Testimony" (*Shemos* 38:21). Rashi asks, What is the reason for the Torah's double use here of the word "Mishkan"? He answers that it alludes to the future Beis Hamikdash, which was twice taken as "collateral" in its destruction, because of the sins of Yisrael.

Rav Yaakov Kamenetsky[38] gives the following insight into this verse. If one falls on hard times, he will sell the luxuries of his house — the grand piano, the marble coffee table — before selling the more essential items, such as his refrigerator or bed. If things get really bad, then rather than sell his necessities, he will borrow money and give these items as security for the loan. However, he will not give up these items completely.

The Jewish people had a commandment to build the Mishkan. This was meant to be only a temporary structure, because in the pre-golden-calf era they were meant to arrive in the Land of Israel within a very short period of time. Therefore, they could have reasoned that the Mishkan should be built with cheaper materials, since it was only a temporary structure. They could have rationalized, Why spend the money on the

Mishkan? After all, if one goes traveling, one doesn't build one's tent out of the most expensive materials, since it's used for only a short period of time. Since *bnei Yisrael* still hastened to give their silver and gold, it showed that they regarded the Mishkan as a necessity and not as a luxury. Therefore, Hashem said that He too would regard it as a necessity, and when it was to be taken away — that is, when the Beis Hamikdash was destroyed — it was taken only as collateral and therefore had to be returned.

Into Africa

Why does the future destruction of the Beis Hamikdash have to be mentioned here, just when the Mishkan is being inaugurated? It is like a rav under the *chuppah* who looks at the beautiful writing on the *kesubah* and says to the *chasan*, "If ever you need another *kesubah*, be sure to go only to this *sofer*." Why did the factor of its destruction have to be mentioned particularly on this day?

To explain why, the *sefer Kemotzei Shallal Rav* cites the following parable. There was once a man who needed to go on a dangerous journey into the depths of Africa to meet with one of the tribes. Before he left he instructed the members of his household to check thoroughly that he was not taking with him any valuables or jewelery. He changed his watch from his nice Rolex to a cheap digital, and emptied his wallet of all his money except the minimum he would need for the journey. The man went on his way, praying he would arrive back safely.

Despite these preparations, sure enough, when he got to his first destination he opened up his suitcase and found a gold ring with an expensive stone set in it. He was extremely angry with his family for allowing this to go unnoticed, but he had no choice but to take it with him. It so happened that as he continued his journey, he didn't encounter any robbers, but he did fall ill with a dangerous ailment that required expensive treatment. Luckily, he had this ring with him and was able to offer it as a pledge to one of the local businessmen. The large sum of money he received for it enabled him to hire a local doctor, who cared for him fully until he recovered. He then went out to finish his business and made such a great profit that he was able to retrieve his ring. Only then did he realize that he had needed the ring, and that it was indeed *hashgachah pratis* that he had taken it with him, as it had saved his life.

A Time for Song?

It is the same with the Beis Hamikdash. The verse says, "A song of Assaf. Hashem, nations come into Your inheritance" (*Tehillim* 79:1). Why is it called a "song" when it talks about the destruction of the Beis Hamikdash? Shouldn't it be called a "lament"? The answer is that the song was said over the fact that Hashem vented His wrath on the sticks and stones of the Beis Hamikdash rather than on His people. If not for the Beis Hamikdash He would have had to obliterate the Jewish people.

Thus, the "song of Assaf" is like our traveler, who rejoiced that the ring had saved him from death. So too, through the destruction of the Beis Hamikdash we were saved. Now we can fully answer the question why the destruction is mentioned at the Mishkan's inauguration. Through the mention of its destruction here, we learn that although the Beis Hamikdash would be taken as a pledge, we are promised that at a later date the pledge will be redeemed and it will be rebuilt.

I Want It Now

Once, a student asked Rav Yosef Chaim Sonnenfeld,[39] "Since Hashem has taken away the Beis Hamikdash for the sins of

Yisrael, why won't He return it to us, especially as we long for it so much?" Rav Yosef Chaim answered, "There is a law in the Torah that if a lender has to take a pledge — such as a poor man's blanket — for a loan as security, and it is the poor man's only blanket, the pledge must be returned to the borrower every night. If the poor man has another blanket to use, then the lender can hold on to it until the debt is paid. Why then hasn't Hashem returned our pledge — the Beis Hamikdash — to us? The answer is that most Jews are more comfortable in exile. They have wealth, luxury and prestige, so why give it all up and come to the Middle East? They are happy with their situation and can do without Hashem returning the Beis Hamikdash and resting His Presence there. Unfortunately, there is no requirement that the pledge should be returned yet."

The verse says, "Her gates have been sunk into the ground" (*Eichah* 2:9). This alludes to the fact that before the Beis Hamikdash was destroyed, the doors came off and were hidden in the ground. What was the significance of their being hidden? It is also interesting that in the last five *parashos* we have read, all deal with the Mishkan and its construction in one way or another. That is about 10 percent of the entire Torah. Yet we are told that in the future, the Beis Hamikdash will descend complete from Heaven. In other words, although much of the Torah deals with the building of the Mishkan, in the future we will have no further part in its construction. Why then is its construction dealt with in such detail?

The Maharil Diskin[40] answers by citing the *gemara* (*Bava Basra* 53b) that says if one builds a palace on the property of a deceased convert (with no inheritors), and then another person comes along and makes doors for that palace, it is the second person who acquires the property. (The reasoning is that one needs an active legal method of *chazakah* [acquiring property].) One acquires the land beneath a structure not through building that structure but through creating the finished enclosure.

In like manner, Hashem was about to destroy the Beis Hamikdash, but He was only taking it on collateral, and would later on send down a third Beis Hamikdash. Hashem knew that the third one would be sent complete and that the people would not have a part in its construction. Therefore, through our adding the finishing touches, putting on the doors, it will be as if we have built it, and we will thereby acquire it.

This is seen in what we say in *mussaf* on *yom tov*: "Show us its building and gladden us with its establishment." "Show us its building" refers to the fact that the Beis Hamikdash will arrive almost complete. But we will be disappointed that we were not able to take part in its construction. Therefore, we continue, "gladden us with its establishment"; that is, we will be truly happy when we add the doors and have the opportunity to do some of the building.

Basic Math

Following the completion of the work of the Mishkan, the verse says, "And Moshe blessed them" (*Shemos* 39:43). What was the blessing that he gave them? The Midrash provides the answer. It informs us that Moshe said, "May Hashem...increase you and bless you one thousandfold."

The Panim Yafos explains why this particular blessing was appropriate. The Midrash tells us that on the day the Mishkan was erected, all the Jewish adult males stood in its courtyard within a space of 50 *amos* length and 50 *amos* breadth, and each person was able to prostrate himself within 4 *amos* going forward. The Gemara (*Sukkah* 7b) says that a person seated takes up 1 *amah* width. Thus, the courtyard of the Mishkan, with its 50 *amos* length, would have held 50 people across, with each person needing 4 *amos* forward to prostrate himself. Therefore, there was room forward for only 12 rows of people (since 12 multiplied by 4 *amos* is 48 *amos* in length, 2 *amos* short of the 50-*amos*-long courtyard), which means it could have held 600 people (12 multiplied by 50). The miracle was that in fact 600,000 people filled this space, a blessing of a thousandfold.

However, what about the remaining 2 *amos* left after the first 48 *amos* were taken up by the first 12 rows of people? These 2 *amos* multiplied by their width of 50 gives a total area of 100 square *amos*, room enough for 25 people. With the thousandfold miracle this meant an extra 25,000 could be held.

The exact count of the Jewish people was 603,000, plus the *levi'im* who numbered 22,000, making a total of 625,000. Therefore, with Moshe's blessing of multiplying a thousandfold, the 50 square *amos* of the Mishkan's courtyard held all the people.

The accountings of the Mishkan are interrupted by the verse "And Betzalel...made all that Hashem had commanded Moshe" (*Shemos* 38:22). As was mentioned, the Beis Hamikdash was destroyed because of the sins of Yisrael. The Divrei Shaul[41] says that it was possible to destroy it only because it was Betzalel who "made" the Mishkan. In other words, because it was built by man, it was not meant to be everlasting. This is seen in the verse "Do good in your favor to Tzion," that Hashem Himself should "build the walls of Yerushalayim" (*Tehillim* 51:20). When Hashem builds the next Beis Hamikdash personally, it will no longer be a pledge but will be everlasting. May we see it built speedily and in our days.

Vayikra

Big and Small
(Gaavah, Part 1)

I n our previous volume we spoke about the distinctive fea-
ture of the first word of *Sefer Vayikra*: "And He called
(*vayikra*) [to Moshe]." The letter aleph at the end of the word
vayikra is written small. The Baal Haturim comments that at the
time Moshe was writing down the Torah, he wanted to write the
word *vayakar* instead of *vayikra*. That term was used regarding
the prophecy of Bilaam, showing that Hashem merely chanced
upon him, making a coincidental appearance. This is in contrast
to *vayikra*, which, as Rashi explains, is an expression of affection.
Moshe, in his humility, wanted to downplay the compliment
and use the word *vayakar*. Hashem told him he was not to do so.
Instead, Moshe went ahead and wrote *vayikra* but with a small
aleph at the end of the word, indicating his wish to downplay its
significance.

With Good Reason

The Torah tells us, "Now the man Moshe was exceedingly
humble" (*Bemidbar* 12:3). One may have thought that Moshe

would have had reason to feel good about himself. After all, he spoke directly to Hashem, face-to-face, which no other prophet ever did. Perhaps he could have given himself a pat on the back for being the one chosen to communicate with Hashem. The Torah tells us otherwise: not only did he stay humble, but he was the most humble man who ever lived!

Rav Simchah Bunim of Peshischa[1] cites the following parable. A man once went up to the top of a mountain which was higher than all the surrounding mountains. He looked at all the villages in the valley and thought to himself, "Wow! I'm so high, more special and great than any of the village people down there!" Any sane man would know that his height is only a function of the mountain he is standing on. Similarly, Moshe had reached the greatest of peaks, having spoken to Hashem face-to-face. The small aleph tells us that despite this he still retained his humility.

Taking out the Garbage

At the beginning of *parashas Tzav* the *kohen* is given the mitzvah to remove the pile of ashes that accumulated on the altar from the previous day's offerings. This was to be done at the beginning of every day. Why did this have to be performed then? Shouldn't the *kohen* perform a more glorious task to begin the day with? One answer is that the Torah is teaching us a lesson about *gaavah* (pride), that one should not become haughty and arrogant. The *kohen gadol* is one of the select few who are privileged to perform the holy service on behalf of all of the Jewish people. To prevent his appointment to this holy task from going to his head, the Torah gives him this commandment to perform...first thing in the morning, and every morning.

On a related note, someone once said to his wife, "Isn't it a bit beneath my dignity as a *kohen* to take out the garbage?" to which his wife replied, "Isn't it beneath a *kohen*'s dignity to be without a wife?"

The verse says, "Any meal offering...you shall not cause to go up in smoke any leaven or honey" (*Vayikra* 2:11). In other words, the Torah forbids us from giving an offering that contains *chametz* or honey. Why are these two items in particular forbidden?

The Ridbaz[2] says that these items are symbolic of two character traits which are hazardous to one's spiritual health. *Chametz* (leaven) is caused by adding yeast to flour and water. The yeast makes the dough puffy. This is symbolic of *gaavah*, the puffy ego which inflates a person's importance in his own eyes. The way yeast expands corresponds to how the ego expands — very easily. Honey symbolizes *taavah*, one's lusts. Just like honey drips slowly from place to place, spreading its sticky mess, so too *taavah* is something which slowly spreads, making a person desire more and more. Both of these traits are seen in the verse "One with haughty eyes and an expansive heart, him I cannot bear" (*Tehillim* 101:5). Although the language seems harsh, we learn from the verse that one who follows the ways of Hashem controls his lusts and desires, as well as taming his ego and realizing who he really is.

What then are the problems with *gaavah*? In *Orchos Tzaddikim*, the author writes about nearly thirty different topics, and yet out of all of them he chooses to open with the trait of *gaavah*. He writes that the reason for this is "because man has an obligation to separate from this [trait], for it is the gateway to many evils, and amongst all the other traits we have not seen anything as evil...a man must be careful and reject it whenever it is not in its proper place."

What are the sources in Scripture for the prohibition against *gaavah*, what are the evils associated with *gaavah* and why is there so much emphasis on it?

A Source of Pride

There are various sources for the prohibition against *gaavah* that are cited in the classical ethical works. Interestingly, of all the traits mentioned in these works, only a few of them are explicitly mentioned in the Torah, and *gaavah* is one of them. The *Orchos Tzaddikim* cites two Scriptural sources. The first source is the verse "Beware that you don't forget Hashem your God...when you have eaten and are satisfied and build good houses...and your silver and gold increases for you...and your heart be lifted up and you forget Hashem your God...and say in your heart, 'My strength and power of my hands made for me this wealth'" (*Devarim* 8:11-14, 17). The Sifsei Chaim[3] explains that from these verses we see that *gaavah* characterizes a person who glorifies himself by thinking that all he has earned, accomplished and achieved comes from the sweat of his own hands. He does not realize that ultimately everything comes from Hashem, and that He is the Source of all blessing, without which all his labor would be for naught.

The Sifsei Chaim cites the Sma, who says that *gaavah* is at the root of the denial of the good that Hashem has done. A person views himself as too big, thinking all he accomplishes is due to "My strength and power of my hands," and that he does not need any input from Hashem. We see from the beginning of these verses that the root cause of *gaavah* is too much abundance. When things are going well materially, a person then prides himself on the fact that he was the one who made the fortune, and he forgets who the real Source of it is.

A second Scriptural source for the prohibition against *gaavah* is found in the commandments to a king. A king is given certain restrictions and guidelines, such as not having too many horses or too many wives. The Torah then says that the reason for all these prohibitions is "that his heart not be lifted up from his brothers" (*Devarim* 17:20).

This is an interesting commandment. The king is the one person for whom there seems to be good reason for his heart to swell with pride. He is the one with the crown and the royal family. Why not let him feel a bit of pride? Yet the Torah gives us an explicit commandment that he has to remain humble, despite the advantages of throne and wealth.

The Ramban[4] says that if the king, in his exalted position, is given such a charge, then how much more so does it apply to others of a lesser stature. He says that *gaavah*, even in a king, is such an abominable trait in Hashem's eyes because it is only Hashem Who has real greatness, and only He Who is worthy of praise. He points out that Hashem hates *gaavah*, as the verse says, "Every haughty heart is the abomination of Hashem" (*Mishlei* 16:5). Why are they an abomination, particularly before Hashem? Because only He is truly great and worthy of praise.

In his famous letter, the Ramban wrote, "And now, my son, know and see that those who pride their hearts against people are rebelling against the Kingship of Hashem. They glorify themselves in the clothing of Heavenly Kingship, as it says, 'Hashem reigns, He is clothed with majesty' (*Tehillim* 93:1)...how can they glorify themselves in the honor of Hashem?" It follows that one who uses the King's clothes and glory is rebelling against the King.

The Mesillas Yesharim lists various degrees of *gaavah* and ends by saying that pride sets back sages, makes foolish their minds and perverts the hearts of the highest in wisdom. He says that even students whose eyes are just opened to Torah suddenly think of themselves as great scholars. To cleanse oneself of this trait, he continues, one has to understand that pride is blindness itself, and that man's reason cannot see his defects and realize his lowliness. If he could he would depart from this evil, destructive trait and remove himself very far from it.

The Mesillas Yesharim is informing us that when *gaavah* sets in it deceives a person, telling him how great he is. As mentioned, much of the problem is what it does to one's imagination. When he has a slight talent for something, suddenly in his eyes he is the world's greatest authority on the subject. To cite an example, a chazzan once came to Rav Yisrael Salanter and asked him how he could stop feeling pride about his great talents and about the compliments he got from the congregation. Rav Yisrael replied, "It's easy. Just take the tallis off your head and see how they are laughing at you."

Parashas Tzav

Giving Thanks

In *parashas Vayikra* all the information regarding the different forms of sacrifices was given to Moshe, yet one sacrifice was omitted. The *korban todah* (thanksgiving offering) is mentioned only this week. What is the reason for this?

Rav Yosef Chaim Sonnenfeld[5] explains. He first defines the exact nature of the *korban todah*. Rashi says that one would bring a thanksgiving offering "in recognition of a miraculous deliverance from harm, such as those who travel at sea, the desert, are freed from prison, or recover from illness." These are all events where one sees Hashem's hand in the world, His kindness and salvation. They are incidents which one perceives as miraculous, and bring one to thanksgiving.

The *kohanim*, however, were on a different level. They saw Hashem's Presence in the world more often, as they saw the miracles in the Beis Hamikdash on a daily basis. It follows that a thanksgiving offering would be more applicable to them, as they were accustomed to seeing these miracles and would thus be more in tune with Hashem's intervention in our daily lives, in seemingly normal events. Therefore, the details of the thanksgiving offering were left for *parashas Tzav*, which speaks directly with the *kohanim* rather than the rest of the people.

The First Thanks?

Rav Sonnenfeld provides another answer. When Leah gave birth to her fourth son, Yehudah, she said, "This time I will thank Hashem" (*Bereishis* 29:35). The Gemara (*Berachos* 7b) says that from the time Hashem created the world, there was no one who gave thanks to Him until Leah came along.

How can the Gemara say this? Adam gave thanks, as indicated in certain chapters of *Tehillim*, which he authored. Noach offered sacrifices after the flood; surely they were offered as a way of giving thanks. The answer is that indeed Adam and Noach were giving thanks, yet they did it only as a result of some miraculous event. Leah, however, was the first to thank Hashem for a seemingly natural event such as childbirth.

We can use this explanation to answer our question why the thanksgiving offering was left until *Tzav*. *Tzav* speaks specifically to *kohanim*, who, because of their constant devotion to the Divine service, are, like Leah, more spiritually sensitive and more perceptive regarding the hidden way Hashem orchestrates what are seemingly natural events. Therefore, it is they who would be most likely to express their feelings of thanks through a *korban todah*.

A daughter was once born to an *avreich* a year after his wedding. He asked Rav Shach whether it was fitting to make a Kiddush out of thanks to Hashem. Rav Shach answered, "If she had been born after eight years of marriage, would you ask? You would have understood to praise Him and offer thanks. Now that Hashem has helped you and saved you many years of sorrow, is your obligation to give thanks any less?"[6]

How to Improve Health

As mentioned above, Rashi says that one specifically thanks Hashem for a miracle that occurred, or for some other deliverance. But before we go further, there is a philosophical question that needs to be answered. Why do we have an obligation to thank Hashem when He certainly has no need for our thanks or praise? Obviously, when we thank Hashem we are not providing any benefit to Him. We can say Hallel all day and Hashem won't benefit. Rather, *we* need to praise Him.

Rebbi Akiva Eiger[7] says that man has no means whatsoever to repay Hashem for the good he receives. We are constantly living in debt for the daily, hourly and moment-to-moment kindnesses bestowed upon us. We say in Hallel, "What can I return to Hashem, all of Whose bounty has been given to me?" Yet the fact is that just because we cannot offer Him anything does not free us from the obligation to thank Him. We are required to acknowledge and thank Hashem through the *berachos* we recite and thanksgiving offerings we gave when it was possible.

Rebbi Akiva Eiger continues by saying that usually, when one gives thanks to someone sincerely, the giver is motivated to give again at a later stage. On the other hand, when the beneficiary does not appreciate what he is given, the giver will not be inclined to give anytime soon. The same is true of the relationship between Hashem and His people. When we recognize the blessing that Hashem gives us, then He continues to provide more. If we are ungrateful, then Hashem withholds His blessings.

There are various *segulos* for wealth, health, and so on. One of them is making *berachos* with just a little more intent than before. In *bentching*, if one examines the text, one sees that it is all about appreciating the bounty Hashem has provided, and a prayer that He continue to do so. Similarly, in the *berachah Asher Yatzar* we thank Hashem for making our bodies function properly, enabling us to remain healthy. Therefore, if we increase our understanding and concentration in these areas we may see our desires fulfilled and health improved.

I'll Teach You How to Thank...

The following parable[8] will help illustrate this point. There was once a man who raised an orphan in his home for many years, at the same time struggling over his own existence. The orphan treated the home as his own and didn't pay attention to the fact that the man had been doing a great *chessed* for him for all these years. One day a poor person came to the man's door, and he gave him a generous donation, after which the poor man didn't stop praising and blessing him for his great kindness. Following this incident, his wife asked him, "Why is it that the poor man, who you did a kindness for only once, thanked you so much, yet the orphan, whom we have raised for many years, has never thanked us at all?"

The husband answered her, "I know how to get him to thank us." He called to the orphan and said to him, "We've raised you this long, and we are happy that Hashem has given us the chance to do this mitzvah, but now you are older and it is possible for you to stand on your own two feet. Therefore, it's time you left our house and tried to make a living on your own." These words shocked the orphan, but, having no choice, he packed up his belongings and left.

He tried to find somewhere to live, and a place to work, but sadly, fortune was not on his side. Hungry and feeling low, he roamed the streets. While his former guardian was out walking one day, he saw the orphan in this state. He said to him that he saw that it isn't working out for him and that he would be happy to accept him back. From that time on the orphan knew how to thank his benefactor. Because he had fallen so low, he now appreciated the constant kindness that was provided for him.

The Ben Ish Chai explains that a person lives in the world and Hashem provides *chessed* constantly. When one gets too used to it he forgets Hashem and doesn't thank Him for all the goodness He bestows on him. When, God forbid, something bad happens to him, only then does he understand that all his life he had been living with the goodness and blessings of Hashem. At that time he realizes that he has to thank Hashem for the constant *chessed* that He does for us. Now we can better understand why by making the *berachos* with more *kavanah* and reciting *Birkas Hamazon* with more intent, we show our appreciation to Hashem.

Once there was a rich man who bought a house for a thousand gold pieces. He then found a buyer who bought it from him for two thousand gold pieces. He was very happy that Hashem had made him such a profit. Later on that day someone approached him and offered him three thousand gold pieces for the house which was now sold. He became angry at himself and at Hashem that he had lost a thousand gold pieces, and ended the day feeling sad.

In contrast, once a poor person went to the market in search of work in order to have bread to eat. After waiting half the day and finding no work, he became despondent, worrying that perhaps he would return home with an empty purse. At that point a merchant came up to him, asking him if he would be interested in bringing many sacks of flour from the mill for pay. He eagerly accepted the offer, and when he finished he ran home to his wife and gave her the coins he had earned so that they could buy bread. He was grateful to Hashem for having brought money his way, and he thanked Him with a full heart.

The poor person thanked Hashem even for a few coins, while the rich man could not thank Hashem even for a profit of a thousand gold pieces. The Chafetz Chaim explains that every day of our lives we receive gifts from Hashem; He showers us with life and fulfills all our needs. A person has to recognize the good of Hashem and thank Him for everything, small as well as large. We should not be like that rich person who, in his pride, doesn't understand that goodness comes from Hashem, and thinks that the whole world is his. Rather, we have to see that the amount we receive is determined by Hashem, and we must thank Him for it, along with all the other blessings, both hidden and revealed.

When Separating Brings Closer

T here is an interesting contrast between the language used when Hashem instructed Noach to take the animals with him into the ark, and that which is used in our *parashah* when explaining the laws of kashrus. Regarding Noach, the Torah says, "and of the beast that is not clean, two" (*Bereishis* 7:2). Scripture uses a nonderogatory term — "not clean" — for the impure animals, effectively adding letters to the Torah, yet in our *parashah* it refers to these animals as *tamei* (unclean), a shorter form. How can we account for this difference?

The Dubno Maggid⁹ cites a parable to answer our question. In a certain town lived two people who were both called Yosel. One was a wise man, well versed in Torah, while the other was completely ignorant, and was known as Yosel the Boar, to distinguish him from the other Yosel. One day a man came to the house of the learned Yosel and asked his servant if he knew where the other Yosel could be found. The servant replied, "You mean Yosel the Boor?"

When his master heard him talking like that he reprimanded him. "You must not call any man a boor," he said. "People only call him that to distinguish between us, but in my house there is no excuse for this. I will not have people think I look down on one of my neighbors."

A while later a *shadchan* came to the scholarly Yosel, suggesting a *shidduch* between his daughter and the son of the ignorant Yosel. Yosel was furious at him even for suggesting it. "My daughter, married to the son of Yosel the Boor?" he exclaimed. "Not while I'm alive."

After the *shadchan* left, the servant asked his master why a while earlier his master had reprimanded him for calling his neighbor Yosel the Boor, yet the master himself had used such uncomplimentary terms. Yosel explained the difference. "If someone asks you where someone lives, you are not required to give any information about his character; simply giving the address will do. When I receive an undesirable marriage proposal for my daughter, I have to be straight and to the point about why I object. It is my duty to explain to the *shadchan* that my daughter will not marry the son of one who is known for being an ignoramus."

The same applies in the Torah. With Noach, the impure animals were being listed only for the purpose of information, to identify who should and shouldn't go into the ark. Therefore, it was sufficient to use the terms clean and not clean. In our *parashah*, the laws of kashrus are set out, and a line is being drawn between what is and what isn't permissible. Yisrael has a special status and has to retain holiness; therefore, the Torah has to be blunt and call the nonclean animals what they are: *tamei*.

With All Due Respect?

A student once asked Rav Elchanan Wasserman[10] why he used such harsh words for those he considered wicked. He asked, "If the Torah used extra letters (as above) in order to avoid impure expressions, wouldn't it oblige the Rav to do so, with all due respect?" Rav Elchanan answered with the above idea, that when the Torah wanted to tell Yisrael which animals were fit to be eaten, it called them *tamei*, without trying to use a gentler expression. So too, when it is time to defend *Yiddishkeit* against the destroyers and underminers of religion, there is no reason to try and be more polite. He is quoted as saying, "This is especially true at a time when there are those who seek to purify that which is *treif*. It is obligatory to point out that the Torah considers them impure."

Greek Wisdom Within

Rav Yosef Chaim Sonnenfeld[11] spent much effort trying to counter the inroads being made into Judaism by non-Orthodox elements. He cited the following Gemara (*Bava Kamma* 82b). The Hasmoneans were undergoing internal warfare at the same time that the Temple was under siege, with each sect undermining the efforts of the other. Every day they would lower a basket over the Temple wall with some money, and animals for the offerings would be sent up. One day, someone who was familiar with Greek wisdom advised the Greeks that as long as the Jews were offering up the animals, they would not be victorious over them. The next day, when the money was lowered, the enemy switched the animal and sent up a pig instead of a sheep. When the pig was halfway up the Temple walls it dug its claws into the stones and made such a screech that the entire Land of Israel trembled. Because of this incident the Sages declared, "Cursed is the man who teaches his children Greek wisdom."

This Gemara poses several difficulties. Why did they specifically send up a pig rather than any other animal? What is the significance of its digging its claws into the Temple walls? What is the meaning of the entire land trembling? Rav Yosef Chaim explains that at the time of this *gemara*, besides the division between the various groups within the Hasmonean family, there was a cultural war as well. There were those who thought that Greek culture had a lot to offer Judaism, and that it was appropriate to reform it with some Greek improvements. Then there were those who wanted to preserve Judaism in its undiluted form, as the word of God.

The pig is a very unique animal. It is the only animal that has the inner sign of impurity — it doesn't chew the cud — but possesses the outer pure sign of having split hooves. It is often used as a metaphor for hypocrisy, as it stretches its hooves outward, as if to say, "Look at me. I'm kosher. Come and eat me," yet its inner self is as *treif* as can be. Similarly, the Hellenists of old tried hard to show how their brand of Judaism was "kosher." They tried to prove that it was an improvement, that Greek culture had a lot to offer them. However, what the Hellenists tried to create was intrinsically *treif*. Just like the pig, it tried to flout its external qualities, yet inside, its culture was putrid and filthy. (This also explains why the man who chose the pig was referred to as a "man familiar with Greek wisdom.")

With this we can also understand why the pig dug its claws into the wall of the Temple. In other words, the Hellenists tried to claw their way into the holy of holies of Jewish life. Because of the threats posed to the Jewish people, the sound of this impurity shook the land to its very core. Rav Yosef Chaim continued by saying that the threat to Jewish life by those within who seek to make their own convenient improvements, is far greater than the threats posed from outside.

Another incident which illustrates this kind of threat to Judaism occurred in the Volozhin Yeshivah,[12] which received orders from the government that they were to introduce some secular subjects into the yeshivah or else face closure. The Netziv, who was the *rosh yeshivah* at the time, called a meeting of the leaders of the generation to decide what to do. Most of those in attendance felt that the least damaging option would be to give in to the request, which would at least keep the yeshivah open. Then came the turn of the Beis Halevi. He stood up, and with tears in his eyes said, "It is not up to us to worry on Hashem's behalf or to build Him yeshivos. If we can operate yeshivos in the way that has been handed down to us from previous generations, then let us do so. If we cannot, then the responsibility is not in our hands. He Who gave the Torah will ensure that the Torah continues to be taught." Because of his speech, the Volozhin Yeshivah, with its four hundred students, was closed and its students dispersed. In Volozhin's place, other centers began to flourish — Slobodka, Telshe, Mir, Radin, to name a few. All were yeshivos established in the purity of undiluted Torah study.

Rav Chaim Berlin wrote in a letter about his father, the Netziv, that he literally sacrificed himself for the sake of his yeshivah and as a result of its closing he fell victim to an illness from which he did not recover. Rav Chaim wrote: "I was commanded by my father not to allow in any way or form to agree to this (the introduction of secular studies into the yeshivah). My father told me that this is alluded to in the Torah, where it says, 'To separate between the holy and the profane' (*Vayikra* 10:10). Whenever you have anything secular mixed with holy, not only do the secular matters not become permeated with holiness, but the holy matters become profaned by the secular." The Netziv concluded that "This matter caused me to depart from the world and to close the yeshivah, for this matter is worth sacrificing one's life for."

Parashas Tazria

Thinking like a Donkey (Gaavah, Part 2)

There was once a donkey[13] that was loaded with sacks of fragrant spices. When it would pass through the streets everyone would move nearer to smell the spices. When it returned from its travels it boasted to its fellow donkeys, "Who is like me? Everyone who passes is attracted to me!" The next day this donkey was loaded with sacks of manure to be taken to the local dump. Whoever would pass by would run away as fast as he could. When it returned from the journey it said to its fellow donkeys, "Today the fear of me fell on all the people. Not only do they all love me, but now they all fear me."

When the fox heard his words, he said, "Foolish donkey! Yesterday you were carrying fragrant spices. Everyone came close to you not because they loved you but because they loved the smell of the spices. And today it wasn't you that they feared; it was the manure that they ran from. How can you be prideful?"

This rather amusing parable shows us how *gaavah* (pride, arrogance) can cause a person to think that everyone around him is so impressed by his special qualities and uniqueness, when in reality something else entirely is going on.

The Big War

The Orchos Tzaddikim describes how one's evil inclination is his greatest enemy when it comes to fighting *gaavah*. It constantly works at his mind, trying to convince him about how great he is, and at the same time leads to his downfall in this world.

He cites the following story to illustrate his point. Once a soldier was returning from a war when someone came up to him and said, "You've returned from the small war, yet the great war still awaits you."

The soldier asked, "What do you mean? We've just overcome great enemies? What could be a greater war?"

The man replied, "The great war is against the evil inclination and its battalions."

Why is this battle called "the great war"? He answers that usually, when one is victorious, the enemy leaves you alone once and for all. With the evil inclination, even if you defeat it a hundred times it still rears its ugly head, as it says in *Avos* (2:4), "And do not trust yourself until the day of your death." Every day it lies in ambush, waiting to catch you off guard.

The Orchos Tzaddikim continues, "Since pride is the root of many bad traits, and the evil inclination is an active partner in a man's heart; since the intent of the evil inclination is to falsify the truth and place the stamp of truth on falsity, teaching man to be proud and presenting him with ways to rationalize it, therefore you must strive to outsmart it."

"Broigez" with the Prophet

Unfortunately, this is not always the case. In the haftarah this week we read the story of Naaman, who was a general of the army of Aram. He was afflicted with *tzaraas* and needed a cure. Someone told him about the prophet Elisha, who had the power to affect a cure. He traveled to the prophet's house with his grand entourage of chariots and horses. Elisha was told of his arrival and sent out the message that he should immerse in the river Jordan seven times and then he would be cured. On hearing this he declared, " 'Behold, I thought he would come to me, that he would stand and call out in the Name of Hashem...and lift up his hands...and the afflicted one would be healed. Are not...the rivers of Damascus better than all the waters of Israel? Can I not immerse in them and be healed?' And he left in a rage" (II *Melachim* 5:11-12).

Rav Yehudah Ze'ev Segal[14] says that at first one may have thought that Naaman was angry because he felt that this was a ridiculous cure, that there are bigger rivers than the Jordan. Yet on closer examination, it is his opening remarks that give him away: "I thought he would come to me." (This phrase may sound familiar.) The Metzudos explains that he was saying, "I thought that because of my importance he would come to me and stand erect in the way of honor that people give esteemed officers."

This whole incident is bizarre. Here we have a man for whom there is no cure through medication and who was consequently dependent on the prophet. He then stormed home because he felt he was not given the honor that was due him, despite the fact that he would have to continue to live with the disease. Rav Segal then cites the Mesillas Yesharim, who says, "One who is bound up in the chains of his evil inclination cannot see or perceive the truth because he is blinded, literally." When one is tied up in pursuing his honor, even an affliction of *tzaraas* will seem trivial to him. He would rather keep the *tzaraas* and not forgo the honor.

Is That a Nice Way to Talk?

The Gemara (*Nedarim* 9b) tells of a *Nazir* who came to Rabbi Shimon Hatzaddik and told him that he had taken on this vow because once he saw his reflection in a spring of water and became prideful because of his good looks. The man knew the danger of being prideful and immediately said to himself, "Wicked one, why do you pride yourself in a world that isn't yours?" Rabbi Shimon got up and kissed him on his head. What he was so impressed by was his realization that a man's physical appearance is not of his doing, and therefore one cannot pride oneself on it.

The Sifsei Chaim[15] says that just like a bird cannot feel pride because it has wings, which are just a part of its nature, so too with us. With all things that a man seeks to pride himself on, he has to constantly say to himself, "Wicked one, why do you pride yourself in a world that isn't yours?" When a person is tending towards pride in his looks or wealth or even in his learning, he has to take a step back and realize that everything comes from Hashem. Furthermore, he has to understand that although he has been given these gifts, perhaps he hasn't used them in the capacity he otherwise could have and has therefore wasted the potential he was given.

The Chafetz Chaim[16] says that we learn from *tzaraas* what an abomination Hashem considers *gaavah* to be, and on the other hand, how pleasing the trait of humility is.

Hashem told Eliyahu to go down and meet Achav and tell him, "In the place where the dogs licked the blood of Navot, shall the dogs lick your blood" (*I Melachim* 21:19). Since Achav tore his garments and placed sackcloth on himself and fasted, Hashem said to Eliyahu, "See how Achav humbles himself before Me; I will not bring the evil in his days" (ibid., 28). The Chafetz Chaim says that from here we have a clear proof that when one humbles himself before Hashem, one can turn a decree of death into life.

The law of the *metzora* is that he has to dwell alone outside the camp, and even other afflicted people may not dwell with him. This is meant to bring him to repentance for his great sins. By going through such a humiliating experience, his heart will be humbled.

One of the ironies of *tzaraas* is that if the one afflicted has turned a pure white, he is declared pure, yet if he is afflicted in only one place, he is declared impure. The reason is that in the case where a person gets only a small affliction, he may reason that perhaps it was a chance occurrence and that he was in fact pure. His heart would become stubborn and he would not repent for his sins. Therefore, to counter this, the Torah says that even with one single bad spot, he is sent out of the camp to dwell alone, so that he should realize his errors and return for the better. He will have time to contemplate that the affliction comes from Hashem.

On the other hand, if one is covered from head to toe in the white affliction, his heart is already broken and he doesn't need to be sent out of the camp. He knows it's not by chance and will already be examining his deeds. By humbling himself he will be forgiven and cured.

If one looks at certain influences beneath the surface, one realizes that there are certain industries which are based entirely on the trait of *gaavah*. When one looks at what *gaavah* may lead to one understands why the Sages spoke about its harmful effects and how it can lead one totally astray.

The Sifsei Chaim says that *gaavah* could well be the affliction of the generation. The one of arrogant spirit is always looking at what the other has. He is pained when others have more than he has, for he feels he deserves all they have, and more. He says that this illness even finds its way into *frum* homes, when Yidden are not satisfied with what they have. When one sees what his neighbor drives, he wants to keep up with the Joneses (or Cohens) and buy the same thing. The Sifsei Chaim says that this attitude brings one to all forms of sin — namely jealousy, hatred and arguments — and it disrupts *shalom bayis*, as it causes dissatisfaction with what one has, which leads to arguments.

What then is the cure? To humble oneself. By lowering oneself from his pedestal, he will be satisfied with his lot and will then also view others with a generous eye.

The Solution? (Gaavah, Part 3)

The Gemara (*Arachin* 16a) lists seven causes of *tzaraas*, and amongst them are *lashon hara* and *tzaras ayin* (literally, narrowness of the eye). However, the Sifsei Chaim[17] says that in fact, the Torah also alludes to another cause of *tzaraas*, namely *gaavah*.

The verse describes what the afflicted had to do to be cured: "And the *kohen* shall instruct, and for the person being purified there shall be taken two live, clean birds, cedarwood, crimson thread and hyssop" (*Vayikra* 14:4). Rashi explains what each ingredient symbolizes. The bird represents that the plague came because of *lashon hara*, which is an act of verbal twittering. Therefore, the purification of the afflicted person requires birds, which constantly twitter. The cedarwood symbolizes that the plague came because of a haughty and arrogant spirit. The crimson thread (*solaas*) and hyssop signify that the afflicted person should lower himself from his arrogance like a worm (*solaas*).

A Good Eye?

The Torah is telling us that the way to be cured from the affliction is by humbling oneself. The causes mentioned in the

Gemara, *tzaraas ayin* and *lashon hara*, both stem from *gaavah*.

What is this "narrowness of the eye"? One person looks at another, eyeing him up and down, looking only for the faults in that person (as if he is so perfect himself, and faults are found only in others). Alternatively, he looks at everything the other possesses and is jealous, thinking that these things should belong to him. All these are characteristic of one who is full of an arrogant, haughty spirit. In contrast, one of humble spirit hasn't got guilty feelings when he sees someone acting correctly. He looks at the positive aspects in everyone, with a good eye, interpreting acts he sees for the good. Also, he is not bothered when others have more than he has, since he appreciates the lot that Hashem has given him.

The Sifsei Chaim says that a generous eye and a humble spirit are very much connected, while, on the other hand, arrogance brings one to *tzaras ayin*, and this causes him to speak *lashon hara* about his fellow. Because of arrogance, he cannot bear the good in others and will speak *lashon hara* about them. He has to search for the faults in others in order to show how great he (thinks he) is.

Worms and Wood

What then is the arrogant person's cure? Not only his actions need atoning for, but also his frame of mind has to be altered. The source of the illness is purely spiritual and has to be dealt with as such. The above Rashi is saying that to be healed he has to lower himself from his pride like a worm and hyssop. Just like a worm is the lowest of all living things, hyssop is the lowest type of vegetation. Hyssop is satisfied with very little; it grows around stones and rocks. So too, should he be satisfied with less, which will cause him to have a humble spirit.

The birds that are brought because of the twittering of *lashon hara*, and the cedarwood, which represents haughtiness, are connected in that *gaavah* is the source of *lashon hara* and *tzaras ayin*. The arrogant person needs to heal the sources of his affliction by humbling himself to one who is as low as hyssop and worms. Through this he will view everyone with a generous eye, looking at their pluses, and at his own minuses.

A Lonely Time

Other laws of the treatment of the *metzora* show us that the cure is very much related to the roots of the disease. The *metzora* has to sit outside of the camp with his garments torn and his head unshaven and call out, "*Tamei, tamei*, I am impure." As he sits in isolation outside the camp, passersby will look at him in this state as he goes through the humiliating process of saying, "*Tamei, tamei*" loud and clear. If this won't get him down off his high horse, then what will!

Chazal comment (*Moed Katan* 5a) on the repetition of the word *tamei*. The first time it is said to warn people to keep away from him, and the second time it is said to make others aware of his pain, to ensure that they have mercy and beseech Heaven for mercy on his behalf. The man of *gaavah*, who saw himself as being above his peers, is now forced to need their help to pray on his behalf.

The Sifsei Chaim adds that the Torah's intention is certainly not to embarrass him and take away his *kavod*, but rather, to heal his disease and the sources that led him to speak *lashon hara* in the first place. Only through this medicine will he be healed of his spiritual disease.

Who Needs More Belts?

As mentioned, the afflicted had to call out, "*Tamei, tamei*" so that people would know that he was impure and should distance themselves from him. Rav Shach[18] relates that during the month of Elul, his uncle, Rav Isser Zalman Meltzer, would give over words of *mussar* which would go out from his pure heart and pierce the hearts of those listening, causing even the toughest of people to cry. One time he gave a particularly moving speech. "When a *sefer Torah* carries a mistake," he said, "it is wrapped up and a belt is placed around it so that people should know it is unfit and shouldn't read from it." Rav Isser Zalman then raised a great cry and continued, "If so, how many belts do we need to wear on the outside so that people should know we are unfit and that they shouldn't learn from us?" By now the entire audience was crying uncontrollably.

How To...

The Sifsei Chaim goes on to cite various suggestions to help tackle *gaavah*, which is the key to attaining wholeness. The first suggestion is to put things in their proper perspective. If one would only realize that he is blinded, then he would already have come a long way. In one's imagination, every small good trait that he has is magnified in his eyes, while the good traits which others possess are downgraded. Similarly, he reads his shortcomings as insignificant and unimportant, while other people's shortcomings are terrible, and *lashon hara* must be spoken about them. He needs to change his outlook, to emphasize the positive qualities of others and lessen the importance of his own. He then needs to realize how far he is from where he could be, and he will then realize that he has little to be prideful about.

The Sifsei Chaim's second suggestion involves one's examining where one is holding by looking only at oneself and not in comparison to others. A person usually thinks of himself as just a normal person going about his daily affairs. If he does have any bad traits, he reasons, they are not that important anyway. And even if they are, surely he is better than the person across the street, for example, who doesn't keep Shabbos.

The Sifsei Chaim questions whether it is a valid approach to compare oneself to weaker people, who, as in the example above, never grew up knowing what Shabbos is. The first problem with this attitude is that a person could be asked why he reached only that level and didn't get further. The second problem is, why compare oneself to weaker elements and be prideful that he is better than they are?

This can be compared to one who walks into a home for people with poor mental health. When he sees that each resident has some mental disease, he begins to praise himself for being healthy. So too, even one who is surrounded by people whom he is stronger than in various areas should not be prideful because of it. Rather, he has to ask himself if he is using his strengths in the maximum possible way.

Meet Azazel

O ne of the most mysterious sections of the Yom Kippur service was when the *kohen* would take two he-goats, identical in size and appearance, and lots would be drawn to determine which of the two would be offered on the altar, *laShem* (for Hashem), while the second would be drawn *la'Azazel* (for Azazel). Perhaps this is where the word "scape-goat" comes from, since the *kohen* would stand by the latter and confess all of the sins of Israel. It would then be led outside the city, taking the sins with it, and thrown off a cliff to a bloody death below. What is the deeper meaning and significance of this ritual?

Great Secrets

The verse says, "Aharon should place lots upon the two he-goats, one lot 'for Hashem' and one lot 'for Azazel' " (*Vayikra* 16:8). Ibn Ezra makes a mysterious comment regarding this ritual: "If you are able to understand the secret after the word 'Azazel,' you will understand its secret and the secret of its name...I will reveal part of its secret by allusion: when you are thirty-three you will understand it."

It is fascinating that the Ibn Ezra speaks like this, and we actually find that the Ramban says he will reveal its secret. According to the Ramban, the number thirty-three alludes to the thirty-third verse following the above verse, where it says, "And they will no longer bring their sacrifices to the demons" (*Vayikra* 17:7). Yisrael often fell into idolatry, which the Torah warns against many times, yet the Ramban quotes Pirkei D'Rabi Eliezer, who says that we are to send a bribe to Samael on Yom Kippur. It should be sent to him, he says, "as he rules over the desolate places and has the authority to bring destruction, desolation and war to the world. It is fitting that this be brought to him, as he has the powers for all of this." What we have to be wary of is that we not think, God forbid, that we are offering a sacrifice to Samael, but we are to do this simply because it is the will of Hashem.

The Ramban cites the following parable to illustrate his point. There was once a man who prepared a banquet for the king. The king commanded the host to send a portion to one of his servants. The host does not send this portion in order to give that servant any respect; rather, he does it all for the king, who is giving reward to the servant. The host is only showing his loyalty to the king by carrying out his command. On the other hand, the king, in his compassion for the host, wants his servant to benefit, so that the servant should only praise the host.

In like manner, Hashem is telling us to give a portion to His servant (Samael), in the hope that the servant will not bring accusations against us. It is for this reason that the goats are divided by lottery. If the *kohen* would designate each one, it would appear that he was offering something in his own name. Instead, both were placed before Hashem, and through the lottery, Hashem chose which one was for Him and which for His servant. Therefore, we do not even slaughter the goat; we only pass it on to His servant. We follow this procedure because on Yom

Kippur we want the accuser to remain silent and refrain from condemning Yisrael.

Where Does He Belong?

Rav Shimshon Raphael Hirsch[19] explains what the two goats symbolize. Each one of us is faced with free choice. One can oppose his evil inclination, resisting the evil it offers him. By doing so one comes closer to Hashem. On the other hand, one who gives in to his desires and the dictates of his heart is *l'Azazel*. Rav Hirsch describes at great length that free will is such a crucial factor of our existence that it places us over the lower elements: "The whole height and dignity and worth of human beings lies in the ability to sin...in the sphere of the primitive and organic world there can be no sin, but just on that account no virtue, no morality." He then continues, saying that "if everything good was sweet and everything bad was bitter," then we would be deprived of free will and would be unable to make an active choice to be *laShem* or *l'Azazel*.

We all face a choice whether to sacrifice ourselves for the sake of being *laShem*, having to control our desires, and to follow His Torah and mitzvos. Only then can we enter the holy of holies. On the other hand, there, at the entrance to the holy of holies, one can scorn the choice offered to him, opting for a life of "the uncontrolled might of sensuality, which has no place in the Sanctuary." This has to be sent away into the barren wilderness, for it belongs in the wild, "where this earthly world does not become elevated." It is precisely because one has free will that this decision has value, yet one has to face this choice, which will determine his present and future existence.

Two Inclinations

Rav Yisrael Salanter[20] says that the two goats represent the two types of *yetzer hara* that must be combated. The first acts when a person's natural impulse tempts him to sin. The second type actually persuades him to believe that what he is doing is right. *Chazal* say that the first type actually has to be used in the service of Hashem, as the verse says, "and you shall serve Him with all your heart," referring to the good and bad inclinations, which can both be used to serve the Creator. For instance, jealousy is generally not a good trait, but if it leads a man to learn Torah even more diligently than he had learned before, it may have a positive benefit. On the other hand, one has to flee as far as possible from the *yetzer* that deceives him and makes him believe what he is doing is right. This is alluded to in the following verse. Regarding the slaughtered goat it says, "that you shall offer it 'in front of Hashem.' " In other words, one can use this first type of *yetzer* in front of Hashem for the better. The second goat, "you shall send to Azazel, in the desert," that is, there is no remedy for this second type of *yetzer* and it has to be banished.

Another way of looking at the symbolism of the two goats[21] regards the direction that people take in life. Two people can be doing exactly the same actions on the surface, yet if one were to look at the motivation of each, or where each one hopes these actions will take him, their deeds couldn't be further apart. This can be compared to two trains at a station, each identical. One pulls out in a westerly direction, while the other heads eastward. The further they move, the more they are traveling apart; while each has traveled only, say fifty miles, they are now one hundred miles apart.

Thus, two people may appear to be doing the same actions, yet on closer inspection their real intentions and where they are heading are entirely different from each other. What is the reason for the difference? Because at the beginning each were facing different directions. Although they are doing the same thing, slowly they move further and further apart.

Parashas Kedoshim

No Surprises There

av Yaakov Neimann[22] cites the following *gemara* (*Berachos* 28b). When Rebi Eliezer was ill, his students went up to visit him. They said to him, "Our master, teach us the path of life with which to merit the World to Come." One of the pieces of advice that he gave was "Be careful of the honor of your friend."

Why is it that Rebi Eliezer's students waited until he was about to die to ask him this question? What else had he been teaching them all these years if not the path to life? The answer is that every day Rebi Eliezer was going up a level, and the next day another level. They wanted to know what the highest level was that he had reached and then that would be the highest that they would strive for.

What is surprising is that Rebi Eliezer did not teach his students something profound and esoteric; instead, the best piece of advice he had was to be careful about the honor due to their fellows. Through this simple advice they would become more and more elevated. The idea is that if one wants to reach high levels of spirituality, one does not need to seek supernatural means to achieve this. Rather, one can attain great heights through more obvious, earthly deeds (see *The Wisdom Within, Parashas Acharei Mos-Kedoshim* for more on this). In particular, let us examine how his advice manifests itself through the mitzvos of our *parashah*.

Pale From...

Once, Rav Baruch Ber[23] had finished davening when his son-in-law noticed that he looked very pale. He asked him if everything was in order, to which he replied that he was afraid that he had invalidated a bill of divorce. What was the problem? He was going through his suitcase and he came upon a book that bore a stamp belonging to a certain shul that he had passed, and since he hadn't returned the book at that time, he felt that he was considered a thief. A few days prior to this he had been a witness on a bill of divorce and was worried that in retrospect it was invalid, as he was a nonkosher witness.

Rav Baruch's son-in-law tried to prove to him that the halachah does not follow this opinion, but Rav Baruch would not accept his reasoning. He only calmed down when he recalled that on a trip to Minsk, highwaymen had attacked his coach, and in fear of his life he had recited *vidui* (confession) for his sins. Although he was still obligated to return the book, the confession had meant that he was no longer considered a sinner. He was a kosher witness and the bill of divorce was valid.

One More Trick up His Sleeve

The verse says, "You shall surely rebuke your fellow and you shall not bear a sin" (*Vayikra* 19:17). The Ben Ish Chai[24] cites a beautiful parable that illustrates this point. There was once a king who decreed that a certain robber should be hanged. The thief said that he accepted the judgment, but that the king should wait while he performed a wondrous feat for him. Since the thief claimed that he was the only one in the world that could perform the feat, should he be killed so would his wondrous act.

The thief explained that he would take a single seed, prepare it in a magic potion, place it in the ground, and after half a year it would grow into a large tree full of fruit. His curiosity piqued, the king took his second-in-command as well as his finance minister into the royal garden to observe the act. The king gave the thief a seed, and the thief coated it in a special potion and waited half an hour until it was time to plant it. When the half hour had passed he told his audience that the seed would grow only if the one who planted it had hands that were free from all traces of robbery, and therefore perhaps someone else would oblige, as he was a convicted robber.

He asked the second-in-command to plant it, but he replied that he couldn't, as when he was younger he cared for the estate of his father and he may have spent more than necessary, so it was better if someone else would do it. He turned to the finance minister, who replied that as finance minister, much money passed through his hands and he may have made a mistake somewhere along the line. He then turned to the king himself, who said that when he was younger he had stolen a golden thread from his father and therefore his hands were not totally clean.

When the thief heard this he fell to the feet of the king and said, "First I asked the second-in-command, and then the finance minister, but their hands are not clean. Not even you, the king, have clean hands. Why then are you hanging me? I only stole because I was hungry for bread."

The king knew that the thief had done all of this deliberately. He had proved his point and the king forgave him. The idea is that before one rebukes his friend he has to look at himself first and see that he is free of these negative traits. That is why the verse says, "You shall surely rebuke (*hochei'ach tochi'ach*) your fellow," using a repetition. It teaches us that when one comes to rebuke his fellow, he has to rebuke himself first. Only once he is free of that trait can he rebuke others. Then he will not "bear a sin" over it.

Coming Back to Haunt You

The verse says, "With justice you shall judge your fellow" (*Vayikra* 19:15). One interpretation[25] is that you have to judge others meritoriously and assume that what they are doing is correct, even if on the surface it could seem otherwise. *Chazal* say that the way one judges others is the way that he will be treated in Heaven. This is seen in *Avos* (3:20), where it says that a person receives punishment "in ways that he knows about and in ways that he does not know about." The idea is that if one sees another doing something questionable and one comes to the conclusion that he is sinning, he himself will be judged like that in the next world.

Regarding this idea, Rav Avraham Pam cites the story of David Hamelech. David was married to Batsheva, whose husband Uriyah had been killed on the front lines (and had indeed been placed there by the king). After Uriyah was killed, the prophet Nassan came and told David a story of a rich and poor man. The rich man had everything and the poor man had only one sheep, which the rich man took away. Nassan asked David Hamelech what he thought should happen, to which he answered that such a man should be put to death. Nassan then told David that indeed he was that guilty man, as he himself had married Batsheva.

The Baal Shem Tov says that this is what will happen in the next world. We will come before the Heavenly Court and will be given cases to judge. We will say he should be punished this way, another a different way, until it is revealed that in fact we are the ones who committed the crimes and we have declared our own fate.

This treatment stems from our inability to give others the benefit of the doubt. The Gemara (*Shabbos* 127b) says that one who judges others favorably will himself be judged favorably. How we judge others is how we will be judged, measure for measure. We have to avoid jumping to conclusions about the worthiness of others and judge people favorably, or our negative attitude may come back to haunt us.

Going against the Grain

The verse says, "You shall not hate your brother in your heart" (*Vayikra* 19:17). Rav Yaakov Neimann[26] says that it is obvious that when someone does evil to another, it is forbidden for the victim to take revenge on that person. One has to forgive him and remove the hatred from his heart. The question is, how can the Torah make such an instruction, requiring one to go against his natural emotions? He cites a principle of Rav Yisrael Salanter, which says when a person has done wrong to one, one should do something good for that person. This idea may sound strange, yet it is similar to what we mentioned in *parashas Bereishis*, that when one gives to another person, he actually becomes closer to him. Therefore, when one gives to a person who has wronged him, one's hatred for him will be removed from his heart. Also, the "friend" will come to see the good done for him and will have regrets over what he has done. Someone possessing a quiet nature may keep the hatred within him, as he doesn't want to make a big deal out of it, yet inside it bothers him. Should such a person follow Rav Yisrael Salanter's advice, he will eradicate the hatred from his heart.

These ideas are perhaps summarized by the following explanation of Rav Yehudah Ze'ev Segal,[27] who says that there is a connection between not taking revenge and the commandment to love one's fellow Jew as oneself. The Yerushalmi offers a parable. If one used a knife to cut one of his hands with the other hand, would he take revenge on the hand that inflicted the wound? Surely he is only hurting his other hand more. Similarly, if one sees the Jewish people as a whole, he will not seek revenge or bear a grudge against others.

The Chafetz Chaim says that when the seventy people went down with Yaakov to Egypt they were called *nefesh* (a soul). The verse that we recite on Shabbos during *minchah* says, "Who is like Your people Yisrael, one nation on earth?" (I *Divrei Hayamim* 17:21). The Jewish nation is a whole. Therefore, says the Chafetz Chaim, taking revenge or bearing a grudge is really doing damage to oneself.

Parashas Emor

The Lesson of the Clock

A certain rav once gave a *shiur* in which he posed the following question: What is the most valuable commodity in the world? One person answered, "Diamonds," another, "Love," another, "Money," another "Happiness," and so on. Finally he revealed what the great secret was: "The most valuable commodity in the world is...time." This sort of answer may seem rather surprising at first, but when we look at some of the lessons in this week's *parashah*, and in particular the counting of the Omer, it may not seem so strange.

Rav Chaim of Volozhin[28] would say that there is one *mussar sefer* which is not counted amongst the classics, yet it has a great deal to teach us. What is it? The clock. If one were to look at the hands of his watch going round and round, and realize how each second is lost, and each minute and hour has passed without anything productive being accomplished, he would be awakened to the value of time and devote more attention to matters of Heaven.

Rav Zalman Sorotzkin says that this idea is seen in the verse "So teach us to number our days, that we may get a heart of wisdom" (*Tehillim* 90:12). If a person would count his days so that they should not go to waste, then the wisdom within his heart would be increased.

Similarly, we have a mitzvah in this week's *parashah* to count the Omer. By counting aloud, "Today is day..." we realize that each day has to be used productively in order to place us on a higher spiritual level than the day before. One realizes that there are fewer and fewer days until the receiving of the Torah and will be inspired to greater alacrity in one's Divine service. We shall return to this idea later.

Unspecified

The verse[29] says that on Shavuos "you shall offer a new meal offering to Hashem" (*Vayikra* 23:16). This particular offering alludes to the day of the giving of the Torah, in that just like when we stood at Sinai all the laws of the Torah were new and fresh, every day a person has to feel that the Torah is fresh, as if he had received it that day. One has to find ways of maintaining his enthusiasm, and feel the attractiveness of learning something new, rather than letting it become stale to him.

Why is it that in this passage dealing with Shavuos, no mention is made of the giving of the Torah? Rather, we have to make the calculation ourselves. Why does the Torah hide this connection? The answer is that the Torah did not wish to fix a specific date to our receiving the Torah, as every single day one has to feel like we are receiving it anew. The *Sifri* says that every day has to be considered as new and not as something which one is repulsed by because he is doing the same old thing. This idea is alluded to in the fact that on Shavuos, a *minchah chadashah* is offered, a meal offering of the new crops. In addition, two loaves are brought, which allude to the *yetzer hara*, which is symbolized by the puffy appearance of leaven. This shows us that although there is the evil inclination, there is also the Torah which is used to counter it.

The following parable[30] illustrates this point. Two people enter a house. One is a regular there. He goes in every day and stays for several hours. The second visits infrequently and for shorter amounts of time. Each one of them has an advantage over his fellow. The former, who spends more time there, is considered a more permanent resident and feels that it is like home. On the other hand, when the infrequent visitor comes it is a fresh and new experience each time. He sees things that he did not notice before and feels excited about coming.

This is seen in the verse that King David said: "One thing I request...to dwell in the House of Hashem...and to visit in His Sanctuary" (*Tehillim* 27:4). He was asking that even though he wanted to always dwell in the House of Hashem, he also wanted to have the status of a visitor, that he should feel the freshness and excitement of being there and learning Hashem's Torah as if it were given today.

Barley versus Wheat

There is a great difference between Pesach, when we offer the Omer offering, which consists of barley, and the Shavuos offering, which is made of grain. How can we account for this difference? When the Jews were in Egypt they were one step away from the lowest level of impurity, and were bereft of mitzvos. Therefore, the offering on Pesach is made of barley, which is an animal fodder, to show us that a person without Torah and mitzvos is like an animal. On the other hand, the offering of Shavuos is wheat, a food for human consumption. This teaches us that only after receiving the Torah are we truly more refined and above simply following our animal instincts.

Let us examine an approach of Rav Shimshon Pinkus.[31] He

says that with every mitzvah we have some understanding of the reasoning behind it and what it is supposed to achieve. For example, one of the reasons behind sitting in the sukkah is to remind us of Hashem's constant supervision of and protection over us. Yet with the mitzvah to count the Omer, the reasons are somewhat unclear. The Torah has told us to count days, yet what is the nature and purpose of it, and why is it counted in a particular way, starting from one and ending with forty-nine, rather than counting downwards?

Rav Pinkus quotes the *Sefer Hachinnuch*, which enlightens us regarding some of these issues. The *Sefer Hachinnuch* says that the root of the mitzvah stems from the fact that the essence of the Jewish people is their adherence to Torah. Their going from slavery to freedom wasn't just to attain freedom for its own sake, but in order to receive the Torah. Therefore, we are commanded to count from the second day of Pesach until the day of the giving of the Torah, to show our will, desire and enthusiasm for the receiving of the Torah.

Long Time or Short Time

The question remains: If one strongly desires something, he counts the days that are left until the great event. Why is it that here we count the days that have passed?

Rav Pinkus cites an idea of Rav Aharon Kotler, which we mentioned in *parashas Vayeitzei*. Yaakov had to wait seven years before he could marry Rachel, yet, as the Torah describes it, "and they were in his eyes like a few days in his love for her" (*Bereishis* 29:20). Surely conventional thinking would suggest that the more one desires something, the longer it would seem to take to obtain it. Each day should then have seemed to Yaakov like seven years. Rav Aharon answers that Yaakov wasn't spending the days thinking about his future marriage. Rather, he was purifying and sanctifying himself for the purpose of building *Klal Yisrael.*

To illustrate this point, Rav Pinkus goes on to cite the following parable. A certain person was destined to receive a million dollars in a hundred days. If he were told that he would receive the money without any exertion on his part, he would be very happy, but every day of the wait would seem to last a lifetime. On the other hand, if he were given set tasks to do each day in order to attain the money at the end of the hundred days, then each day would be worth ten thousand dollars to him and would consequently pass much more quickly.

What then is the difference? In the former instance, when the person has to do nothing to receive the money, his one hundred days are spent empty of all content. Since he is only looking forward to the final day, each day is just an interruption between now and the money. In contrast, in the second instance, where the person spends each day fruitfully, time will pass much more quickly. He realizes each day's worth, as without it the final amount will be deficient.

It was the same with Yaakov. He spent those seven years before his marriage building himself spiritually, and consequently, each day was spent happily and productively. That is why they seemed like only a few days to him.

The same principle applies to the counting of the Omer. There are fifty days from Pesach to Shavuos. If we were to count down from fifty to one it would appear as if each day was just a burden without purpose. By counting upwards, we show that each day is one of building and preparing ourselves for the receiving of the Torah.

Just Ask the Land

The verse says, "And you will fulfill My statutes...and you shall dwell on the land in security...and you shall dwell upon it in security" (*Vayikra* 25:18-19). The second half of the verse seems to be merely a repetition of what has already been stated. The Meshech Chochmah offers an explanation for this. When there is strife between two nations, it usually takes one of two forms: either hatred based on religious differences, or hatred based on jealousy, perhaps of the other country's material success. The Torah repeats the above promise to teach us that it is within our power to remain protected from both causes of hatred.

This is seen in the verse "And you will fulfill My statutes and observe My commandments." Adherence to the Torah is the key to our dwelling securely. One would have thought that since the Jews have practices unlike any other nation, then the nations should detest us. Therefore, the Torah points out that firstly, Yisrael will dwell securely on the land, meaning that if they follow the correct path there will not be religious hatred, and secondly, there will not be hatred based on jealousy. Furthermore, "the land shall give you its fruit and you will eat to your satisfaction."

As long as the Jews follow Hashem's Torah, there will be only peace with their neighbors.

Kicked Out

The Gemara (*Shabbos* 33a) says that the punishment for failing to observe the *shemittah* is exile. Why is this punishment appropriate? The Kli Yakar says that when one doesn't observe the *shemittah*, he is indicating that he lacks faith in the promise of Hashem to provide enough food in the sixth year to last him for three years until the next crop is ready. Eretz Yisrael is particular, so to speak, that this miracle be performed through it. When one lets his field rest he demonstrates firstly that one must have faith in Hashem, as He is the Source of all, regardless of one's own efforts, and secondly, that he knows he is not the true owner of the land, but ultimately it all belongs to Hashem. Eretz Yisrael has this second desire as well, to be recognized as the property of Hashem. Therefore, when one fails to observe these laws, he is offending the land, so the most appropriate punishment is banishing him from it.

On this point, Rav Shlomo Bloch[32] observes that the first exile, which was caused by Israel's failure to observe the *shemittah*, lasted only seventy years, yet the second exile, which was caused by baseless hatred, has to date lasted two thousand years. He explains that this is an indication of Hashem's mercy. The *shemittah* is a difficult mitzvah to observe, and consequently, people who observe it are described as "mighty warriors who fulfill His word" (*Tehillim* 103:26). Great faith is required to meet this daunting challenge; therefore, the first exile lasted only seventy years. On the other hand, the current exile, which began because of baseless hatred, is within our power to restrict. Therefore, its punishment is more severe.

Whose Is It, Anyway?

Rav Moshe Feinstein[33] says that there is another lesson to be learned from *shemittah*. By releasing one's land every seven years, one demonstrates that really one's ownership of it is limited and that it is ultimately Hashem's. During the *shemittah* he has to open his gates and let everyone in to enjoy the fruits of his fields. Then in the Yovel year (occurring every fifty years), certain fields and houses are returned to their ancestral heritage. This demonstrates Hashem's will and control over everything, as it says, "And the land shall not be sold forever, for the land is Mine, for you are strangers and sojourners with Me" (*Vayikra* 25:23).

Two people once came to Reb Chaim of Volozhin,[34] each claiming that they owned a piece of land. After presenting their arguments, much to their astonishment, they watched Reb Chaim bend down to the ground. Seeing their surprised expressions, he said to them, "Each one of you is claiming the land, so I decided to see what the land had to say. Do you know what it said? That both of you belong to Him."

Well, Anyway...

The Torah says, "And if you will say, 'What shall we eat in the seventh year...?' and I will command My blessing to you in the sixth year" (*Vayikra* 25:20). Rav Yaakov Neimann[35] asks the following question on this verse. The Torah need only tell us that Hashem would give His blessing and then there would be no room for the question "What shall we eat?" Why does it have to mention the question as well?

Rav Neimann answers that really it is inappropriate to ask the question "What shall we eat?" This is because even without the promise of extra blessing one would still have to observe the mitzvah of Hashem. Rather, the question "What shall we eat?"

applies to one who has not taken upon himself the yoke of Torah and mitzvos and belief in Hashem. Therefore, it is said to him, "and I will command My blessing."

The proof of this is that nowadays, since the exile, many are of the opinion that *shemittah* is rabbinical in nature, and the promise of extra blessing does not apply, yet we are still obligated to observe it and endure the hardships it entails. Therefore, those who observe the *shemittah* are testifying to the Kingship of Hashem, since they are prepared to do the will of the King even without the promises of plenty. If one would have been lacking in faith (during the times when the *shemittah* was Biblically ordained), the answer to him is prepared: "and I will command My blessing to you in the sixth year." However, to ask such a question in the first place demonstrates a lack of faith.

Rav Moshe Feinstein[36] says that in fact the question is totally inappropriate. The verse says that they are asking what they will eat in the seventh year, but in fact in that year they would still have food to eat from the crop of the sixth year. The question would be appropriate to ask only in the eighth year, when they would really be lacking. Thus, the verse is indicating that their request is inappropriate, as they are asking what they will eat when they still have food in front of them. Since they see the food before them, they should know that it comes from Hashem and that He can provide them with everything, even should nothing sprout. Therefore, the question is based on a lack of faith.

Maybe Not Bad?

I saw another interpretation[37] of the question "What shall we eat?" which describes the question positively. Throughout the other six years of the *shemittah* cycle the people would be involved in many land-related mitzvos: *leket, shichechah, pe'ah, terumos* and *maasros*. By performing these mitzvos, the farmer would increase the holiness in his work, which would lead to blessing from Hashem. However, in the seventh year, when the farmers let the land lie fallow, they couldn't perform these mitzvos. This would lead to an absence of holiness, as well as an absence of the blessings that the holiness would bring. Thus, the question "What shall we eat?" in fact expresses the concern that from the lack of these mitzvos, people would think that they would not receive blessing. Therefore, the Torah says "and I will command My blessing to you," meaning that the produce of the sixth year would suffice for the next three years.

Elsewhere, Rav Moshe Feinstein comments on the connection between the mitzvah of *shemittah* and the commandment "a man shall not cheat his brother" (*Vayikra* 25:14), which is mentioned right in the middle of the portion dealing with *shemittah*. He says that one refrains from cheating, lying and robbing his fellow man because one believes that his *parnassah* is ordained from Heaven and is not due to any more or less effort on his part. Therefore, one will have no interest in what one's fellow has. As we have mentioned, *shemittah* also requires great strength to perform. Therefore, should a person have this level of faith, he will not stumble by cheating. The same person who will express a lack of faith in Hashem by attempting to steal, will also ask in the *shemittah,* "What shall we eat?"

Standing on Two Feet

T his week's *parashah* contains the *tochachah* (rebuke) and enumerates the consequences the Jewish people will suffer should they disobey the Torah's laws. The verse says, "and you will be smitten before your enemies; they that hate you shall rule over you" (*Vayikra* 26:17). Rav Baruch of Kosov[38] cites the following parable. Reuven was fighting Shimon and was punching him while he was lying on the floor. Shimon should have been the one crying out. Yet Reuven, in his wisdom, not only punches him, but he cries out that Shimon is beating him so that others can hear. This is a double blow for Shimon: not only is he being smitten, but he is also being incited against, as if he were the one smiting his fellow.

The verse says in *Tehillim* (22:14), "They gape upon me with their mouths, like a raving and roaring lion." What is the connection between the first and second parts of the verse? The Jewish people complain that not only do the nations fight us physically, but even at the time of fighting they open their mouths and say that it is Yisrael who is the roaring lion, the aggressor.

Rav Baruch explains that in every generation, the nations rise up against the Jews and claim that they are in the right, as if the real enemies and aggressors are the Jews. It is for this double blow that we cry out to Hashem.

Great Kindness!

When the Noda BeYehudah[39] was the Rav in Prague, a decree was promulgated that Jews be drafted into the army. In 1789 the first group left for service. The Noda BeYehudah accompanied them for part of the way, offering them support and words of consolation. Before parting from them he instructed them that they must continue praying daily, and that they should volunteer for extra duty on Sundays so that their fellow soldiers might relieve them of their duties on Shabbos.

When the Rav returned to Prague he related to his congregants the following insight. Towards the end of the *tochachah* it says, "But despite all this, while they will be in the land of their enemies, I will not have been abhorred by them, nor will I have rejected them to destroy them...to annul My covenant with them" (*Vayikra* 26:44). Why does the verse say, "despite all this"? This verse introduces the words of comfort. Why then does it mention that it was despite all that had happened?

He continued that the emperor's decree drafting Jews into the army had been somewhat beneficial for the Jews, in that they were being treated as equal to all citizens of the empire. The Jewish soldiers were told that they too would rise through the ranks and gain honor. However, this rise in prominence would bring with it a great problem. When the verse says, "But despite all this," it tells us that there is one more curse left that would visit the Jewish people at the end of days. When they will be "in the land of their enemies," there will be a time when they will dwell in peace and serenity, they will not be abhorred by the nations and will have equal rights. However, we have to beware that their intention in befriending us is to bring us to the point where the Jewish faith is endangered. The nations want the Jews to act like them, so that they will be unrecognizable as Jews, severing their relationship with Hashem. The nations will try to "annul My covenant with them." This is the final test to beware of.

Rav Nachum Ze'ev,[40] the son of the Alter of Kelm, cites the following parable. When a group of people are sitting around a table eating and drinking, the distinctions between them are somewhat blurred. After the meal all of them get up and go, except for one who remains seated. The reason only becomes clear when one looks beneath the table and sees that the man has no legs. Originally, they all appeared the same, yet when it is time to go the differences rise to the surface. Similarly, there are people who sit in yeshivah, and when all of them are learning, there doesn't appear to be any distinction between them. Yet when they leave yeshivah, then the differences become apparent, and one can see who has or hasn't got feet to stand on. There are those whom the slightest winds knock off, while there are others whom even the strongest winds in the world will not move.

In the opening of this week's *parashah*, the verse says, "If you will go (*teileichu*) in My decrees" (*Vayikra* 26:3). The "going" refers to going with the Torah, meaning that one has to stand firmly on his feet and not be ashamed before those who scoff and try to point him in other directions.

Hitting the Target

Chazal say (*Sanhedrin* 60a) that the verse "If you will go in My decrees" (*Vayikra* 26:3) means "the decrees that I have set for you already." What is the meaning of this statement?

Rav Yosef Shaul Nathanson[41] cites the following parable. When one wants to teach soldiers how to shoot arrows, one first paints a center point to aim at and then draws rings around it. If one were to shoot at the wall and then draw rings around where the arrow lands, it would be a rather fruitless exercise. The same is true of mitzvos. We are obligated to follow the Torah as Hashem gave it to Moshe at Sinai. Heaven forbid were we to draw our own road map of what we want to do. This is the intention of the Gemara. "If you will go in My decrees": you have to follow the decrees which Hashem has already set out. Hashem has already painted the target, and it's not the other way round.

Rav Moshe Feinstein[42] says that the words "go in My decrees" instruct us to go on the path that will bring us to fulfill the Torah and mitzvos, and not to seek alternative paths. The verse says, "Happy is the man who does not go in the counsel of the wicked (*Tehillim* 1:1). The verse is telling us that the wicked do not explicitly tell us to transgress the Torah and not to fulfill its laws, because they know that no one will listen to them. Rather, they suggest ways that are seemingly in accordance with the Torah, but are really aimed at pushing people further away from it. We learn from here that the only true path is to follow in His ways, with learning Torah, doing mitzvos and working on one's character traits.

It's All There

Rav Aharon Kotler[43] cites some very fundamental principles which he gleans from our *parashah*. His essay is entitled "Everything Is Included in the Torah," referring to the fact that all aspects of human endeavor, all events, have their source in the Torah. The Torah has said, "from the ends of the land to the ends of the land" (*Devarim* 28:64), referring to the fact that throughout the exiles, Jews have literally been found in every corner of the world. Think of the most remote place on earth, and you can be sure there are some Jews there, and maybe even a kosher restaurant. Despite this, the Torah has promised us that the people of Israel will never be lost or destroyed completely. This is a most remarkable fact, that despite being scattered everywhere, the people have retained their identity as Jews.

We also find that the Torah uses the past and present interchangeably. The verse says, "That the land shall not spew you out when you defile it, as it has spewed out the nations that were before you" (*Vayikra* 18:28). The irony is that this verse was said in the wilderness, when the seven nations were still in the land, yet it speaks of them as having already been spewed out. This is because Hashem is above time; past and present are viewed together by Him. Therefore, the Torah writes about the nations already being expelled although it had not yet occurred.

Rav Aharon then says that we have to understand that every word in the Torah has worlds contained within it. He cites a *sefer* that gives us an unbelievable insight. Every prophecy that was said to our fathers was fulfilled in the very place that the prophecy was said, many years later. Hashem said to Yaakov, "a nation and a congregation of nations shall be from you" (*Bereishis* 35:11). This was said at a time when the tribes were already born. *Chazal* say that "a nation" refers to the tribe of Binyamin, and "a congregation of nations" refers to Ephraim and Menasheh. This prophecy was said at Beit El, the place which is the common border of those three tribes. Furthermore, the prophecy of "kings shall descend from you" (*Bereishis* 17:6) was said in Chevron, the place where the house of David was born. Similarly, every word in the Torah was fulfilled at the very place where it was said.

Rav Aharon goes on to say that the entire future of *Klal Yisrael*, of every individual, of other nations and creatures, is indeed all in the Torah. The Torah includes everything from creation until the end of days. He says that this has to be understood, especially as there are many voices preaching to the contrary that are making themselves heard. We have to understand that everything is included in the Torah, and we have continuously seen the fulfillment of its prophecies.

The verse says, "The Torah of Hashem is perfect, restoring the soul" (*Tehillim* 19:8). When is it "restoring the soul"? When it is perfect and free of those who distort it. Rav Aharon says that we have the benefit of the holy *Tanna'im*, *Amora'im* and *gedolei Yisrael*, who are able to interpret how the Torah is meant to be understood. Understanding it through any other means can lead one along dangerous paths. Only when the Torah is pure will it draw one into its holy chambers.

Bemidbar

Part of the Whole

This week's *parashah* describes the counting of the tribes. Our discussion will focus on one tribe in particular, the tribe of Levi. Levi was distinguished from the other tribes by, amongst other things, its small size. This week's *parashah* describes the counting of the tribes. Why was the tribe of Levi smaller in number than the other tribes? Various reasons are given for this. The Netziv[1] says that even when they lived in Egypt, the tribe of Levi was set aside for the service of Hashem. While the rest of *bnei Yisrael* kept the Torah only from Sinai onwards, Levi accepted it upon themselves even in Egypt (just like our three forefathers, who observed the Torah even when it was not yet given).

There is a saying that "the closer you are to the fire, the more you get burnt." Hashem deals more strictly with those who are nearer to Him. Therefore, the tribe of Levi was punished when they would transgress the Torah, even though it had not yet been given to *bnei Yisrael*, and these punishments diminished their numbers. On the other hand, the rest of *bnei Yisrael* were not culpable for violating the commandments until the giving of the Torah at Sinai. Therefore, their numbers remained high.

The Ramban provides a different explanation as to why the tribe of Levi was so small. The other tribes were enslaved, and the Egyptians tried to diminish their numbers by subjecting them to hard labor. Hashem performed a miracle to counter this, and they increased and multiplied instead of diminishing. On the other hand, Levi should have increased in the normal fashion, since they weren't being persecuted, and yet they couldn't match the other tribes in numbers and were in fact far less in populaton. The Ramban says that this may have been because of Yaakov's anger towards Shimon and Levi after they wiped out the city of Shechem and his subsequent cursing of their anger. Shimon was the most populous tribe at this stage, yet by the time they entered the land they were greatly diminished due to various plagues meted out as punishments for various sins. Levi was never harmed by the plagues Shimon suffered, but started small and was not blessed with growth when, in contrast, the other tribes were increasing at a supernatural rate.

Being Apart

The Torah says that the tribe of Levi had to be counted separately from the rest of the tribes and not included in their numbering. If one looks at the verses in the first two chapters of *Bemidbar*, one notices that the commandment that the tribe of Levi should not be counted among the other tribes is in fact mentioned three times.

Rav Chaim Shmulevitz[2] examines the reasons for this. He says that this is to emphasize that there is something about the *levi'im* which sets them apart. Rashi cites a *midrash* which says that Hashem looked into the future and saw that there would be a decree on all people over the age of twenty, that they would die in the desert and not merit entering the land. Hashem said that the tribe of Levi should not be included in that group. Had they been in the count along with the rest of *bnei Yisrael*, they too would have been included in the decree.

From this we learn an aspect of how Hashem runs the world. When there is a decree on the whole, it encompasses the entire whole. Even if there are individuals who are not worthy of being punished in that way, nevertheless, they are still included in that group. Therefore, Moshe was instructed not to include Levi in his count of the tribes so that they not suffer the same fate as the remainder of *bnei Yisrael*.

We see an application of this idea in the sentencing of the spies with their punishment. The Ohr Hachaim asks the following question. When the verse says, "And those men that spoke evil about the land died" (*Bemidbar* 14:37), it implies that had they not spoken badly, they would have lived. How can this be, as surely they were over the age of twenty and thus included in the generation that would die in the wilderness? The answer is that because they were the leaders and were assigned this task, they were not included in the regular count of *bnei Yisrael*. Therefore, had they not sinned, they would have survived the decree imposed on the generation of the wilderness as well. On the other hand, Yehoshua and Kalev both lived because they were in this group that was separate from *bnei Yisrael*, yet they passed the test. This is seen in the verse, "And Yehoshua bin Nun and Kalev ben Yefuneh shall live from the men who went to tour out the land" (*Bemidbar* 14:38).

Private and Public

Reb Chaim goes on to explain that there are two ways in which Hashem runs the world. One is that Hashem acts by looking at people as a group, and the world as a whole, and the second is that Hashem acts according to each individual's deeds.

As was mentioned, if punishment is meted out on the whole, then even the righteous cannot avoid it. On the other hand, there are positive aspects to being a part of the whole. Sometimes, if one asks Hashem for mercy as part of a *tzibbur*, then, even if according to his own merits he would not be deemed worthy, he may receive what he requests in the merit of the *tzibbur*.

If one looks at the weekday *Shemoneh Esrei*, all its blessings are in the plural, such as in "Forgive us..." and "Heal us...." Invoking mercy for the whole is a way of invoking mercy for oneself as well. The reasoning behind this idea is that a *tzibbur* is not merely the sum of each individual. Rather, it is a new creation. It has an essence that did not exist before, and therefore, it can achieve things which mere individuals cannot. However, for all of this to happen there has to be unity.

Chazal derive from Scripture that the redemption can come only when *Klal Yisrael* act as one united force. Each individual alone cannot merit the redemption or perceive the Divine Presence, yet when they are all joined together, they become a new entity more powerful than before.

All Together

Bnei Yisrael exhibited this kind of unity at the giving of the Torah. The verse says, "And Yisrael camped opposite the mountain"(*Shemos* 19:20). Rashi says that the Torah uses the singular expression "And Yisrael camped" to show that they camped "like one man with one heart." The Ohr Hachaim says that this was their preparation for receiving the Torah: that they all joined together in unity. The Torah could not be given to individuals; rather, when there was a *tzibbur* they were fit to receive the Torah.

Reb Chaim Shmulevitz explains further that this idea has

ramifications not only for the whole, but also for individuals. The more they join together, the more their strength increases. We see this in last week's *parashah*, where it says that if we follow Hashem's laws, then five men will pursue a hundred enemies, and a hundred will pursue ten thousand. A simple mathematical calculation will show that the latter figures are out of proportion. Yet the answer is that one cannot compare the few who do mitzvos to the many who do mitzvos. The power of the whole is far greater than the sum of individuals.

The verse says, "And Yaakov was left alone and a man fought with him" (*Bereishis* 32:25). Reb Chaim says it was the fact that Yaakov "was left alone" that led to a man fighting with him. We learn from here the danger of being alone. As long as Yaakov was with his sons, he was never in danger. Similarly, when a man is alone, away from the *tzibbur*, his *yetzer hara* tries to attack him. This is seen in the Gemara (*Kiddushin* 30b), where Rebbi Yishmael said to his son, "My son, if that disgusting one (the *yetzer hara*) meets you, drag him into the *beis medrash*." In other words, if he is encountered by his evil inclination when alone, he should bring it into a public place, as the merit of the *tzibbur* will protect him from stumbling.

Reb Chaim adds the following on the subject. We have seen that one included in the *tzibbur* cannot escape Divine punishment. If so, then since the attribute of good is many times greater than the attribute of evil, one should remain with the *tzibbur* in order to merit being blessed along with them. One who separates himself from the *tzibbur* will not merit to receive this blessing with them. He says that this aspect of how Hashem runs the world was evident in the miraculous survival of Yeshivas Mir, which survived the war by moving to Shanghai. Those who stayed with the yeshivah survived, while those who tried their own ways to escape were unfortunately not successful. This idea is also seen in the requirement of a quorum for prayer. The power of ten praying together, even without individual intent, may surpass that of the individual praying with intent. May the merit of the multitude following in the ways of Hashem stand with us.

Inside Out

The famous philosopher Aristotle was once dining at home when some of his students came to his house to discuss philosophy with him. His wife let them in and led them into the dining room where their revered teacher was eating. They were rather surprised to discover that they could not see their teacher's face. He was indulging, head first, in an enormous chicken. They said to him, "Our master, how is it the great one can sink to such depths of baseness?" to which he replied, "When I am out there I am Aristotle, the great philosopher. When I am at home I am but a normal man."

Towards the end of the *parashah* we find the enumeration of each prince's offering for the dedication of the altar in the Mishkan. The whole description is repeated twelve times over, followed by the sum total of what all twelve princes brought. Rashi explains that this teaches us that all of the implements of the Temple were equal individually and when weighed up together, no more and no less.

What is the meaning behind this comment? Rav Moshe Feinstein[3] says that an important message is being conveyed here. A person has to act the same when he is in private and in public. There are some people who are more particular about their actions in public than they are in private, as they think that in public people will learn from them. Therefore, they reason, they need to behave better in public than in private. There are likewise people who are particular about their behavior in private but not in public, as they think other people will view them as haughty. In truth, a person has to be the same inside and outside, in public and in private. Rav Moshe says that this is the way to live in order not to cause damage to one's spirituality. This is seen from the end of our *parashah*, where the vessels were of the same weight, whether taken alone, or whether taken as a group.

I Say, Nice Day...

Once I was taking a tourist friend around to see some of the sights of London. We were at the Tower of London and it was a boiling hot day, so in true, polite English fashion we joined the end of a rather long line to buy a drink. We noticed that the person in front of us was in fact a "beefeater." To the unacquainted, this was a person who would guard the tower and its prisoners hundreds of years ago. Anyway, as part of their efforts to promote tourism, these men walk around the site, giving the tower its authentic feel. We thought that because this beefeater was in front of us, and there was still quite a wait before we would receive our precious drink, it would be the perfect opportunity to have our picture taken with him. We politely asked whether he would mind posing for a photograph with our foreigner, to which he snapped, "When I'm out there you can take as many photos as you like. Now I'm just buying a drink. I'm like any other person."

At first I thought it was rather funny. Was he really forgetting that he was dressed up in garb from the Middle Ages and would therefore attract attention? On reflection, however, I believe there is more than one lesson to be learned from this incident.

A related idea is seen in *Sefer Vayikra*. The verse says, "And any earthenware vessel which something will fall into, all that is in it is impure" (11:33). *Chazal* say that an earthenware vessel has distinct ways of becoming impure. The law is that if an impure object enters the inside of the vessel, even without touching the wall, but only its airspace, the vessel becomes impure. If, on the other hand, the impure object touches the outside of the vessel, the vessel remains pure. The reason for this is that the ability to impart impurity seems to depend on the purpose of the vessel. The earthenware itself has no intrinsic value; rather, its importance is only with respect to what it can contain. Therefore, it becomes impure only when its inside is defiled; its outer side is not what is important. On the other hand, a metal vessel also becomes impure when its outside is touched. This is because the metal itself has intrinsic value, and therefore even the outside is a receptacle for impurity.

On Rosh Hashanah we say that a man is comparable to an earthenware piece. We are like this vessel, whose function is based only on what is on the inside. We are not like metal vessels, whose value is based on external appearances. Instead, a Jew's value is based on what is within and not on how he dresses.

This is seen in the Mishnah (*Avos* 4:27): "Do not look at the jug, but rather that which is inside it," more commonly known as "Never judge a book by its cover." This is a very important lesson for our times. We live in a generation which is accustomed to placing much importance on externals, at the expense of seeing what is really going on. One looks at a person's dress and judges him immediately. How often does it happen that one sees another performing a questionable act and immediately jumps to a conclusion, when a real investigation would reveal otherwise. The lesson of our *parashah* is to see beneath the surface as well.

Not Following the Crowd

The *Sefer Aparion* deals with the above question of why the Torah goes to such great lengths to tell us all the details of the princes' offerings, twelve times over. It would have been enough to describe the first one, and then say that the next prince brought the same one as was brought the day before. It answers by citing the following question. When the Men of the Great Assembly instituted the *Shemoneh Esrei*, why did they write "the God of Avraham, the God of Yitzchak and the God of Yaakov"? It would have been enough to say the God of Avraham, Yitzchak and Yaakov, putting them all together. The answer is that one shouldn't say that only Avraham found Hashem, and that the others just took his word for it. Rather, each of the fathers conducted their own intellectual investigation and came to believe in Hashem.

The same idea is true of the princes. The verse testifies that they didn't just bring their offerings based on what they had seen on the previous day. Instead, when they heard that each of them would be bringing their sacrifices on their own particular day, they came to their own decision to bring these offerings. Furthermore, they were not merely random choices of offerings; instead, each item was specifically chosen because of what it represented (see Rashi for details). This is the reason why each day's offering ends with the words "This is the offering of..." to show that each was an individual choice, made by each prince without his having simply followed something he had seen on previous days.

The Chafetz Chaim[4] takes a different approach. He says that Nesanel ben Suar advised the princes that they should all offer the same offering, that no one should bring more or less than his fellow, since this would have caused jealousy. Hashem gained great satisfaction from this and said, "Just as you do it this way, showing love and respect for each other, therefore I will give you my Shabbos to bring them." Usually a private offering is not brought on the Shabbos, while a public offering is. These offerings were considered private offerings, yet Hashem allowed the seventh offering to override the Shabbos. As a further indication of Hashem's satisfaction with the way they went about their offerings, the Torah lists each one separately.

Sometimes the Torah is very brief with a matter, and sometimes it goes back and repeats information. Because of the princes' respect for one another, the Torah describes each offering at great length, even though each one is the same. This shows Hashem's great love of peace between people. On the other hand, in *parashas Vayakhel*, the princes' offerings for the Mishkan are listed very briefly, with the Torah mentioning only a few words of what they brought. Furthermore, the words there are written in their shortened from, missing various letters. The reason for this is that the princes didn't wish to join together with the people. They said that the people should bring first, and they would bring whatever was left to bring. Hashem was disappointed with them for this, and so the Torah recorded this incident in a different style. The contrast in these two episodes highlights the importance of giving with an outstretched hand, and how great it is when *Klal Yisrael* are at peace with one another.

Parashas Behaalosecha

I'd Like to See the Manager

This week's *parashah* relates several tragic incidents caused by *bnei Yisrael*. Rashi says that the people were intent on angering Hashem, so they started to complain about how tiresome the journey was. The verse says, "The people were like complainers" (*Bemidbar* 11:1). Rashi explains that the word "complainers" means that they were actually looking for something to complain about. Rav Yerucham Levovitz[5] says that the generation that received the Torah not only wanted to separate from following Hashem, but they sought a pretext to do so.

Rav Yerucham cites a parable to explain what a pretext is. Someone asked his friend to deliver some money, but he didn't deliver it to the intended recipient. If the friend would falsely claim that it was lost, this would be a lie but not a pretext. While the matter is false, it is something that could have happened. On the other hand, if the deliverer says that in the middle of the night, the man the money was intended for broke in and took the money, he is casting suspicion on someone who is kosher, and this matter is too unlikely to be true; it is a pretext. In any case, why would the man do such a thing, as he knew the money was on the way?

Rav Yerucham says that the infamous blood libels were also examples of pretexts. Of course they had no logical basis, but they were invented to serve a purpose: to incite people against Jews.

In light of this explanation, the incident in our *parashah* is most unbelievable. *Bnei Yisrael* would make up stories and lies at the very same time that they were sheltered by the cloud of glory and the pillar of fire. How could they do this in the face of Hashem, especially considering the level they were on after witnessing the revelation at Sinai?

Rav Yerucham explains that it all depends on what a person desires. If someone wants something, he will go to any lengths and will bear anything to attain it. King Solomon said, "Many waters cannot quench love, nor can the rivers wash it away" (*Shir Hashirim* 8:7). If a person cannot bear something, and there is a lack of will to even try and put up with it, he will be drawn away for any reason, even the smallest of excuses. For example, there are numerous reasons why one could not learn Torah on any particular day. One could say it's too hot, it's too cold, he's too tired, he's a bit under the weather, and so forth. The problem is that eventually one has to be honest with oneself and ask himself whether they are just excuses or whether they are based on truth. In this case, the people had no desire to follow Hashem. Therefore, they resorted to looking for pretexts to justify not following His will.

We Want Melons

Immediately after this, a further troublesome incident occurs: "And the rabble that was within them desired a desire...And *bnei Yisrael* also wept and said, 'Who will give us meat to eat? We remember the fish which we ate in Egypt for free, the cucumbers, and the melons, and the leeks, and the onions and the garlic' " (*Bemidbar* 11:4-5). The first thing we notice is the repetition in the words "desired a desire." We learn from here that they actually sought to activate this desire within themselves. After all, they had all the food they could want in the form of manna. Thus, they just sought something to complain about.

How can the verse say that they remembered the fish which they ate "for free"? The Egyptians didn't even give them straw, so surely they didn't treat them to fish. The answer is that the word "free" refers to when they were free of Torah and mitzvos. They were revealing their inner desires. Their complaint was not really about the food, but about freeing themselves from the yoke of Hashem's Torah. They viewed life as much better in the olden days of slavery, when at least they didn't have the restrictions of the Torah.

Coming from Effort

This incident raises many questions. We are dealing with what was called the *Dor De'ah*, the Generation of Knowledge. *Chazal* say that at the splitting of the sea they experienced a level of prophecy not even surpassed by Yechezkel. They heard Hashem speaking from Sinai, with the lightning and thunder accompanying it. How could they suddenly lower themselves to such a level where they were moaning over a few onions and a piece of watermelon?

The *mashgiach* of the Lomza Yeshivah, Rav Moshe Rosenstein,[6] explains as follows. The prophets reached their level through toil and effort and therefore were able to maintain that elevated state all their lives. In contrast, the generation of the wilderness were given prophecy without any effort on their part. Hashem gave it to them as a gift so that they would be fit to receive the Torah. This didn't change their inner selves, and hence, once the prophecy ceased, they resorted to sin.

Rav Yaakov Neimann says from here we learn how even those on a high level can stumble and forget everything for some vegetables. Even if one has achieved great accomplishments, one still has to be careful that he doesn't fall to a low level.

This is seen in the following idea. *Chazal* say, "All who see a *sotah* in her disgrace will take a vow of *nezirus*, prohibiting him from wine." The Alter of Kelm points out that this *chazal* uses the word "all" to tell us that even great scholars and sages are included in this warning. If one sees someone doing a greatly corrupt act, one shouldn't think, "What has that got to do with me? I won't reach such low levels as that." Rather, whoever sees has to set himself boundaries that will prevent him from going down that path. This is because the one performing the act didn't just decide one day to do such evil. Instead, it began with a small act, and slowly his deeds became worse until he was eventually capable of such lowly behavior. Each person has to worry that perhaps he is at the beginning stage of developing into something worse. Therefore, one who saw a *sotah* in her disgrace would take a vow prohibiting him from wine, as that was at the root of the sin.

We Don't Like This System

The Kehillas Yitzchak asks the following: Why was *bnei Yisrael's* sin so great that it provoked the anger of Hashem, resulting in their suffering such harsh punishment? It wasn't *treif* meat that they sought; they just wanted kosher meat to satisfy their desires.

The answer is that behind their complaints lay other motives. The lives of the Jews in the desert were not the same as they are now. They were lacking in free will, as immediately after they would sin, they would be punished. The purpose of its being immediate was to instill in them a true fear of Heaven. They would see the ways of Hashem and acquire a deep awareness of His constant supervision, and this knowledge would benefit future generations as well. When they would enter the land, their free will would be returned to them, once they had the tools to face the challenges and with which to cling to the Divine Presence. Therefore, Hashem sent their food in the form of manna, which would also serve as a tool for punishing them immediately if necessary.

The Gemara (*Yoma* 75a) says that sometimes manna is called bread, sometimes rolled dough, and sometimes it was grain that would have to be ground in a mill. How could all these different descriptions be applied to the same thing? The answer is that for the righteous the manna came as ready-made bread. For the intermediate types it came as dough that they had to bake. Finally, for the wicked, it had to be ground with a mill. The nature of the manna was that if a person would sin on one particular day, the next day his food would be more difficult to come by, as his level had dropped and he would have to exert more effort to prepare it. His family would see that he had sinned, and he also had to wait longer for his food, as he had to grind and bake it himself.

In Broad Daylight

Another feature of the manna was that for the righteous it fell outside their front door, bright and early. The intermediate people had to travel slightly further out to collect it, while the wicked would have to go much further to gather it. This factor constituted an even more severe punishment than the first, for the amount of preparation one had to put into the manna was apparent only to the members of a person's household, whereas if one had to travel far out for the manna, everyone would know why he was there. *Chazal* say that the manna could even be used to determine quarrels between people; it would serve as the litmus test in determining who was right or wrong. *Bnei Yisrael* were thus prevented from sinning, as immediately in the morning it would be revealed who the previous day's sinners were.

The wicked therefore sought a way to avoid the manna, yet if they would cite their embarrassment at the trial as the reason, then people would never have accepted it. So instead, they incited people to demand more earthly food. They wanted to purchase meat from the surrounding nations, and they would then also buy flour, thus ridding themselves of the need for manna once and for all. Their pretense was thus just another attempt at removing the yoke of Heaven. It is for this reason that it provoked the wrath of Hashem.

Parashas Shelach Lecha

With All Due Respect

When the spies returned from Eretz Yisrael they reported, "And in our eyes we were as grasshoppers, and so we were in their eyes" (*Bemidbar* 13:33). Rashi says that they told everyone that the inhabitants of the land were saying about them, "In the vineyard there are ants that look like men." In another version cited by Rashi, it says that the inhabitants were in fact saying, "There are grasshoppers that look like men."

The Chasam Sofer[7] says that there is really no contradiction between these two different versions cited by Rashi. A person usually exaggerates his good qualities, both in his own eyes and when reporting them to others. However, when speaking about others he focuses on and exaggerates their bad traits. The spies heard the people saying they were like ants, yet reported back a bit more positively that they were at least like grasshoppers.

Rav Yaakov Kamenetsky[8] says that the reason the spies looked so small to the inhabitants of the land was because they saw themselves as small in their own eyes. If one views himself as nothing, then others will also do so. If he thinks he has no chance of conquering, others will think likewise, and the reality will change accordingly and he will indeed have no chance.

Before Yehoshua brought the people into the land, he insti-tuted the *Aleinu* prayer, in which we thank Hashem that "He did not make our portion as their portion and did not make us like the families of the earth." In this prayer we are thanking Hashem for the differences between ourselves and the nations, who worship mere sticks and stones, who "bow down to vanity and nothingness, to a god that will not save." In contrast, we bow down only to "the King, the King of kings."

With this attitude Yehoshua and the people could go in and do battle with the nations. The old generation had a certain in-feriority complex when they viewed the nations. They saw themselves as ants and grasshoppers. However, once they gained the confidence that they were special, and appreciated that they had a bond with Hashem and His Torah and were en-tering a special land, then they were ready for war.

Coming Up for Air

Rav Yaakov Neimann[9] explains that when the spies said that it was a land that consumed its inhabitants, they were not lying. Before *bnei Yisrael* arrived there it did indeed consume them. When Hashem said that the land was "good," the good refers to the Torah. Rav Neimann compares it to one who enters a certain house which has been closed up for some time and finds the air musty and unpleasant. He cries out, "How is it possible for me to dwell in this house?" His friend then says to him, "Fool! Can't you see that the house is good? It's big and tall. The reason the air isn't good is because it has been sealed up until now. Open the doors and windows and air it out and the place will be good."

The same is true of the Land of Israel. Without Torah, there is no air in the land; therefore, it consumes its inhabitants. When *bnei Yisrael* entered the land, they brought with it the Torah, and this caused a change of air. Says Rav Neimann, the air of the land is Torah, and without it it's impossible to dwell there; it reverts to a land that consumes its inhabitants. When there are people learning Torah in the land, even though there are others who are not learning it, they are also able to live there because of the change of air.

Immediately following the pronouncement of their sentence of forty years of wandering in the desert, some people rebelled against the decree and said, "Now we shall go up to the place that Hashem has said" (*Bemidbar* 14:40). How is it that there was such pandemonium among the people when the spies came back with their report, that they were ready to go back to Egypt, yet suddenly, once Hashem made known their punishment, they were mourning their fate and ready to go up to the land immediately?

The Alter of Kelm explains that when a person is instructed to do something, it becomes harder to do it of his own free will. As long as *bnei Yisrael* were instructed to enter the land, the *yetzer hara* seduced them so that they didn't want to enter and they even cried about having left Egypt. As soon as Hashem annulled the commandment to enter the land, the evil inclination released its hold on them. They returned to their straight thinking and saw that the land really was good for them, and they even put themselves at great risk trying to enter it.

Can I Have a Word?

The Melo Ha'Omer points out that there is a contradiction in the way the spies reported their tale. The verse says, "And they went and came to Moshe and Aharon and to the entire congregation...and they told him" (*Bemidbar* 13:26-27). The verse says that they came to many people, but then reports that they told it only to "him," that is, to Moshe. How can we account for the fact that they began by telling all the people, but then spoke only to Moshe?

When they returned from Eretz Yisrael, they began telling everyone how wonderful the land is. However, they made it clear that there was something that they wished to tell only Moshe. This made people afraid that they were hiding something about the land, and all was not as they were saying publicly.

The same holds true when one speaks negatively about someone. He makes out as if he really doesn't want to say what he is saying. He pretends it is painful for him to say it, or that he is not saying everything he could. A person might say, "With all due respect...," and use it as license to then say whatever he likes about a person. With these tricks he is trying to enhance the credibility of the slander he is spreading. Similarly, the spies were seen going off with Moshe alone so that no one would hear, yet the people began to suspect the worst, and they no longer desired to enter the land.

The spies reported back, "and it also is flowing with milk and honey" (*Bemidbar* 13:27). Rashi comments that a lie cannot stand in the end unless it starts with some truth. The Ohr Torah[10] points out that Rashi's words are extremely precise. When Moshe sent the spies, he told them first to see the strength of the people, depending on what sorts of cities they dwelled in. Only afterwards did he tell them to take note of the quality of the land, whether it is fertile or not. However, when the spies returned they reported in the reverse order, saying first that the land indeed did flow with milk and honey, and only afterwards mentioning that the inhabitants were mighty and frightening and that they could not defeat them.

Why did the spies change the order? The answer lies in the above Rashi. To make their false views acceptable, they had to begin the report by stating some truths. Therefore, first they stated what was true — the physical praises of the land — and then they continued with the falsehoods, saying that the land could not be conquered.

Shooting Arrows

In a similar vein, Yirmeyahu rebuked the nation, "Their tongue is a sharpened arrow speaking deceit; their mouth speaks peace to their friend, but their heart lies in wait to ambush him" (*Yirmeyahu* 9:7). The Vilna Gaon[11] asks, Why is the heart compared to an arrow? When one shoots an arrow, first one pulls the string towards him, and then he lets go, and off the arrow goes. The laws of physics say that the further towards one it is pulled, the further it will then fly. The same is true of those who speak *lashon hara*. First they speak some praise about their target, and then they unleash the dirt. The more praises they say at the outset, the more chance that what they say later will be believed.

I heard the following from a friend. What exactly was the sin of the spies? After all, they were sent to spy out the land. Weren't they right to point out both its advantages and disadvantages?

The answer lies in the way the spies reported the bad. One single word was enough to undo everything. "But, for the inhabitants of the land are strong" (*Bemidbar* 13:25). By saying "but," they cast aspersions even on what good they had mentioned until then.

The Ramban, cited by the Chafetz Chaim, says that the "but" implied that the problem they were about to point out was something which they had no way of overcoming under any circumstances. It was as if they were saying, "All that's very nice, except none of it is going to help you." That was the undoing of the spies.

Thus is the power of such reporting, and with this we can understand why the Chafetz Chaim places such emphasis on the laws of *lashon hara*. Even mixing the simplest word into one's speech, or raising the eyebrows at a certain time, are enough to undo all one's praises of a subject.

The First Human Rights Activist

Many years ago[12] a villager went to the nearest city and brought back the very latest invention for his family — a watch. When he arrived home, all his neighbors gathered round to see this great wonder, the likes of which had never been seen there before.

One of the local women became jealous and asked her husband to get her one. The husband replied, "Why do I want to acquire for myself a master? When I'm hungry I go and eat. When I'm tired I go to bed. When I'm ready I get up. No one tells me what to do. If I would buy a watch, when I want to eat I will have to look at it and see if it's the right time to eat. When I want to go to bed, I'll have to check to see if it's the right time to sleep. Why do I want to trouble myself with this?"

When his wife heard these wise words, she ran back to point this out to the villager. "Why do you want such a thing, placing over yourselves a master and a ruler?" she asked.

When the villager heard this, he said to her, "Do you think I didn't think of this beforehand? When I bought it, the merchant taught me a trick. He showed me how to move the hands of the watch forwards and backwards. When I'm hungry, if I look at my watch and it's not time to eat, I don't let that watch tell me what to do. I move the hands forward so that then it is time to eat. The watch doesn't rule me; I rule it."

The *sefer Vayedaber Moshe* explains that a rav is comparable to a watch, which teaches us the time. In each generation the rav teaches us how to act in accordance with Hashem's Torah. One follows the rav, appreciating that he has superior knowledge and involvement in Torah, and that gives him license to rule on halachic matters. The rav is able to show the way, teach and advise, and others should not merely teach him what to say. If one wants the rav to rule according to his own "superior" views, he annuls the whole purpose of the watch.

Each a Cause

There are two *gemaras* which cite seemingly contradictory reasons for the destruction of the Beis Hamikdash. In *Shabbos* (119b) it says the destruction occurred because the people made no distinction between small people and great people, yet in *Yoma* (9b), it says that the destruction occurred because of baseless hatred.

The Be'er Moshe[13] says that on the surface these two reasons may seem to contradict one another. If the people weren't making distinctions between one another, there should have been peace. Everyone was equal; they all had mutual respect and were seeking equality. How then can the Gemara say that there was strife and baseless hatred at the same time that equality was being sought?

The answer is that such a drive for equality is not always in one's best interests. When society considers small people the same as big people, one loses respect for those that are truly great. Someone who is ignorant of Torah will say, "I'm also great. Who is that rabbi to tell me what to do?" In such a situation, anyone can offer an opinion on complex matters of halachah, whether or not one is qualified to do so. People will want *daas Torah* to be democratic, following what is popular, but not what is right. This will generate strife, as the common folk will constantly be trying to assert their views, and consequently unity will be lost.

Real Reason

When Korach said, "For the entire assembly, all of them are holy," he was saying that every one of them is holy; no one is greater or smaller than the other. That being so, he asked Moshe, "Why do you exalt yourselves?" (*Bemidbar* 16:3). As we shall see, there were other motives behind his drive for equality: jealousy, hatred and the thirst for honor and status.

Rashi says that Korach's rebellion started when he became jealous that someone else was the Divinely appointed head of the tribe of Levi, since he felt the position should have been his. The Steipler[14] says that the whole incident is recorded in the Torah to show how strife continuously grows, and it should be studied so that people will avoid future *machlokes*. In fact, a commandment came from it: "Do not be like Korach and his congregation" (*Bemidbar* 17:5).

This Rashi clearly shows us that the whole rebellion was rooted in jealousy and the drive for glory and power, yet when Korach started it, he concealed his true motives. His manifesto was that he was against people ruling over others. He was fighting for the weak and underprivileged. It was time for equality: "It is too much for you. For the entire assembly, all of them are holy...why do you exalt yourselves over the congregation of Hashem?" (*Bemidbar* 16:3).

Korach was telling the nation that he was the new champion

of their rights...only that he would be that leader. Korach knew that if he would reveal his real motives, he would give away his game and no one would follow him. Therefore, he fought under a different banner. The fact is that he felt he was next in line and should have been prince, but because of his extreme desire for leadership, he was merely a pursuer of honor. Thus, he was most unsuitable for the task anyway and had to be overlooked by Hashem.

It is ironic that the same person who accused Moshe of ruling over other people sought to rule over others. The Steipler says that this is the way of those who cause strife. They pretend they are acting for some common good, when really, in their hearts, there is something else entirely going on.

Under the Influence

There is another lesson to be learned from this incident.[15] Although Korach tried to hide his true motives, his followers realized what was going on. Yet despite this, they continued to side with him. This is the nature of those involved in strife. Even though they know the apple is rotten, since they have chosen to follow that path, they cannot tear themselves away from it. Come what may, they will follow that path to wherever it will lead them.

The story of Onn ben Peles, cited in the Gemara, proves this point. His wife said to him, "What's the purpose of your being involved? If Moshe wins you'll be subordinate to him. If Korach wins you'll be subordinate to him." Onn's response wasn't, "But human rights are at stake. That Moshe needs to be taught a lesson. Korach is championing the cause of the underdog." Rather, his response was "What can I do? I already swore allegiance."

Then there is the case of the suicide fire pans. You have 250 people all prepared to offer incense on the holy altar. The punishment for offering foreign incense is death. Against them is Aharon, the established high priest. Did they really think they had a chance of overcoming him? Yet this is what happens when people are caught up in *machlokes*.

Everyone knew that Korach was only out for himself. However, since they were already involved and had taken sides, they could not back out. These are the dangers of being associated with people involved in strife, and we see from this *parashah* how one has to distance himself from it.

Moshe tried to summon two of the main instigators, Dasan and Aviram, but they sent back the message, "Even if you would gouge out the eyes of those men, we shall not go up" (*Bemidbar* 16:14). They were saying that even if they would be punished with having their eyes pulled out for not going up, they still would not go up. The Chafetz Chaim says that we see from here how far the fire of *machlokes* burns. They were so mired in the strife that they didn't realize what they were saying. Would any rational person be willing to walk around blind for the rest of his life, just to prove a point? But when one is so enmeshed in the quarrel, rationality flies out the window.

Victory Is Not Ours

The following story was related by Rav Yissachar Frand. Two people once had an argument that grew larger and larger. It became extremely ugly and affected all aspects of their lives. Mysteriously, the children of the two people started dying. The Chafetz Chaim[16] went to one of the parties involved and asked, "Don't you think it is time to stop? This is harming your children already!" Incredibly, the person answered: "I will bury every one of them, but I am going to win." This is the lesson of Korach. Just as he was swallowed up, and his family and property were obliterated, those involved in *machlokes* will have their lives destroyed. As the Steipler said, we should read this *parashah* and learn the lessons of what *machlokes* can do.

Just Checking

There is one more lesson that can be learned from this week's *parashah*. Moshe prayed to Hashem that He should not be appeased by the offering of the sinners, and then he said, "Not one donkey did I take from them, and I didn't harm one of them" (*Bemidbar* 16:15). Rashi explains that Moshe was referring to the fact that when he traveled from Midian, he could have taken one of their donkeys, as he was traveling on behalf of *bnei Yisrael*. Nevertheless, he went beyond the letter of the law and used only his own.

Moshe heard the complaint of Dasan and Aviram against him: "You seek to dominate us, even to dominate further?" (*Bemidbar* 16:13). Rav Yerucham Levovitz[17] says that we see something remarkable from this incident. These men accused Moshe of being the exact opposite of what he was, the humblest of all men. What is remarkable is that Moshe didn't say to them, "What are you talking about? You're lying." Instead, he actually reviewed his own actions to see if there was any truth in what they were saying. Only after he searched his actions, and reviewed the incident of the donkeys, could he counter, "Not one donkey did I take from them." Once he was absolved of their claims against them, he then felt he could pray to Hashem not to accept their offering. Rav Yerucham continues, saying that we see from here how much a person has to examine his own actions, and accept rebuke, even if it comes from his enemies. When he is accused of something, he has to do some soul-searching to see whether he is guilty or not.

Fiery Snakes

There is a section of historical interest in our *parashah*. The Jewish people wanted to travel through the land of Sichon, the king of the Emorites. When permission for free passage was denied, *bnei Yisrael* went to war and defeated them in battle. One of the cities they captured was called Cheshbon. The Torah relates that Cheshbon used to be in Moav's territory, yet now they conquered it from Sichon. The verse says, "Therefore, those who speak in parables (*moshlim*) say, 'Come to Cheshbon; let the city of Sichon be built and established'" (*Bemidbar* 21:27).

The Gemara in *Bava Basra* (78b) explains this verse as alluding to something else entirely. The word *moshlim* can also mean "those who rule." Here it means "those who rule over their inclinations." When the verse continues, "Come to Cheshbon," the word *cheshbon* means "to take an accounting." The verse is saying that they should come and take an accounting of the world. In other words, measure the loss for not performing a mitzvah against what can be gained from committing a sin, compared to what one stands to lose. If one does this then he will "be built" in this world, and be "established" in the World to Come.

Why does the Torah use this incident to teach us this lesson? Originally, Cheshbon was in the territory of Moav, but *bnei Yisrael* have a commandment not to wage war with them, and it was therefore off-limits. However, Sichon went and conquered Cheshbon. Now that it was under their domain, *bnei Yisrael* were allowed to conquer it. In other words, because of what Sichon did — it helped to rid the land of the previous occupants — that land was now suitable to be taken by *bnei Yisrael*.

Rav Elya Lopian[18] says that at this place it is appropriate to tell people of the lesson of taking account of the world, because of what occurred there. Sichon had just waged a successful campaign against Moav and had been celebrating his victory. What he didn't realize was that he was just a pawn in Hashem's grand plan for the Jewish people. Hashem wanted *bnei Yisrael* to have Cheshbon, but it belonged to Moav, whom they couldn't attack, so He let Sichon take it from Moav, to enable His people to inherit it.

This is the irony of history. We cannot fathom why events happen as they do. History is replete with many ironies, and we have to realize that we are unable to control it. Rather, all that we can do is to examine our ways and make sure we do what is right.

In Broad Daylight

The Dubno Maggid[19] cites the following parable. A merchant was passing through a town and stopped for the night at an inn. While he was staying there he couldn't rest. Every few hours he went outside to see if his wares were all right. In the morning he woke up early, paid his host the full price and set off on his way.

A while later a second merchant at the same inn stopped by. He made sure that his host provided everything for him, yet he didn't pay attention to his own goods, not checking them even once. In the morning he set off...without paying. The owner said to himself that he had now discovered a way to tell about a merchant's character. If the merchant would check on the status of his goods, then that indicates it is his, and he must be a wealthy man and not a thief. If he doesn't go to check it, it proves that he is a thief. He doesn't care about the status of his merchandise, since stolen goods have less importance in his eyes.

It is the same with a person in this world. If he lives making a *cheshbon*, a proper accounting of his deeds, then he is living properly. If he doesn't, then he is merely a thief and is stealing and sinning all his life.

What Does It Create?

The Jewish people were once again complaining, this time against not only Moshe, but also Hashem. "And Hashem sent amongst the people fiery serpents" (*Bemidbar* 21:6). The Ohr Hachaim deals with the question of why Hashem sent snakes in particular, and why they were also fiery. He says that when one commits a sin, he creates something which is similar in kind to the particular sin performed. The Gemara (*Eiruvin* 15b) says that the snake was asked the following: "A lion claws its victim and then eats it; so too a bear. But you, after you bite, what pleasure do you get?" The snake answered, "And what pleasure is gained by someone who speaks *lashon hara*?"

What is going on in this *gemara*? The answer is that the snake is symbolic of *lashon hara*. In fact, it exists only because of it. There were two punishments going on here: first, that there were snakes, and in addition, that they were fiery. When one sins, the punishment comes not out of revenge. Rather, it comes from the very sin itself; it is an outgrowth of it. The snakes came because *bnei Yisrael* spoke *lashon hara* against Moshe.

Chazal say that whoever speaks *lashon hara* — and all the more so one who speaks against his teacher — should be bitten by a snake. A snake was therefore the natural consequence of their slander. Furthermore, when they spoke against Hashem, the snakes became fiery. This was symbolic of the burning of something metaphysical, namely, the destruction of the soul which they were causing.

The Chafetz Chaim[20] poses three questions regarding the incident of the fiery snakes. Firstly, why does it say that they bit "the people," but then uses a different expression when it says that they killed many "from Yisrael"? Secondly, why did Moshe pray that "the snake" should be removed, as if there was only one snake, when we are told that there were many "fiery snakes"? Thirdly, why didn't Moshe's prayer help in this instance? Instead, he had to build a bronze snake for the people to look at?

The snakes came because of the sin of *lashon hara*, as it says, "and the people spoke about Hashem and against Moshe" (*Bemidbar* 21:5). The Chafetz Chaim says that when one commits a sin it creates an accusing angel. This angel doesn't have to actually say anything; his presence is the accusation. When the sinner reaches judgment day, that angel will be there. The sin of *lashon hara*, however, is different. The accusing angel works measure for measure and has the power to actually speak and accuse, verbally spelling out the severity of the sin. The Midrash says that Hashem does not have too much pity on those that speak *lashon hara*, and that the only solution is not to speak it in the first place.

Just Hide

The Sifrei Zuta says that Hashem said, "For all suffering that comes I can save you, but for *lashon hara* you will have to hide yourselves." This idea can be explained with the following para- ble. A wealthy man had a friend who lived in the city. The wealthy man went to visit his city friend, and found in the mid- dle of the city a mad dog biting and killing people. The wealthy man said to his friend, "If you owe anyone money you don't have to hide, as I'll pay your debt. But if that dog comes near you, just hide."

It is the same with *lashon hara*. The verse says, "From six trou- bles Hashem will redeem you...but from the scourge of the tongue you must hide" (*Iyov* 5:19-20). The *Zohar* says that Hashem is forgiving of all sins, except for *lashon hara*. If accusers come before the Heavenly throne for other sins, Hashem will in His mercy remove those sins. While Hashem usually likes to have mercy, here, because of the noise of the accusers created by the *lashon hara*, in the Heavenly Court, the sin of *lashon hara* cannot be merely swept away; rather, justice has to be done.

With this understanding we can answer the three questions the Chafetz Chaim poses. At first *bnei Yisrael* are called "'the peo- ple," who complained because of the journey. However, the sin then became one of "Yisrael," because the leaders should have prevented them from going so far as to speak against Hashem and Moshe. As to the question why Moshe prayed for the re- moval of "the snake," when there were in fact many snakes, the answer is that he was praying not just for the removal of the physical snakes, but for the removal of the snake represented by the prosecutor in Heaven. Finally, regarding why Moshe's prayer didn't help and he had to build a bronze snake, the an- swer is that Hashem said that it was impossible to remove this type of accuser, so He provided a solution — namely, that they build a bronze snake and whoever would look at it would live.

The Mishnah in *Rosh Hashanah* (29a) says that it wasn't the act of looking at the snake that made people live or die. Rather, they would look upwards and set their hearts to Heaven, and then they would not come to stumble through improper speech.

I would like to add one final comment on this subject. On the one hand, there are the physical snakes, which killed many people, and on the other hand, there is the bronze snake, which had the power to cure people. Its power to heal was so great that, according to the Meshech Chochmah, whoever had any other illness and would look at it, would also be cured.

As mentioned, *lashon hara* is symbolized by a snake. We see from this that just as in this incident the snake had the power of life and death, so too, speech also holds the power of life and death. *Chazal* say that life and death is in the power of the tongue. There are many stories about the tremendous *yeshuos* and healings that were brought about by taking on further commitment to the laws of *lashon hara*. May we gain the strength to improve our adherence to the laws in this area, and see more *yeshuos* in *Klal Yisrael.*

Parashas Balak

Out There for a Profit

I n this week's *parashah* King Balak was worried about the approaching Jewish people and felt they were a threat to his land, so he called for Bilaam, the gentile prophet, to curse them and prevent their advance. The verse describes how the elders of Moav went with the elders of Midian, the latter taking their charms with them. Rashi says that the word "charms" means that they took a sign along with them from which they could tell whether Bilaam would be successful. The sign is described as follows: "If he will come now, there is substance to him. If he will push us off, there is no purpose in him. When he said that they should stay the night they said that there is no hope."

The Vilna Gaon[21] examines the language used in this charm. The claim of Moav was that they needed Bilaam to be greater than Moshe. Moshe was the greatest of all prophets, able to converse with Hashem at any time. Bilaam's marketing strategy was to say that he was above Moshe, that he "knows the mind of the Supreme One" (*Bemidbar* 24:16). He claimed that he didn't need to ask from Hashem; rather, he already knows His mind.

Thus, this is what the elders of Midian were saying: "If he will come now," and it is true what he is saying and he doesn't even need to inquire of Hashem, then "there is substance to him," and he is greater than Moshe, who needs to inquire of Hashem. "If he will push us off" — in other words, if he needs to wait to find out the word of Hashem — then he is of the same status as Moshe and "there is no purpose in him," because they are equal and we don't know that he will be victorious. Therefore, when Bilaam said "that they should stay the night," they understood that he was of a lesser status than Moshe, as Hashem revealed Himself to Bilaam only at night, whereas Moshe could converse with Him at any time. Therefore, they said "that there is no hope"; Moshe is obviously greater. Hence, the elders of Midian abandoned Bilaam, leaving the elders of Moav alone.

Why the Difference?

As mentioned, Bilaam requested that the messengers of Balak stay overnight so that he could see whether Hashem would allow him to thwart *bnei Yisrael*. Regarding Hashem's responses to Bilaam's request, there is a discrepancy between the first and second times Hashem answered him. During the night, Hashem said to him, "Do not go with them. Do not curse the nation, for it is blessed" (*Bemidbar* 22:12). When Balak heard that Bilaam would not go, he sent more important messengers and a greater promise: "I will honor you greatly and everything you tell me I will do" (*Bemidbar* 22:17). Bilaam waited a second time to hear the response of Hashem, Who this time said, "If these men come to call you, rise up and go with them. And only that word which I shall speak to you shall you do" (*Bemidbar* 22:20).

How can we account for this change? First Hashem refused to allow Bilaam to go, but the second time, He allowed him to go — and Bilaam then got the blame? In explanation, Rashi comments that the words "If these men come to call you" mean as follows: If they are coming to give you payment — in other words, there is something for you to gain from this — then you may go. The first time they came they didn't specify any offer, so Hashem said, "Do not go." However, once they came with promises of great wealth, Hashem said Bilaam could go. What difference did his being paid make to the decision of whether or not he was allowed to go?

Rav Yissachar Frand quoted the following idea from Rav Shimon Schwab. One of the greatest, most powerful forces in the world is when something is done *lishmah*, for its own sake, without any ulterior motives. On the other hand, something which is done for other motives has a weaker force. Rav Schwab cited one application of this. We have seen the popularity, and the downfall, of the communist system. At its peak a billion and a half people lived under it. Originally it was done *lishmah*, to make the world a better place, with equality for all. In more recent times, it was discovered that many Swiss bank accounts were growing in this communist system, and corruption was abundant. Somehow it lost its *lishmah* element and collapsed.

The same is true of other "isms" which have arisen and then disappeared into history. When they started out they were done *lishmah*, and nothing could stop them. When the idealism waned and money became the motive, the idea failed and was abandoned.

Likewise, when the messengers came and didn't offer Bilaam anything for his services, this was a dangerous proposition. Bilaam was motivated only *lishmah* to the cause of destroying the Jews. Therefore, Hashem didn't let him go. Once Balak offered him money and wealth, his motives would necessarily become less pure. If he was cursing them merely for his own financial benefit, then it was not dangerous, and if he really wanted to, he could go.

At What Price?

The Mishnah (*Avos* 6:9) tells us that once Rav Yosi ben Kisma was traveling, when he was greeted by a man who inquired where he was from. He told him that he came from a great city of Torah scholars and sages. The man then made him an offer. He would give him thousands of gold dinarim, pearls and precious stones if only he would move to his town. Rav Yosi gave the famous answer: "If you would give me all the silver and gold, all the pearls and precious stones in the world, I would dwell nowhere but in a place of Torah."

Bilaam spoke in a similar way: If Balak would give me his house filled with silver and gold, I would not be able to transgress the word of Hashem" (*Bemidbar* 22:18). What then is the difference between the two answers? Perhaps Bilaam was also righteous.

The Torah Temimah[22] says that Rav Yosi was responding to a genuine offer of precious metals and stones. Therefore, his answer was in the same wording as the offer, that if the man would give him all the silver and gold in the world, he would still only live in a place of Torah. With Bilaam, however, Balak's messengers didn't actually make any specific offer. Rather, he made the suggestion that even if they were to offer him abundant riches he could not go. Why then did he actually state these things? Because all he really wanted was wealth. Since a person always speaks what's on his mind, his words revealed what he was really about.

Rav Leib Chasman[23] notes a difference between the language of Bilaam and that of Rav Yosi. Rav Yosi said, "I would dwell nowhere but in a place of Torah." He just wouldn't go anywhere without Torah, however great the offer. To him wealth wasn't important; only Torah mattered. This is seen in the verse "The Torah of Your mouth is more precious to me than gold and silver in the thousands" (*Tehillim* 119). In contrast, Bilaam said, "I would not be able to transgress" the will of Hashem. Wealth was very important to him, but he was constrained. He was saying that he would have liked to go against the will of Hashem and receive all the treasures. It was just that he was being prevented from doing so.

The *Tosafos Berachah* says that when Rav Yosi spoke of all the silver and gold in the world, he obviously wasn't referring to such an amount. How could anyone gather all the gold in the world? Rather, he was teaching him a lesson: just as it is impossible for you to give me all the wealth in the world, so too, it is impossible for me to live in a place without Torah.

Recorded for Posterity

Sixty years ago,[24] the Mir Yeshivah was taking refuge in Shanghai from the war raging in Europe. The *mashgiach*, Rav Yechezkel Levenstein, got up and spoke about the need to remember the miracles Hashem performed for them daily. He quoted for them the haftarah "My people, remember now what Balak, king of Moav, plotted and what Bilaam...answered him...that you may know the righteousness of Hashem" (*Michah* 6:5).

From here we learn that we have a duty to realize and remember the miracles performed for Yisrael. We must remember on one hand what was "plotted," and on the other hand what was "answered" — in other words, how Bilaam failed. Through remembering this, one will come to "know the righteousness of Hashem."

Rav Yechezkel mentioned the venom of the evil führer, and cited the verse "Grant not, Hashem, the desires of the wicked one; do not grant his conspiracy fruition" (*Tehillim* 140:9). *Chazal* say that this verse refers to Germania, which is Edom, who could try and destroy the world.

Rav Yechezkel then recounted the open miracles that had occurred on their journeys after they had fled Vilna, and the miracle that occurred when they reached Shanghai and found a *beis medrash* ready for them to occupy. He went on to explain that the problem is that "the person benefiting from the miracle doesn't always recognize the miracle." When one is constantly living with miracles, eventually they seem to him like natural occurrences. He therefore instructed all of his students to write down in a diary what they were experiencing, so that in future, more peaceful times they would remember the dangerous situation they were in and would know "the righteousness of Hashem" and recognize His greatness.

Parashas Pinchas

Daughters of Tzelofechad

In this week's *parashah*, the five daughters of Tzelofechad came to Moshe with a problem. Their father had died and had left no sons. The Torah rules that a son inherits from his father to the exclusion of his sisters. Therefore, they saw that their family would lose out, and so they wanted to receive their father's portion in the Land of Israel. Moshe took this problem to Hashem for a ruling, following which it was ruled that if there are no sons, indeed a daughter inherits.

Rav Shach[25] cites the *midrash* that says that in the generation of the wilderness, the women filled in that which the men had breached. In the sin of the golden calf, it was the men who rushed to pull off their wives' earrings. However, the women didn't want to give them; they had to be taken against their will. Furthermore, they played no part in the sin of the spies. The men didn't want to enter the land, yet here, with the daughters of Tzelofechad, it was the women who approached Moshe for their share in the land. This explains the reason for the placing of this incident next to the census taken following Hashem's decree that that generation was destined to die in the wilderness because of their lack of desire to enter the land. Here, the women filled in the breach.

This section is similar to the chapter in *parashas Behaalosecha* about Pesach Sheini. These laws were given at that particular point because the people who were unable to bring offerings the first time due to impurity didn't want to miss out. So too here, the desire for Eretz Yisrael on the part of the daughters of Tzelofechad provided the impetus for the portion on the laws of inheritance found in this *parashah.*

Taking It All

Rav Yissachar Frand cites a *midrash* that says that sometimes an individual can take the reward for an entire generation. Noach in his righteousness took the reward of all his generation, and so did Avraham in his. Lot took the entire reward destined for Sodom. The *midrash* finishes by saying that the daughters of Tzelofechad took the reward of their entire generation.

What was the great act the daughters of Tzelofechad performed for which they deserved such acclaim? Noach had to fight off his generation for 120 years. Avraham jumped into the fiery furnace for his beliefs. Lot had to withstand the baseness of Sodom. Yet what was so great about these women claiming an inheritance?

The *midrash* says that we have to consider this incident in the proper historical perspective. *Sefer Bemidbar* is full of the nation's complaints and problems. Many times, the claim "We want to go back to Egypt" was heard. Yet, the daughters of Tzelofechad came and showed how great their desire for Eretz Yisrael was. They weren't influenced by what was going on around them. Rather, they stood up and said that their future and that of their descendants lay in Eretz Yisrael. Usually going into court over an inheritance wouldn't be considered a noble act, yet here, considering its context, it was most praiseworthy.

The daughters said, "Our father died in the wilderness, but he was not among...the assembly of Korach" (*Bemidbar* 27:3). The Meshech Chochmah points out that we see from here that they were wise. They knew the halachah that the property of one who is killed by the king goes to the king's estate, while the property of one put to death by *beis din* goes to his heirs. Moshe was considered the king, as in the verse "And there was in Yeshuran a king" (*Devarim* 33:5). Therefore, had their father been involved in the rebellion against Moshe, they would not have been entitled to his property. Since their father would have consequently fallen under the category of one who is killed by the king (Moshe), his property would have gone to the estate of Moshe. Since "he died in his sin" (*Bemidbar* 27:3), which is equivalent to one put to death by *beis din*, therefore, they were entitled to inherit.

One or the Other

Rashi cites two opinions of what Tzelofechad's sin was. One says that he was the "gatherer" of wood on Shabbos, while the other says that he was of the people who, following the decree of forty years' wandering in the wilderness, tried to enter the land, but were slaughtered upon entry.

The question is, from where do these opinions derive their sources? The Divrei Shaul says that from the words "he died in his sin," we learn that he didn't do *teshuvah* or confess for his sin before he died. How is this known? According to the opinion that he was the wood gatherer, it is known that he acted for the sake of Heaven, one explanation being that he sacrificed his life for the sake of showing people the severity of transgressing laws of Shabbos. Therefore, he didn't confess, as he thought what he was doing was right. Hence, "he died in his sin." According to the opinion that he was of those who ascended into the land, they were felled by the Amalekites and must have died without the opportunity to do *teshuvah*.

Disqualified

Rashi says that Moshe had to consult with Hashem regarding the question of the daughters of Tzelofechad because the halachah was hidden from him. The Chafetz Chaim[26] says that he wasn't able to judge this case because he felt he was biased in this instance. The daughters of Tzelofechad had said that there father "was not among...the assembly of Korach." Although on the one hand they had to mention this point to show that they were still entitled to the property, as explained above, Moshe realized that they were clever women and may have been trying to influence him. After all, of the many sins committed by the people in the desert, perhaps none was more detestable to Moshe than the incident of Korach. A judge is not allowed to take even the slightest favor from a litigant. Therefore, as soon as he heard their words, he took the judgment straight to Hashem.

Once a case was taken to the Minchas Chinnuch.[27] As he was listening to one of the litigants, he was told, "I remember Rebbe's father, who was *mesader kiddushin* at my wedding."

Hearing this, the Minchas Chinnuch turned to the other litigant and asked, "Was my father also *mesader kiddushin* at your wedding?" When he answered no, he immediately said, "If so, I am disqualified to judge this case. Perhaps I am biased towards the one who had close ties with my father."

The prophet Shemuel was once crossing a bridge when someone extended a hand to help him. He asked him who he was, to which the man replied, "A litigant in a case you are soon to judge."

Shemuel replied, "If that's the case, I have just become unfit to judge it."

The Torah tells us several times about the need for judges who can rule in an unbiased manner. Because Moshe believed that what the daughters of Tzelofechad said was a form of bribery, he felt he could not rule here.

All the Way Back

The verse cites the lineage of the daughters of Tzelofechad. They were "of the family of Menasheh, son of Yosef" (*Bemidbar* 27:1). Why does the verse have to add that Menasheh was the son of Yosef? This is obvious. The answer is that just as Yosef loved Eretz Yisrael, so did the daughters of Tzelofechad.

The Chasam Sofer asks: If Hashem would have given any other land to the Jews, they certainly would have also asked for a portion in it. How then does their request illustrate their great love for the Land of Israel in particular?

The answer is that they were from the tribe of Menasheh. We know from next week's *parashah* that half of Menasheh was to settle across the Jordan, and half within the land. Therefore, the daughters said, "Give us a holding amongst the brothers of our father"; they wanted to be among the majority of the Jewish people, in Israel proper. Even though they would have had a greater-sized portion in the vast lands across the Jordan, they wanted to be in the land of the fathers. This shows that the Land of Israel was indeed dear to them, and it wasn't just the inheritance they were after. Similarly, their lineage was traced back to Yosef because he insisted on having his bones bought up from Egypt to be buried in Eretz Yisrael, showing his great love of the land.

Rav Avraham Mordechai of Gur[28] gave another answer as to how we know the land was dear to the daughters of Tzelofechad, and that they weren't just interested in the inheritance. According to the two opinions cited regarding what their father's sin had been, we have a tradition that he must have died within the first two years of their going out of Egypt. If they were only interested in the money, why did they wait nearly forty years before making their claim? Their father must have had other property, such as that collected at the sea, yet they were not interested in that. Only when the land was being divided up did they speak up.

Parashas Mattos-Massei

On the Road

The verse says, "Moshe wrote their goings forth according to their journeys, by the mouth of Hashem, and these were their journeys according to their goings forth" (*Bemidbar* 33:2). First the verse mentions their "goings forth" and then their "journeys," while at the end of the verse it mentions first their "journeys" and then their "goings forth." Why does the verse reverse the order in this way? Also, why does the first half mention that their journeys were "by the mouth of Hashem," while the second half doesn't mention this?

The Dubno Maggid[29] answers with a parable. There was once a boy whose mother died. His father remarried, but the son and stepmother did not get along at all, and she made life very difficult for him. When the boy grew up he became engaged to a fine girl, the daughter of a prominent *talmid chacham*. The son was overjoyed not only at the *shidduch*, but at the prospect of leaving his awful stepmother.

The father and son set out by wagon for the long journey to the wedding. After a while, the son asked the wagon driver, "How far are we from the town we left?"

The father, on the other hand, asked the driver, "How far are we from our destination?"

The son was surprised at his father's question and asked him, "Why do you only ask how far we are from my future father-in-law's house? Why don't you ask how far we are from where we left?"

The father explained his question to him. "I know your in-laws, what fine people they are and how fortunate you are to marry into their family. I can't wait to meet them. Therefore, I want to know how far we are from our destination and how long it will take us to get there. You aren't familiar with who your in-laws really are. You are only pleased to get away from my new wife, which is why you only ask about how far away we have traveled."

Similarly, Moshe knew the importance and beauty of Eretz Yisrael. He wished desperately to see it. That is why he mentions first their "goings forth" as a means to the "journeys" which would take them there. When the verse continues with the words "and these," it refers to the attitude of *bnei Yisrael*. They didn't have a feel for the land. They weren't aware of its qualities. Their journey was just to get away from Egypt. That is why here the verse first mentions their "journeys" merely "according to their goings forth."

The Kli Yakar gives three answers to the above question of why the order of the words of the verse is reversed, and they also provide us with additional insights into *bnei Yisrael*'s journeys in the desert. Some of the journeys were in a forward direction, towards their destination, while others went backwards. The forward journeys were positive ones, their aim being to reach Eretz Yisrael. They are described as "goings forth according to their journeys." *Bnei Yisrael* turned away from the place they came from and looked only towards what they would encounter in the future. These are described as being "by the mouth of Hashem." The backward journeys, on the other hand, were usually a result of the sins they had committed. These are mentioned in the second half of the verse and were not described as being by the mouth of Hashem. They are "journeys according to their goings forth," meaning that they turned backwards towards the direction they came from, and were heading towards Egypt.

Fleeing or Leaving?

The second explanation of the Kli Yakar is based on a fascinating difference between the beginning and end of another verse, which immediately follows our verse in *Bemidbar*: "They journeyed from Rameses...on the day after the Pesach offering *bnei Yisrael* went forth with an upraised hand," (33:3). Two question can be posed on this verse. Firstly, why does only the second part mention that it was *bnei Yisrael* who journeyed, while the first part does not? Secondly, here it says that Hashem took them out from Egypt at daytime, while elsewhere it describes that they went out at night?

The Kli Yakar answers that only the *erev rav* (the mixed multitude) fled at night. They fled from Egypt as fast as they could, as the verse says, "And it was told to the king of Egypt that the people had fled" (*Shemos* 14:5). They are merely referred to there as "the people." They are mentioned in the first half of the above verse in *Bemidbar* when it says, "They journeyed from Rameses," and are not given any formal title. On the other hand, the rest of *bnei Yisrael* went out from Egypt in broad daylight, as the verse continues, "on the day after the Pesach offering *bnei Yisrael* went forth with an upraised hand"; they went in full view of the Egyptians. We see that while the mixed multitude was called "the people," the main group was referred to as *bnei Yisrael*.

This understanding helps us answer our question regarding the difference in order in the previous verse. When it says, "their goings forth according to their journeys, by the mouth of

Hashem," it refers to how *bnei Yisrael*, not the *erev rav*, jour-
neyed. Their purpose was to leave Egypt — that is, "their goings
forth," — and head towards Eretz Yisrael, as mentioned by
"their journeys." This journeying is described as being "by the
mouth of Hashem." On the other hand, the mixed multitude
didn't journey "by the mouth of Hashem." They continuously
desired to return to Egypt. This is seen in the words "their jour-
neys according to their goings forth"; their intent was to go back
to their place of origin.

The Kli Yakar's third explanation is based on the fact that
had *bnei Yisrael* not sinned, they would have journeyed without
interruption to Eretz Yisrael. When the verse says, "their goings
forth according to their journeys," it refers to the fact that there
was supposed to be only one such journey, for the purpose of go-
ing straight to their destination, "by the mouth of Hashem."
Since *bnei Yisrael* sinned, the Torah wrote, "and these were their
journeys according to their goings forth," indicating that they
had to journey through some of the places they had already
been to. Hashem's Name is not ascribed to this half of the verse,
as this was not His original plan for *bnei Yisrael*.

Living on Miracles

Much of *parashas Massei* is taken up describing the exact en-
campments and journeys of *bnei Yisrael* in the desert. What is
the reason for all the description? The Ramban says that it is to
enable future generations to know about the miracles that sus-
tained *bnei Yisrael* in the desert. While the generation that left
Egypt would know of the great miracles performed for them,
subsequent generations would say, "Their dwelling in the desert
wasn't such a great miracle. Nowadays there are nomads and
bedouin who live in the desert. They have what they need out
there, and some of them anyway are close to settlements."

In order to dispel the thoughts of those who wish to deny the truth of the miracle, the Torah detailed the journeys to teach us that this was not like other deserts, where it was dry and barren, but certain useful things could be found. This desert was also full of snakes and scorpions, and the cloud that accompanied *bnei Yisrael* dispelled them. Furthermore, this desert was completely barren, as *bnei Yisrael* complained, "Why did you bring us...it is not a place of seed, or fig tree...and there is no water to drink" (*Bemidbar* 20:5). Ordinarily a person could not have survived a single day there, never mind such a vast number of people, and for no less than forty years. Therefore, the Torah wrote about the journeys so that people would say that in such and such a place, *bnei Yisrael* were sustained by the miracles of Hashem.

Rashi says the reason all the places *bnei Yisrael* journeyed to are mentioned is to show the great kindness of Hashem. Although it was decreed that they wander for forty years, Hashem had mercy on them and let them stay in each place for long periods of time. They did not travel day and night endlessly, like travelers, but had some serenity. In all, there were forty-two journeys in forty years. In the first year they made fourteen journeys, and in the last year, after Aharon died, they journeyed eight times. Therefore, in the remaining thirty-eight years, they journeyed only twenty times. In addition, they dwelt for nineteen years at Kadesh, so in the remaining nineteen years they journeyed only nineteen times. Some of these journeys only involved an overnight stay. Therefore, we see that for all those years they did have some tranquility and were not always on the move.

How It Was Then...

Rabbeinu Bachaya says that the redemption from Egypt has many similarities with the future redemption. Just as the Exodus from Egypt involved a journey through the desert, so will the future redemption also involve such a journey. He relates that this is seen in the repetition of the words "goings out," once referring to the past redemption, and once to the future redemption.

The Malbim[30] questions why the verse says, "These are the journeys of *bnei Yisrael* who went forth from the land of Egypt" (*Bemidbar* 33:1). It apparently should have said, "their journeys to Eretz Yisrael," since the purpose of their journey was to reach their destination. He answers that in order to purify themselves to the point where they would be able to enter the land, they needed to go through all these journeys. Through each one they lost more of the impurity of Egypt. Each journey was a part of leaving behind Egypt's impurity.

The Skulener Rebbe[31] comments that this *parashah* is always read in the three weeks before Tishah B'Av. Just as all the journeys were for the purpose of enabling them to reach Eretz Yisrael, we need to know that all the journeys of our present, bitter exile are for the purpose of enabling us to merit and reach the *geulah sheleimah*. May we see it speedily, in our days.

Devarim

Who Wrote It?

S*efer Devarim* is somewhat different from the other four *sefarim*. It is known as *Mishneh Torah*, a repetition of the Torah, which alludes to the fact that many of the laws mentioned in the first four books are repeated there.

The Hakesav Vehakabbalah notes that in the first five verses of the book, the fact that Moshe was speaking is mentioned no less than three times. The book begins, "These are the words that Moshe spoke" (*Devarim* 1:1); then it says, "...when Moshe spoke to *bnei Yisrael*" (ibid., 3); and finally it says, "Moshe began clarifying this Torah" (ibid., 5).

What is the meaning of this apparent repetition? The Hakesav Vehakabbalah answers that *Sefer Devarim* is in fact divided up into three parts. The first section is from the beginning until the Ten Commandments in chapter five. In this section, Moshe rebukes *bnei Yisrael* for the events that took place in the desert. The second section is from the Ten Commandments until the blessings and curses. This part contains the mitzvos, many of which are repeated, but also many of which are given over for the first time. One can see from the Gemara that even though some of the descriptions of the mitzvos seem repetitious, nevertheless, we can derive many new laws and details from the way they were written. The final part is from the blessings and the curses until the end of the Torah, where Moshe gives his final speech to *bnei Yisrael*, encouraging them to be strong in their adherence to Hashem's Torah.

A Change

Sefer Devarim begins, "These are the words which Moshe spoke." The Ohr Hachaim comments that the word "these" serves to exclude the words written up until this point. This tells us that there is a major difference between the Torah until this point and the remainder. Until *Devarim*, Hashem dictated and Moshe wrote it down. However, from *Devarim* onwards, the words originated from Moshe. Hashem did not command him to say these words; they were spoken on his own accord. This is seen in the verse, "Moshe began clarifying this Torah" (*Devarim* 1:5). Moshe repeated various laws, as well as giving rebuke to the people.

The Klei Chemdah elaborates on this idea. He cites the Gaon of Kinsk, who asks the following: We have a *gemara* in *Bava Basra* (16a) that explicitly says that the verse "and Moshe died there" (*Devarim* 34:5) teaches us that until that point, Hashem spoke and Moshe wrote, while from then on, Hashem spoke and Moshe wrote with tears. This implies that the entire Torah was said by Hashem. How then can the Ohr Hachaim possibly say that the words came from Moshe?

The Klei Chemdah answers with a fascinating idea. Indeed, the first four books of the Torah were said word for word by Hashem. The fifth book evolved differently. Moshe gave over his speech to *bnei Yisrael* as they were about to enter the land. He reexamined many of the mitzvos already given, exhorting the people to follow the ways of Hashem, and offering rebuke. He wanted to teach the people that their stay upon the land was completely dependent upon their following Hashem's Torah and mitzvos. However, once the words came out of Moshe's mouth, Hashem agreed with them and repeated back to Moshe the words that Moshe had said, for them to be transmitted to *bnei Yisrael*. They now acquired the same level of divinity and holiness as the words in the other four books, having received Hashem's stamp of approval.

Chronology

With this idea, we can understand a *machlokes* in the Gemara (*Yevamos* 4a) regarding from which books in the Torah we can learn *semuchim*. *Semuchim* refers to the ability to learn a law from the fact that two verses are adjacent to one another. The rule is based on there being a time frame in which the two laws were said one after the other. Only because the verses were said one after the other can they be expounded using this rule. For example, the verse says, "You shall not wear *shaatnez*, wool and linen, together" (*Devarim* 22:11). The very next verse says, "Twisted threads you shall make for yourselves on the four corners of your garment." The Gemara learns from their being placed next to each other, that while one usually cannot wear wool and linen together, on a pair of tzitzis one can. This sort of derivation is known as *semuchim* and can be derived from two verses only because of their being issued in chronological order.

The Gemara says that while there is a dispute as to whether we learn *semuchim* in the first four books of the Torah, everyone agrees that we do in *Sefer Devarim*. How can we account for this difference? The Maharav Ransburg (cited at the side of the Gemara) says that the rest of the Torah originated from Hashem, and we are not aware of its exact chronology. This lack of chronology in the Torah is a well-known and important principle and explains why certain parts of the Torah seem to be nonsequential. It is not to say that events are described randomly; we simply don't have a tradition explaining why they are arranged as such, and therefore we cannot expound the rest of the Torah using *semuchim*. On the other hand, *Sefer Devarim*, at least in origin, came from Moshe. Therefore, when he spoke, everything was said in order, and in fact he gave over many laws there — some hidden, some more obvious. He gave over the Torah in such a way — with the Divine seal of approval — that laws would be derived in the future using the rules with which the Torah is expounded. This is why everyone agrees that we employ *semuchim* in *Sefer Devarim*.

Why This?

Let us examine an event described much later on in *Sefer Devarim*. Once every seven years all of *bnei Yisrael* would gather in Jerusalem for the *hakhel* ceremony. The highlight of this ceremony was the king's reading from the Torah. On the verse "you shall read this Torah before all Yisrael" (*Devarim* 31:11), Rashi and the Ramban both say that this means he would read from the beginning of *Sefer Devarim*. Rav Yaakov Kamenetsky[1] asks why this book in particular was chosen. What makes it more special than the other books?

Describing the *hakhel* ceremony, the verse in *Nechemiah* (13:1) says, "On that day, the Book of Moshe was read in the ears of the people." Why is the expression "The Book of Moshe" used here? We never find such wording anywhere else. Rav Yaakov explains that this phrase is unique to *Sefer Devarim*. We have seen that Moshe had some involvement in determining which words appeared in the Torah, as we learn in the Gemara (*Bava Basra* 88b), where it says, "Come and see how the attributes of man are different from those of Hashem. Hashem blessed the people with twenty-two blessings and cursed with eight, while Moshe blessed with eight and cursed with twenty-two." This indicates that some of the curses mentioned in *Sefer Devarim* actually originated from Moshe. Earlier on in the same tractate it says, "Moshe wrote his book, the *parashah* of Bilaam and the Book of Iyov" (ibid., 14b). The book mentioned here is *Sefer Devarim*.

This is all particularly difficult to understand in light of a third *gemara* (ibid., 15a) that says that Moshe was merely a *sofer*; Hashem would dictate and he would write. How can we account for these seeming contradictions?

We can use the above principle to answer these questions. Moshe initiated the Book of *Devarim* through his speech. That is why it is called "his book." Indeed, it was Moshe who chose to warn the people about the curses. Regarding the *gemara* that says Hashem dictated, and Moshe was the *sofer*, we can say the following: Even the fifth book, which originated from him, was relayed back to him by Hashem. So in this aspect *Devarim* is consistent with all the other books of the *Chumash*.

Keep a Copy Handy

With this we can understand why *Sefer Devarim* was chosen to be read by the king. It says regarding a king that "he shall write for himself two copies of this Torah in a book" (*Devarim* 17:18). It is derived from here that he was to have a separate scroll containing only *Sefer Devarim*. Because Moshe initiated *Sefer Devarim* when *bnei Yisrael* were waiting to enter Eretz Yisrael, he gathered in this *sefer* many of the laws that were relevant to their entry into the land. These laws included the laws of a prophet, the laws of an *ir hanidachas* (a city condemned to be destroyed for the sin of idol worship), the laws regarding priestly gifts relevant to Eretz Yisrael, the laws of a king, the laws of war, the laws of a *yefas toar* (woman captive), the laws concerning erasing Amalek, the laws of *bikkurim*, and so on. For this reason, despite its being a repetition of much of the other four books, none of the laws of sacrifices, and other laws pertaining only to priests, are mentioned in *Sefer Devarim*. This is because it was meant for all of *bnei Yisrael* and was to deal with what was relevant to the entire people. In particular, the laws of the king were especially relevant, as he would lead them and had responsibility for the conduct and spiritual welfare of the people. It also taught them that their stay on the land that they were about to enter was contingent upon their keeping the Torah and its mitzvos. Moshe arranged this *sefer* so that it would be laid out for the king to use, to guide him on how to lead the people.

Similarly, we find in the Book of *Yehoshua* that when they stood at the entrance to Eretz Yisrael and Yehoshua took over the mantle of leadership from Moshe, Hashem said to him, "This book of the Torah," *Sefer Devarim*, "shall not move from your mouth." This book in particular, with its laws of kingship, Yehoshua should "contemplate on it day and night" (*Yehoshua* 1:8), as it would be his guidebook on how to lead.

Jewish Wisdom

It is related that the Vilna Gaon[2] had acquired the keys to what is known as "the seven types of wisdom," with the exception of the wisdom related to medicine, which his father had disallowed him to learn. Someone once asked the Vilna Gaon how he managed to acquire all these other wisdoms, since one has to learn Torah and do mitzvos with his time.

The Gaon answered by first citing the verse "She makes a cloak and sells it, and gives a belt to the peddler" (*Mishlei* 31:24). It is interesting to note that the verse starts with a sale, but ends with a gift. The Gaon then cited the following parable. A man once entered a shop and saw a merchant selecting many goods and then paying for them. The shopkeeper wrapped up all the goods with string and then packaged them. The shopkeeper saw the man observing this and asked how he could help him, to which the man asked, "Did that merchant pay for the string and packaging?" The shopkeeper replied that indeed he had given it to him for free. "If so, can I have the same amount of string and packaging?"

The shopkeeper replied, "Fine. The price is ten rubles."

The man was surprised. "I don't understand," he said. "You gave it to him free."

To this the shopkeeper replied, "Of course I did. He bought many items and does a lot of business with me. One who wants the packaging alone has to pay its full worth."

Similarly, one who wants to learn other wisdoms will indeed have to spend much time and use diligence to acquire them; in fact, many years of study will be necessary for him to achieve this goal. However, one who puts all his energies into Torah learning, focusing only on its wisdom, will be given the keys to the other wisdoms as a gift. His eyes will be opened and he will see how all the wisdoms are included within the Torah.

One example that comes to mind is that certain *gemaros* in tractates *Eruvin* and *Sukkah* contain mathematical calculations. Yet there is no requirement to have a PhD in math in order to learn Torah. Rather, if his efforts are directed toward learning Torah, he will acquire these other wisdoms "by the way." This idea is seen in the above verse: "She makes a cloak and sells it." First one has to acquire Torah with effort and hard work; he has to acquire it. Only then Hashem "gives a belt to the peddler"; all the keys to other wisdoms will be given, free of charge.

The "Wonders" of Modern Technology

The beginning of the twentieth century was characterized by the introduction of many fascinating and novel inventions that would change the world forever. Yet one man was not impressed. Rav Yosef Chaim Sonnenfeld[3] would say that our sages already knew the principles behind these inventions, yet the time was not yet right for their production and their being introduced to mankind. Once, in 1927, a German zeppelin appeared over the skies of Jerusalem. Everyone — men, women, young and old — rushed to their rooftops to see the flying marvel. Rav

Yosef Chaim didn't get up from his chair or even take his head out of his books for a moment. He just declared, "How great are Your works, Hashem; You have made all of them with wisdom" (*Tehillim* 104:24). On the other hand, when someone would tell him an interesting Torah insight or a new approach to a *gemara*, his excitement was visible.

When They Have a Good Laugh

The verse says, "See, I have taught you decrees and ordinances...You shall safeguard and perform them, for it is your wisdom and understanding in the eyes of the nations" (*Devarim* 4:5-6). Rav Yonasan Eibeschutz[4] says that Moshe was telling *bnei Yisrael* that even amongst the nations they have to keep the Torah and its laws. They should not say, "How can we fulfill them? Surely the nations will laugh at us." Rather, on the contrary, "it is your wisdom and understanding in the eyes of the nations." Precisely through learning and keeping the Torah is Israel more valued and respected, for, as the Torah continues, "For which is a great nation that has Hashem close to it...whenever we call to Him?" (*Devarim* 4:7).

There is a certain feeling one gets when walking in the streets of London on Sukkos. By now the gentiles are probably used to seeing a Jew with tzitzis out, but one wonders what they are thinking when they see us carrying a *lulav*! Yet Reb Yonasan teaches us that we must not be embarrassed and hide our identity, because this "is your wisdom."

History has shown how the nations have often scorned those who forsook the traditions of their forefathers, and often, the Jews who retained their identities were treated better than the assimilated ones were. A non-Jew often doesn't mind a Jew who practices his own faith. It is when the Jew creeps into the non-Jew's territory that animosity is aroused.

This is seen in Rav Elchanan Wasserman's famous essay "The Epoch of the Messiah," which he wrote just before the Holocaust. He writes, "It is said that it is hard to be a Jew. Now a miracle has happened in recent times: it is harder still to be a non-Jew." He continues that there is by definition a borderline between Jews and the nations, and "if the Jews drift too near then the nations thrust back."

When We're Held in Esteem

The verse (*Devarim* 4:6) says that the nations shall hear "all these statutes," and then they will say, "Surely this great nation is only a wise and understanding people." "Statutes" refers to those laws of the Torah whose reasons are unknown to us. We have to keep them purely because they are the word of Hashem. Examples include laws of *shaatnez* and kashrus, for which there is no reason that humans can understand.

Why is it that these statutes are the cause for the nations to remark how wonderful the Jews are? One would think that it is for these that they laugh at us. Rabbeinu Bachaya explains that indeed this is the case. The nations see the Jews keeping many laws which do fit in with human logic, laws which keep people on the straight and narrow and lead to a society which functions in harmony. The nations then conclude that even the statutes whose reasons are not so well known must also contain great wisdom, except that the reasons are hidden. For this, the nations themselves praise Yisrael, calling them "only a wise and understanding people," with the word "only" serving specifically to exclude all the other nations. The corollary of this is that it is only when we practice the laws in their entirety that the nations hold us in such esteem, even for the statutes whose reasons are hidden. When we make a mockery of those laws that can be understood, the nations will indeed scorn us and mock the statutes as well.

Miscalculating?

The Gemara (*Shabbos* 85a) explains that "wisdom and understanding" refers to the knowledge necessary for intercalating the calendar. The Steipler[5] says that if one looks back through history, one observes that the nations were not able to reach the level of wisdom referred to in the Gemara because many times they revised and changed their calendars to ensure their accuracy. It is a source of amazement to the nations that the Gemara's calculation (*Rosh Hashanah* 25a) that the lunar cycle is precisely 29 days, 12 hours and 793 *chalakim* has been proven correct by recent astronomical studies.

Parashas Eikev

A Good Meal

The verse cites the fruits for which the Land of Israel is praised: "A land of wheat, barley, grape, fig and pomegranate; a land of oil-olives and date honey" (*Devarim* 8:8). Many commentators question why the word "land" is repeated twice in the verse, to separate the fruits into two groups. The Meshech Chochmah says that the final two fruit products were unique in that they were not available in Egypt, while the first five were.

How do we know that olives and dates were unavailable there? The answer is that when Yaakov sent fruits with his sons for the viceroy, Yosef, he instructed them, "Take of the land's glory...a bit of honey" (*Bereishis* 43:11). Yaakov would send to Egypt only a tribute which was something of value that could not be obtained there. Later on, in the wilderness, when the people were complaining about the lack of food, they said, "And why did you have us ascend from Egypt to bring us to this evil place? Not a place of seed, or fig, or grape, or pomegranate" (*Bemidbar* 20:5). Since they left out olives and dates in their complaint, it must be that they did not have them in Egypt.

What One Desires

Food is in fact the subject of a portion of our *parashah*. The verse says, "And you shall eat and you will be satisfied and bless Hashem" (*Devarim* 8:10). The Gemara (*Berachos* 48b) says that from this verse we learn that one is required to say a blessing after eating. The Gemara says that if you make a blessing after eating, how much more so is one obligated to make a blessing before eating.

This is in contrast to the requirement to make a blessing over Torah study. The Gemara (ibid., 21a) says that the source for making a blessing before Torah study is a verse; therefore, how much more so must one make a blessing after Torah study.

Why is it that regarding food, we use a source in Scripture for learning that we must make a blessing after eating, while regarding Torah learning, we rely on a source in Scripture for making a blessing before learning? The Vilna Gaon[6] says that this is a result of the differences between physical and spiritual pleasures. The feelings for physical pleasure are stronger before one partakes of the pleasure. The anticipation and hunger is stronger than the satisfaction afterwards. Therefore, the Gemara says that it is deduced that one needs to make a blessing beforehand, because if the Torah says that one needs to make a blessing after eating, then surely he needs to make one beforehand. Regarding spiritual pleasures, however, one has little desire for them beforehand. Only after one has toiled does one appreciate their sweetness. Therefore, Scripture had to provide an actual source for a blessing before learning. Then it can be deduced that if one needs to make a blessing beforehand, of course when he actually has experienced such pleasure he needs to make a blessing afterwards.

The Meshech Chochmah also cites this *gemara* when he says that the necessity for making a blessing on Torah is in itself derived from a logical deduction. If one has to make a blessing on worldly things, then how much more so does one have to bless on that which brings him to the World to Come. He goes on to say that while the Gemara has discussed that the main reason for making blessings is out of thanks and gratitude to Hashem for the good He does, there is another major factor at play here. When one eats and is satisfied, then one may come to rebel against Hashem. Indeed, the very next verse after the commandment to bless Hashem says, "Take care lest you forget Hashem...lest you eat and be satisfied...and you build good houses...and you increase silver and gold for yourselves...and your heart will become haughty and you will forget Hashem" (*Devarim* 8:11-14). We see that the Torah associates having too much abundance with forgetting Hashem. Perhaps this is because when a person is enjoying the bounty, he gets carried away and is somewhat haughty in his own success. He begins to believe that he was the chief architect of his success, when in fact all he has is purely due to Hashem's blessing. Therefore, the Torah requires that precisely at that moment when one is satisfied, "Then you shall remember Hashem...that it was He Who gave you strength to make wealth" (*Devarim* 8:18).

Some of My Best Friends

The Gemara says that whoever benefits from this world without making a blessing is an acquaintance of Yeravam ben Nevat, who corrupted Yisrael and led them away from Hashem. The question is, Why do we compare such a person to Yerovam ben Nevat rather than anyone else?

The author of *Ner Lamaor*[7] says that Yerovam's sin was with the golden calf that he made, which was a sin similar to the one committed through the original golden calf. Yerovam ben Nevat was of the opinion, not that there is no God, but that He keeps to Himself up in the heavens, while the earth was given to mankind for its own purposes without any Heavenly interference. Through this belief he came to idol worship.

The Gemara itself asks a question. The verse says, "Hashem's is the earth and its fullness" (*Tehillim* 24:1), but later, another verse says, "The heavens are Hashem's, but the earth He has given to man" (*Tehillim* 115:16). What is going on here? Is the earth Hashem's or has He given it to man?

The Gemara resolves this contradiction as follows. It explains that the first verse speaks about the state of things before one makes a blessing. Then the earth is all Hashem's property. The second verse, on the other hand, speaks about the state of things after one makes a blessing. Then the earth is considered legitimate for man to enjoy. It follows that one who believes that he doesn't need to make a blessing before eating is of the opinion that the world is given over to man, and Hashem should remain only in the heavens and not interfere with our business. This being the case, such a person is now engrossed in Yerovam ben Nevat's sin. In his eyes, "the heavens are Hashem's." He will think, "That's fine as long as He doesn't bother me," as long as "the earth He has given to man." That is why one who benefits from the world without making a blessing is called a friend of Yerovam ben Nevat.

Secret Ingredients

The verse says, "not by bread alone does man live, rather by everything that emanates from the mouth of Hashem does man live" (*Devarim* 8:3). Rav Aharon Kotler[8] explains that there is actually a secret aspect of food that not everyone knows about. He says that the strength of bread to nourish is not found in the intrinsic nature of the food. Rather, one has to look at it using spiritual glasses, with which one sees beyond physicality. In this light, one sees that food is imbued with a Divine aspect, "from the mouth of Hashem." This strength is renewed every moment in food, and it is only that aspect which gives it the power to nourish and sustain us.

The Vilna Gaon[9] comments on the portion of creation which deals with food. "I have given to you all herbage yielding seed...every tree that has seed yielding fruit, it shall be yours for food" (*Bereishis* 1:29–30). This statement was in fact the last of the ten statements with which the world was created. With this statement Hashem gave the seed and fruits this power to feed and satisfy people and animals. Even though the seeds were already created, before Hashem made this tenth statement, it was not yet possible to eat them, and they would not fulfill that which a person needs. This statement was thus in itself an act of creation, the creation of the ability to satisfy. Only because Hashem said, "it shall be yours for food" did it acquire this ability.

Breathing Mountain Air

Someone whose family had suffered many tragedies once came before Rav Shach[10] and asked him what he should take upon himself to remove the harsh decrees against them. Rav Shach said to him, "Take upon yourself to do something small, but do it with frequency and always be consistent in it." The man asked for an example and Rav Shach advised him, "When you say *Birkas Hamazon*, recite it from a siddur."

The man was surprised. "Such a small thing?" he asked. "For what purpose?"

Rav Shach said to him, "Listen to the following story. The Brisker Rav once needed to go to Switzerland for his health, where the pure mountain air would help him. The doctor instructed him to walk on a certain path each morning, where he would breathe the air to improve his condition. After a while, the doctor checked the Rav over and found that there was no improvement in his condition. He investigated and found out that the Rav had wanted to get back to his learning each morning, so he rushed the walk so as not to waste any time. However, because of this there was not enough time for the clear mountain air to have an effect on his health. The doctor then advised the Rav to take a *sefer* with him and study it on the way. And so he did. He took a *sefer* and went slowly, absorbing the air along the way. Afterwards, the Rav's condition improved.

"So too," Rav Shach concluded, "if you *bentch* from a siddur, your whole path will be slower and not rushed. The air of the blessing will be clear and you will absorb its blessing."

If we examine the text of *Birkas Hamazon*, we notice that the first part of the text declares that Hashem is the Source of all goodness, and that all blessing and sustenance come only from Him, "Who nourishes and sustains all and benefits all." Then it asks that He further provide for our needs, "but only of Your hand that is full, open.... The Merciful one, may He sustain us in honor." In fact, when recited properly, *Birkas Hamazon* is meant to be a *segulah* for *parnassah* in particular.

Once we understand where everything comes from, may we merit only blessings from Hashem.

Meet Mr. Base, Esq.

There is a well-known *gemara* (*Bava Basra* 10a), in which the evil Turnusrufus asks Rabbi Akiva, "If Hashem loves the poor, why doesn't He provide for them?" The sage replied, "that we may be saved from Gehinnom [by giving them charity]."

Rav Yaakov Neimann[11] asks on this *gemara*, If the purpose of charity is to save us and provide a vehicle through which we can avoid Divine wrath, why did Hashem have to choose this mitzvah and cause the poor suffering? He answers by citing the Alter of Kelm, who says that the mitzvah of giving to charity is not only to give money to the poor. Rather, there is another aspect involved. To fulfill the mitzvah to its completion, through his charity one has to come to also be involved in the commandment "And you shall love your fellow as yourself" (*Vayikra* 19:18).

Rav Neimann then cites what is really an extraordinary *chiddush* (novel teaching): that if one gives *tzedakah* only with the intent to fulfill the Divine instruction of giving to charity, he hasn't fulfilled the mitzvah to its highest level. To fulfill the mitzvah properly, it is as if he has to forget that there is a mitzvah in the first place; he gives because when he sees his friend hungry, he feels his pain. When his fellowman is cold, he feels a degree of suffering too.

When the verse says, "And you shall love your fellow as yourself," it is to be taken literally.

One is commanded to eat and drink when one is hungry, as the verse says, "But you shall greatly beware for your souls" (*Devarim* 4:15), and if you afflict yourself it is a sin. When one is hungry and eats he forgets that it is a mitzvah to do so. It is the hunger that causes him to eat. The same is true with how one should love his fellow. Even though there is a mitzvah to provide for him, he shouldn't do it because of the mitzvah, but because he feels the hunger and suffering of his friend. That is the purpose of charity, to make us feel for our brethren. We shouldn't just give to a needy person and send him on his way; we must put ourselves in his shoes. Because of these feelings that are meant to accompany the mitzvah, Hashem has created the poor, and through giving to them we will "be saved from Gehinnom." Only giving *tzedakah* can have such an effect.

Who Does He Think He Is?

The Torah warns against withholding loans from the poor with the approach of the *shemittah* (where loans become canceled), using a slightly unusual warning: "Beware lest there be a base thought in your heart, saying, 'The seventh year approaches, the *shemittah* year' " (*Devarim* 15:9). The Chafetz Chaim[12] comments on the Torah's choice of expression. If someone were to call someone else a base person, one can imagine how angry he would be. Surely then, if the Torah itself gives a person such a title, he should be aggrieved by it, and contemplate how much shame he will suffer in the next world, the world of truth, all because he chose to close his ears to the pleas of his starving brethren.

The Chafetz Chaim then cites the Midrash, which says that whoever denies the importance of *gemillus chassadim*, it is as if he denies Hashem Himself. Hashem gave us a Torah replete with the kind deeds of our fathers and the commandments to do acts of *chessed*, so that we follow in its ways and it will be good for us. Therefore, if one denies the importance of the sections dealing with *chessed*, it is like he's denying Hashem, Who is behind the commandments of *chessed*. Thus, we must cleave to this trait, performing deeds of kindness as much as possible.

Frozen

The following story is told by Rabbi Pesach Krohn. In Argentina there was a large kosher slaughterhouse. The complex was surrounded by a metal fence, and everyone who entered or left had to pass Domingo the guard. The owner of the plant was the first in and last out every day, and Domingo knew that when he left, it was finally time to lock up.

One day, as the owner was leaving, he called to Domingo, "Good night. You can lock up now."

Domingo replied, "No, not everyone has left yet."

"What do you mean? They all left hours ago," replied the owner.

"No, one of the slaughterers, Rabbi Berkovitz, hasn't left yet," said Domingo.

The boss knew that his guard was reliable, so they went off to look for Rabbi Berkovitz and see what had happened. They ran into the slaughterhouse, and the dressing room, worried that perhaps he had fainted, but there was no sign of him there. They searched the whole complex, but he wasn't to be found.

Finally they came to the door of the huge walk-in freezer.

They opened the door and to their horror they saw the rabbi rolling on the floor, desperately trying to keep warm. They ran in, grabbed him and placed blankets on him to revive him.

The owner was beside himself over what had occurred. "How did you know that he hadn't left yet?" he asked Domingo. "There are over two hundred workers here. You can't possibly know the comings and goings of each one!"

Domingo replied with the most unbelievable lesson: "Every morning when that rabbi comes in, he greets me with a hello. He makes me feel like a person rather than just the guard. Every evening when he leaves he says, 'good evening.' Dozens of other workers pass me and don't say a word to me, but to him I'm a someone. I knew that he came this morning, and I knew he hadn't left yet. I was waiting for his good-bye."

The rabbi's life was saved because of his concern for the feelings of others.

The verse says, "And do not withdraw your hand away from your impoverished brother...for it is because of this that Hashem your God shall bless you" (*Devarim* 15:7–10). Regarding this verse, the Chafetz Chaim[13] cites the following parable. There was a villager who earned his keep by transporting sacks of grain to a storehouse, from where they would be sold. Since the villagers were illiterate, they would make a mark on the wall of the storehouse for each sack that was delivered.

The villager subsequently heard that the people of the town were dishonest and took advantage of the simple villagers, so he demanded another form of accounting. He would place his hat on the table in the office of the warehouse, and every time he delivered a sack of grain, the purchaser would place a coin in the hat. Later he would return to the office and count the coins to work out how much he should be paid. Once, while the purchaser was busy inspecting the grain, the villager thought he would outsmart the purchaser. He crept into the office and took some of the coins from the hat for himself, apparently unaware that in fact he was only cheating himself.

The Chafetz Chaim says that the same is true of people who think they are saving money by taking some of the coins they have set aside for charity. They fail to realize that for every coin they take, they are actually losing sack loads of Divine blessing.

With What to Approach

There are fascinating references to this theme found in the various haftarahs read around this time of year. In *parashas Balak* we read that the prophet is introspecting: "With what shall I approach Hashem? ...Shall I approach Him with burnt offerings?...Will Hashem find favor in thousands of rams?" (*Michah* 6:6–7). He is in fact asking, "What is it I can really do to appease Hashem?" If it is with offerings, this is only a kindness of Hashem that He accepts these, since anyway they are His. The concluding advice is, "He has told you, O man, what is good, and what Hashem seeks from you, only the performance of justice, the love of kindness, and walking humbly with your God" (ibid., 8).

Let us focus on the words "love of kindness." Granted, there are many times when we perform a kindness for another person in our usual way, yet love of kindness means we can't get enough of doing kindness. We run after every opportunity. Love of kindness means we do *chessed* regardless of whether we receive any thanks from the recipient...and when it doesn't come, we don't complain. It means there are no ulterior motives involved.

This is the prophet's conclusion. It isn't to say that sacrifices aren't important. Yet our fellow Jews are Hashem's children, so what is the point of being *frum* towards Hashem, giving Him "thousands of rams," yet neglecting His children? Rather, love of kindness is something that needs to be acquired and refined.

Another example of this idea is found in the haftarah read before Tishah B'Av. That reading is full of the most terrible prophecies, and there are many lessons to be learned from it. "Why do I need your numerous sacrifices...I am satiated with elevation offerings...the blood of birds, sheep and goats I do not desire" (*Yeshayah* 1:11). Again Hashem is asking, What's the point of sacrifices if there is so much evil going on? "Who sought this from your hand to trample My courtyards?" (ibid., 1:12). Hashem is expressing dissatisfaction at the wickedness of the people, who seek to appease Him with mere sacrifices, without changing their ways.

The prophet then seems to offer the solution: "remove the evil of your doings from before My eyes; desist from doing evil. Learn to do good, seek justice, strengthen the victim, do justice for the orphan, take up the cause of the widow" (ibid., 1:16–17). This verse is full of suggestions for improvements that need to be made, and it seems that all the suggestions relate to our personal relationships. The reading ends with the alarming words "Tzion will be redeemed with justice and those that return to her with righteousness" (ibid., 1:27). Interestingly, it says that Tzion will be rebuilt not with external, superficial signs of worship, but rather through improving our relationships with others, doing justice, and acting with righteousness and charity.

Leading and Leaving
the War Effort

The Torah says that before the Jewish people would enter into a war, the officers would stand in front of the people and announce that whoever had either just married, built a new house or planted a new vine were free to go, lest they fall in battle and someone else take over. The officers then continue, "Who is the man who is fearful and fainthearted? Let him go and return to his house, and let him not melt the heart of his fellows like his heart" (*Devarim* 20:8).

Rashi cites a *gemara* that says that in fact the soldiers are fearful of their sins, lest they fall in battle because of them. We see that the Torah allows them to pretend that they are leaving for one of the other reasons to cover up for them, that no one should know that they are leaving because they are worried about their sins.

Rav Yosef Leib Nendik[14] says that from the fact that the Torah made this specific plan to hide the people's sins, we see the greatness of having respect for the honor of other people. Although many important laws are learned out from only perhaps a single word or even an extra letter in the Torah, to save people from embarrassment, the Torah adds several whole verses. From here we realize how severe the prohibition is against causing other people embarrassment, even for their sins.

Not Coming to Shul on Yom Kippur

The passage dealing with war is followed by the laws of the *eglah arufah* (the axed heifer), and the next passage at the beginning of next week's *parashah* again mentions the laws of war. The law of the *eglah arufah* is that if a corpse is found in the fields and it is not known who the murderer is, the elders of the nearest city must come and bring an atonement and declare that they did their duty towards this man, and despite this he was murdered.

Why is this law placed right in the middle of the sections dealing with war? Rav Yaakov Ruderman[15] answers that the Torah is teaching us an important lesson. One of the dark sides of war is that life can become very cheap. Civilians can get trampled upon in the search for the real enemies. The Torah is telling us that whatever situation we are in, we must never underestimate the importance of one human being. The laws of the *eglah arufah* demonstrate that a whole town needs atonement for the loss of one soul. That is why this law is found in the middle of the sections on war.

Rav Yissachar Frand relates the following story. There was once a young boy who was arrested by the czarist government. The boy wasn't a yeshivah student, but in fact a *maskil*, the son of one of the more cultured and enlightened members of Brisk. Reb Chaim Soloveitchik told his community in Brisk that the great mitzvah of *pidyon shevu'im*, (redeeming captives) was at stake here, and that they should raise the money to free this boy. The sum demanded, however, was so huge that the people wondered whether it was appropriate to spend so much on one who never even came to shul. Nonetheless, Reb Chaim declared, "I'm not coming to shul on Yom Kippur unless you raise the money."

Kol Nidrei arrived, and the whole shul was packed and waiting, but the Rav was not to be seen. The elders of the community came to him, and he told them, "I said I'm not coming to shul on Yom Kippur until you raise the money to free the boy. Religious or not, a Jewish soul is a Jewish soul." Indeed, the sum was soon raised.

Returning to the idea of fear, the Rambam says (*Hilchot Melachim* 7:15) that once one is entering the battle he mustn't fear; he has to rely on Hashem, Who saves in times of distress. He says that in fact if one fears he is actually transgressing, as it says, "Let your heart not be faint, do not be afraid, do not panic, and do not be broken before them" (*Devarim* 20:3). Not only this, but the Rambam says that he has responsibility for all of Israel. If one doesn't do battle with all his heart and soul, if he trembles and isn't victorious, it is as if he has spilt the blood of his brethren.

The Rambam then makes an amazing statement. He says that whoever goes into battle with this attitude, without fearing, and has in mind only to sanctify the Name of Hashem through his actions, is guaranteed that no harm or damage will come his way. He will build a fine house in Yisrael, and he and his children will merit the World to Come.

Shema Yisrael

The Kohen's address to the people actually begins with the words "*Shema Yisrael*, Hear O Israel, today you are drawing near to battle with your enemies" (*Devarim* 20:3). The Gemara (*Sotah* 42a) says that from the words *Shema Yisrael* uttered in this verse, the message was that even if they had only the merit of reciting the Shema alone, that would be sufficient for them to be saved in battle.

As mentioned, the later verses say that one who was fearful because of his sins should return from battle. *Chazal* in fact say that even if one was fearful about what was considered a relatively minor sin, he should return, because even for a minor sin one could fall in battle. The Ohr Hachaim says that one who has sins will automatically be trembling and therefore should return from the battlefield. This is seen in the verse "Sinners were afraid in Tzion" (*Yeshayah* 33:14). Even if he doesn't know of any specific sins, the fact that he trembles is a litmus test that he does possess them, and therefore he should leave.

How can we understand this in light of the fact that the merit of saying Shema would protect them? The Vilna Maggid[16] says that there is a difference between the lot of the multitudes and that of the individual. The merit of the Shema would stand by the whole; however, it was still possible for an individual to fall in battle even for a minor sin of his. Thus, if he was fearful he was supposed to leave.

Rav Shlomo Zalman Auerbach[17] examines the precise merit that saying Shema Yisrael had for the war effort. We say twice daily in Tachanun, "Let not Yisrael be destroyed, those who proclaim *Shema Yisrael*. The fact that the officer said only the words *Shema Yisrael*, demonstrates that indeed there must be some merit in the words *Shema Yisrael* alone. How can this be? Isn't the main purpose of the words *Shema Yisrael* in what follows, the declaration of the unity of Hashem's Name and His dominion over us?

Rav Shlomo Zalman answers that this alludes to the fact that there is a specific type of faith in Hashem that is most desirable and preferable: it is a straight, pure and unquestioning faith. This kind of faith is preferable to one which is based on philosophical analysis. This idea is contained in the verse "Hear O Yisrael, Hashem is our God, Hashem is One." The Jewish people are being told, "Hear O Yisrael," you have to believe that

"Hashem is our God, Hashem is One," that this is the foundation of our faith, that we are commanded to believe, so we believe. Therefore, the *kohen* announces only the words *Shema Yisrael*, as if to say that our faith in Hashem is dependent not on inquiries, but on a straight and simple belief, and that the merit of the people in battle is because of this.

Holding Father's Hand

Rav Moshe Aharon Stern[18] cites the following parable to explain the idea of faith. If a child is about to go out into a dark street alone, he is fearful of all the lurking dangers. He thinks about what could be waiting to harm him and how he can stay safe. Most of his fears are just in his imagination and have no basis in reality. Yet when he steps out his heart will be trembling as he just thinks about what could be hiding behind the next corner. Even his own shadow can cause him a fright. On the other hand, if he goes out with his father, he holds his hand and has no fear; he knows his father is there and will protect him.

Rav Stern explains that when a person is lacking in faith and trust in Hashem, he feels that he is going alone in life. Darkness seems to cover the world. Such a person feels that he has to stand on his own two feet through all of this, and he is full of worry as to what could occur. On the other hand, one who trusts in Hashem knows he is under the constant guidance and shadow of Hashem's protection. He knows he is not alone, and he will live a life thanking Hashem for all the good He has given him. Because he knows that he is always under the watchful eye of his Father, he will live in tranquility.

Let us conclude with the following story. Once a group of enlightened, cultured people put on a show in a theater in which they portrayed the scene of the Jews in battle following the Torah's instructions. The officer announced, "Who has built a house...let him go and inaugurate it." Many soldiers were portrayed as leaving the scene at this point. The officer then announced that those who had planted a new vine, and those who were newly married should return. With this, many more people left. Finally he announced, "Who is fearful, let him leave," at which point all the rest of the soldiers left the battlefield, except for two people, one who was portraying the Vilna Gaon, and one the Shaagas Aryeh. Much to the amusement of the audience they acted out a discussion as to who would have the first chance at performing the mitzvah of waging battle against their enemies.

This episode was told to Reb Chaim of Brisk, who said, "Indeed, they are right. This would have happened, yet they left out one detail. These two elders would have actually won the battle." We say daily, "Some with chariots, some with horses, but we, in the Name of Hashem our God, call out" (*Tehillim* 20:8). Our real weapon is Hashem's protection over us. Now more than ever we need to understand this lesson.

Parashas Ki Seitzei

Rejected

The Torah describes how certain foreign nations are restricted regarding marrying into the Jewish nation. An Ammonite or Moavite is forbidden to marry a Jew, while an Edomite or Egyptian may. Why is it that we have such different responses towards these two groups? The Torah actually tells us the reasons for rejecting the Ammonites and Moavites: "they did not greet you with bread and water on the road when you were leaving Egypt, and because he hired Bilaam...to curse you" (*Devarim* 23:5). On the other hand, we are told to accept an Egyptian because "you were a sojourner in his land" (ibid., 8).

This is very difficult to understand. The Egyptians treated the Jewish people with the utmost severity, with slavery and genocide, yet we are willing to forgive and forget, while we reject the Ammonite and Moavite forever because they did not lay out a spread for us? Another question is, why are two separate reasons needed for the rejection of Ammon and Moav. Wouldn't either one alone suffice?

Let us first answer the question of the necessity of having two reasons given for our rejection of the Ammonite and Moavite nations. Firstly, that they didn't greet us with bread and water means that they weren't even willing to sell it to us for a profit. Secondly, they hired Bilaam to curse the Jews. If they wanted to hire Bilaam to destroy the Jews with his curse, what then is the significance of the first reason, reflecting their lack of humanity and dignity? The Dubno Maggid[19] says that the two claims are in fact one. If the Ammonites and Moavites would try and defend themselves by saying that they didn't have enough money to offer *bnei Yisrael* bread and water, how was it then that they could hire Bilaam, who demanded an exorbitant price? We see that both reasons were really one and the same, stemming from their hatred of the Jewish people.

Rav Moshe Feinstein[20] points out that really each nation was at fault for only one of the sins. It was the Ammonites who were faulted for not greeting the Jews with bread and water, and it was the Moavites who hired Bilaam. Why then are both sins seemingly attributed to both nations? The answer is that their main sin was because of their intense hatred for Yisrael. This started with the Ammonites not greeting them with bread and water, and could have ended up with them also wanting to curse through Bilaam in the same way that Moav had done. The two are placed together because of their equally intense hatred.

Far Worse

On this point, Rav Yaakov Ruderman[21] asks, Why were other wicked people, like Nebuchadnezzar and Titus, who destroyed the Beis Hamikdash, ostensibly a far more serious matter, not given such a harsh punishment as Ammon and Moav were? He answers that all punishments that come to Yisrael are ordained by Hashem. Even Nebuchadnezzar and Titus were fulfilling the will of Heaven. Therefore, they weren't punished for that action, but for the wickedness, cruelty, and evil that they otherwise demonstrated. Ammon and Moav, however, were acting against the will of Hashem. So too, Bilaam was going against Hashem's will. Therefore, their punishment was great. Hiring someone to curse another is considered unnatural, while not offering to sell food even for profit reflects an intense hatred. The Torah continues, "But Hashem...refused to listen to Bilaam" (*Devarim* 23:6). This scheme was not a part of the Divine plan, and the parties to it would receive punishment in turn.

Runs in the Family

The Ramban says that for the two above-mentioned sins alone, the Ammonites and Moavites would not have been treated as such. The real sin goes back even further. The mothers of these nations were the two daughters of Lot who were saved by Avraham with the flight from Sodom. Therefore, these nations should have felt some debt of gratitude towards Avraham's descendants. Yet instead, they acted in such an ungrateful manner. Feeling gratitude towards one who does another a favor is deemed so crucial that a nation that is characterized as being ungrateful cannot become part of the Jewish people.

At first glance, Ammon and Moav's refusal to provide food would seem to be out of sync with Lot's behavior. In Sodom, Lot risked his life to protect the angels. His daughter was killed for giving bread to the poor. Hospitality and kindness would then seem to be an inborn trait amongst Lot's descendants, yet they even refused to sell Yisrael food.

The Melitz Yosher[22] says that there are two roots to acts of kindness. There are those who do *chessed* because they know that it is a good thing and their heart tells them to do so. Others perform such acts because they see others doing so, but it is not really an integral part of them. Lot was of this second type. As a nephew of Avraham, he witnessed many acts of kindness. He even reached the level where he almost gave up his life for the sake of doing *chessed*. Yet despite this, it wasn't a natural part of him. There was nothing for his descendants to inherit in this respect, and this manifested itself years later in the desert, when the Ammonites and Moavites didn't even want to sell food to the Jews for a profit.

Bad Manners

Returning to our question of why two reasons are given for the Torah's prohibition against Ammon and Moav marrying into the Jewish nation, Rav Yaakov Neimann[23] gives a different answer. The Torah is telling us that when we see one nation trying to destroy an entire nation, as happened with Moav, one shouldn't think that they descended to such depths in one moment. Rather, it is a slippery slope that begins with a lack of *derech eretz*, namely, their not coming out to greet the weary travelers. If they show that they lack such basic human refinements in the beginning, eventually they will want to murder them.

Along similar lines, *Chazal* say, "All who see a *sotah* in her disgrace will take a vow of *nezirus*, prohibiting him from wine." The Alter of Kelm[24] points out that this *chazal* uses the word "all" to tell us that even great scholars and sages are included in this. If one sees someone doing a greatly corrupt act, one shouldn't think, "What has that got to do with me? I won't reach such low levels as that." Rather, whoever sees has to set himself boundaries that will prevent him from going down that path. This is because the one performing the act didn't just decide one day to commit such evil. Instead, it began with a small act, and slowly his deeds became worse until he sunk to where he is now. One has to worry that perhaps he is at the beginning stage of developing into something worse. Therefore, one who saw a *sotah* in her disgrace would take a vow prohibiting him from drinking wine, as that is the root of the sin.

Once some *yeshivah bachurim* visited the Alter of Slobodka. There was one boy who was known to be especially bright, yet the Alter related afterwards that nothing would sprout from him. What fault did he see in this boy? When the tea was brought out to them, some of the sugar that was served spilled onto the tablecloth. The boy dipped his finger in and put it into his mouth. Having witnessed this, the Alter knew what his end would be. Indeed, in the course of time this boy grew up to become a rabbi, but for various reasons he was forced out and became a lawyer. In the end he made the newspapers, a known crime figure who counterfeited money, ending up in jail. We are not saying that everyone who starts like this will end up as such. The point Rav Neimann is making is that a basic lack of *derech eretz* at the beginning can lead to more severe sins. That is how one goes from not wanting to offer food, to attempted genocide.

Let us now turn to our other question. Why were the Egyptians, who oppressed the Jews for years, allowed to join the Jewish nation after three generations, while the Ammonites and Moavites were never allowed to marry in because they didn't offer food and wanted to curse *bnei Yisrael*? Rav Reuven Melamed[25] explains that because the Jews were spreading throughout Egypt, becoming very prominent, the Egyptians were worried that they would join their enemies and cause Egypt's defeat. Not that this fear justifies full-blown slavery, but the root cause of it is somewhat understandable. Ammon and Moav, however, were never threatened by the Jews. Their refusal to sell food was just because of pure evil and hatred, and therefore the Torah deals with them more strictly.

Let Us Be Broigez

The Torah gives another reason why an Egyptian is treated less harshly than Ammon and Moav: "for you were a stranger in his land" (*Devarim* 23:8). Rashi says that since they provided us with hospitality at a time when we needed it, when there was famine in Canaan and the Jewish people went to reside in Egypt, we owe them a debt of gratitude. This idea is unbelievable. How can it be that after all they did to us, "embittering our lives," not even giving us the raw materials to make bricks, we are still required to have gratitude? One could also say that the Egyptians themselves showed through their behavior that they didn't have any gratitude towards Yosef, who had saved their country from ruin.

Rav Dessler[26] says that we see from here how far the obligation to show gratitude extends. Despite the other person's motivations in helping another, despite what suffering he has caused him, since he once came to his aid, he has to be grateful. Rav Dessler then says that if this is true of those who cause us pain, how much more so is it true of those who perform favors for us, without causing us suffering or discomfort.

Parashas Ki Savo

Missing the Boat

The Torah uses an interesting expression when it says, "and these blessings will come upon you and they will reach you" (*Devarim* 28:2). What is the significance of the expression "and they will reach you"? If you have a blessing "come upon you," then isn't it understood that it reaches you?

The *sefer Beis Av*[27] provides one approach. In *parashas Bechukosai*, on the blessing "and you will eat your bread and be satisfied" (*Vayikra* 26:5), Rashi explains that this means that the food would be blessed inside a person. Even though he would eat a small amount, it would be blessed and be enough to satisfy him. This is the ultimate blessing. If one has eaten a little and is satisfied with what he has, then he is blessed. If, on the other hand, he has great riches but is not happy, and he just wants more and more, thinking that will bring him happiness, then in actuality he is a poor man.

Many people are blessed with children, health and wealth. Yet if one takes them for granted then he will never be happy. He will only see his own needs as constantly multiplying, never appreciating what he has got and deriving no satisfaction from his life.

The Top One Hundred List Revisited

The Mishnah in *Avos* (4:1) says, "Who is a rich man? One who is happy with his lot." We see that the definition of "rich" is not having a seven-figure sum in the bank. If one has wealth and fortune, yet just wants more and more, then he is a poor man according to this *mishnah*. Rather, being rich is based on his outlook towards what he possesses in relation to what he perceives his needs are.

The verse says, "Open Your hand and satisfy all life, with will (*ratzon*)" (*Tehillim* 145:16). What does the word *ratzon* (will) add? The answer is that the recipient will be satisfied with what he receives, not only physically, but also psychologically. With this explanation we can understand the above-mentioned verse. It says, "and these blessings will come upon you." That is the first stage, but it needs to be more than that. "And they will reach you" — the recipient will realize that he has the blessing and will be happy with it.

On the Top

The verse says, "And you will be on the top and not on the bottom" (*Devarim* 28:13). What does this verse mean? It's obvious that if you are at the top, you aren't at the bottom. Rav Tzadok of Lublin[28] cites *Divrei Hayamim* I, where there is a prayer by someone called Yaavetz. In this prayer he says, "If You will bless me and expand my borders" (4:10). Why does he ask for both a blessing and then an expansion? Surely a blessing includes an expansion.

Many people receive great blessing, but they are not well equipped to handle that blessing. How can it be that a sports star at the peak of his career earns an astronomical fee, has fame and fortune, yet by the time he retires he's virtually broke, divorced and maybe in jail? The answer is in the prayer of Yaavetz: May

Hashem bless me, but He should also expand me as a person so I am able to handle that blessing.

The Gemara (*Temurah* 16a) explains the prayer of Yaavetz: "If You will bless me" with Torah, You should "expand my borders" with disciples. The main way one can grow is by having others to whom to impart one's knowledge. By focusing one's efforts outwards, one will have to grow from being a self-centered person, to one involved with and caring for others.

This can be illustrated in the changes a single person undergoes once he gets married and has children. A single person has only himself to look after and is therefore not trained in giving of himself to others. When he becomes a parent, however, and spends his whole day giving to others, he grows outwards.

Rav Tzadok says that this is seen in the famous Talmudic statement "Tithe so that you become wealthy" (*Taanis* 9a). People think this means that as soon as one gives away money, the riches will come flying in through the door. Rather, it means that when one tithes and gives away money, and consequently more people become dependent on him, then he will have to become bigger, so to speak, and Hashem will make sure he has enough to give to those people. The more one makes himself available to others, the more he is given in order to handle it.

This is the meaning of the verse "you will be on the top." Not only will Hashem give you gifts, but He will expand you so that you will be able to handle it. Then there is the second blessing: "and not on the bottom." This means that you will not be ill equipped to handle the blessings, becoming stingy and headed towards disaster. The blessings will not cause you to fall.

Serving with Joy

In the middle of the *tochachah*, the section describing the most horrific curses that will befall the Jewish people should they disobey Hashem, we find the most fascinating verse. After mentioning such terrible punishments, it gives the reason why they were brought upon us: "Because you did not serve Hashem, your God, in joy and with a good heart, because of the abundance of everything" (*Devarim* 28:47). Doesn't it sound a bit harsh that we are punished in such a way for this?

Rabbeinu Bachaya says that a man has to perform all mitzvos with *simchah*. The element of joy is in fact a separate element linked to every mitzvah. A person is rewarded firstly for doing a mitzvah, and then there is a separate reward for doing it with joy.

Rav Moshe Feinstein[29] describes a phenomenon which sheds light on this topic. It is well known that in the early twentieth century the Jews in America faced tremendous challenges regarding Shabbos observance. If one didn't come to work on Saturday, he needn't come on Monday either; he was fired. Despite this great test, many underwent incredible self-sacrifice to keep the Shabbos.

Rav Moshe asked, How was it that the children of these people subsequently forsook religion and did not keep Shabbos, especially after witnessing the self-sacrifice their parents underwent to observe it? He gives a frightening answer. It was precisely because of this self-sacrifice that the children went off the path. When their fathers came home on Friday, they appeared sad, and in a mournful tone they would complain about how terrible the situation was and that they were doing it just for Shabbos. The children got the impression that Shabbos was associated with suffering and was just a burden. They thought that they couldn't undergo such sacrifice themselves, and that it was better to jump ship and abandon the Shabbos altogether.

If their fathers would have come home with joy, expressing gratitude that they were meriting to keep Shabbos in accordance with its laws and saying, "How fortunate are we and how good is our lot that we withstand the trial," then the impression made on the children would have lasted forever. They would have seen the Shabbos as a joy and would have wanted to keep it themselves.

Singing

There is a story about a certain rabbi whose children did not follow in his footsteps. Someone once asked him why this happened, and he answered, "Because I didn't sing Shabbos *zemiros* (songs) at the table."

That this rabbi pinpointed this as the cause is most unbelievable. This element of joy in mitzvos is crucial to our observance. Judaism is meant to be practiced with *simchah*, because one is following the will of his Creator. If we take pleasure in doing the mitzvos, it will enhance our observance. This feeling will rub off on our children as well.

On the other hand, one who fulfills the mitzvos out of compulsion and does them mechanically, with the attitude that he is forfeiting great pleasures by performing them, is obviously missing the boat. Indeed, his own enthusiasm will eventually wane, and what positive feelings will remain that will inspire his children to want to continue doing them? Why will his children want to provide a link in the chain of Shabbos observance if all they saw is that when father went to shul he used the time to discuss the latest in real estate and share prices? Then they came home and their father would rant and rave about how the chazzan was useless and the rabbi took too long. Will those children ever want to set foot in a synagogue again? We are not saying that one has to grin and bear it in a shul that is not to his liking; rather, one should find a shul where it is a pleasure for him to daven. Our service of Hashem has to be with enthusiasm and joy at our lot, and that *simchah* will carry on to the next generation.

Waiting

Rav Zelmele of Volozhin[30] was learning one night in one of the small shuls in Shnipashuk, a village on the other side of the river from Vilna. He needed a *sefer* which could be found only in the larger shuls in Vilna. Undaunted, he set out in the bitter cold of the night to find the *sefer*, completely unaware that ice was forming on his coat and beard as he walked. On his return, people were shocked beyond belief at what he had done. How could he risk his life just to look at a book? He answered with a verse from this week's *parashah* that tells us where the Torah is to be found: "It is not in the heavens...it is not across the sea" (*Devarim* 30:12). He explained that if indeed it were in the heavens, one would have to make the effort to acquire it even from there. Since the Torah was neither in the heavens nor across the sea — it was just over the river — he had no excuse not to make the effort to acquire it.

The verse in *parashas Vayeilech* says that there will come a time when Hashem will hide His face from the Jewish people. It will appear as if they are abandoned, as it says, "and they will find much evil and troubles (*vetzaros*) and they will declare on that day, 'It is because Hashem is not in our midst that these great evils (*ra'os*) have found me' " (*Devarim* 31:17). Nachal Eliyahu[31] says that, using the tool of *gematria*, one sees that this verse alludes to two specific events. The word *ra'os* (evil), has a *gematria* of 676, alluding to the year 5676, i.e., 1916, the time of the First World War. The word *vetzaros* (and troubles) has a *gematria* of 702, alluding to the year 5702, i.e., 1942, which was the year the final solution was passed at the Wannasee Conference.

Forced

The verse says, "And Hashem will return your returnees and have mercy on you, and He will return and gather you from all the nations" (*Devarim* 30:3). The commentators say this is the source in the Torah for the idea of the future redemption and the coming of Mashiach. The Meshech Chochmah comments that the verse is somewhat repetitious, with the second part sounding much like the first. He explains that during the time of exile, many flee from it and seek to return to the Land of Israel. They are mentioned in the first part of the verse: "Hashem will return your returnees and have mercy on you," referring to those who desire to return. On the other hand, there are those who are accustomed to life in the Diaspora and have lost their desire to return. They are referred to at the end of the verse: "He will return and gather you from all the nations," even against your will.

One of the main catalysts for Mashiach's arrival is Torah study. Rav Yosef Chaim Sonnenfeld[32] shows how this is alluded to in a *gematria* in the following verse (*Yeshayah* 1:27): "Tzion will be redeemed through justice" has the numerical equivalent of 1076, which is also the numerical value of the words "Talmud Yerushalmi." The verse continues, "and those who return to her through righteousness," which has a *gematria* of 524, the numerical value of the words "Talmud Bavli."

The Czech ambassador once asked Rav Sonnenfeld why the Jews call the Messiah the *goel tzeddek* (righteous redeemer). Rav Sonnenfeld answered that nowadays world leaders and politicians throw around words like righteousness and justice, yet their actions reveal how hypocritical their words really are. The Jewish people pray for the day when the Messiah will come and be the redeemer of righteousness, as if redeeming the word "righteousness," which has been hijacked by those who distort its real meaning.

On another occasion, someone asked Rav Sonnenfeld about a Gemara that says Mashiach will come only when Israel is unmindful of him, i.e., not thinking about him. How can this be, when our prayers are full of references to how we desire his coming? Rav Sonnenfeld explained what the word "unmindful" means. If someone would run into shul shouting, "Mashiach is here! He's standing on Golders Green Road!" our reaction would be to dismiss it as misinformation and to label that person as mad. This shows how unmindful we really are of Mashiach's imminent arrival.

Main Point

The Rambam[33] writes that we have an obligation to await the arrival of Mashiach. This is in fact one of his Thirteen Principles of Faith. He says that "whoever doesn't believe in him, or doesn't wait for his arrival, it is not only that he denies [belief in] the prophets, but in the Torah and Moshe Rabbeinu, because the Torah itself testifies to this, as it says (*Devarim* 30:3-5), 'Then Hashem your God will bring back your captivity and have mercy on you...If your dispersed will be at the ends of Heaven...Hashem...will bring you." The Brisker Rav says that from this Rambam we learn that it is not enough just to believe in Mashiach's arrival; one has to wait for and anticipate it.

Rav Nachum of Kelm[34] cites the following parable to explain this concept. It can be compared to a situation in which a patient is very ill and is suffering, and whose family calls in the top expert in that field to examine him. They wait for him agitatedly, but he doesn't come. Suddenly there is a knock on the door and they run to answer, convinced it is the doctor. On opening the door they find it is just their neighbor coming to borrow something. When the neighbor leaves they resume waiting for the doctor. Again there is a knock at the door, but when they open it, they see that it is just the mailman with a letter in his hand. This happens again and again, and each time they are disappointed, yet they continue to hope that perhaps the next time it will be the doctor. The reason they don't give up hope is because there is a sick person in the house, and as soon as the doctor comes he will begin to tackle the illness.

Rav Nachum says that similarly, *Klal Yisrael* is suffering from certain illnesses, and we believe that when Mashiach comes he will heal them with the redemption. With this we can understand the inference of the Brisker Rav mentioned above, that one who doesn't wait for Mashiach denies the Torah. It is either because he fails to believe that he could come at any moment, or that he doesn't believe in the necessity of Mashiach to save us from the illnesses from which we are suffering, and therefore it is as if he denies the Torah.

Suddenly

The Chafetz Chaim exemplified this need to wait for Mashiach, as illustrated by the fact that he kept a bag packed so that when Mashiach would come, he could go without delay. He wrote a whole *sefer* (*Torah Ohr*) on the importance of learning *seder Kodshim*, the laws relating to sacrifices, in part because if Mashiach should suddenly arrive, people knowledgeable in those areas would be ready to perform the Divine service.

There is a *gemara* (*Eruvin* 43b) that says if one states, "I am a Nazirite (prohibiting oneself from drinking wine, along with other restrictions) on the day Mashiach comes," he is not allowed to drink wine at any time during the week, as perhaps Mashiach will come on that day. The Chafetz Chaim also cites the Gemara (*Sanhedrin* 22b) that says that the rabbis of Eretz Yisrael forbade *kohanim* from drinking wine at all times, since perhaps the Temple would be rebuilt suddenly, and the law is that one who is intoxicated is not allowed to perform the Temple service. Even according to the opinion that says that they are permitted to drink wine, it is only because there will be time on that day for the effect of the wine to wear off. However, we are still meant to realistically expect that the redemption could come at any time on any day.

The Gemara says that one of the questions one is asked in the world of truth is: "Did you long for the redemption?" We say in our prayers three times a day, "For Your salvation we hope for all day," and in the Aleinu prayer, "therefore we hope for You that it be seen speedily...." How can one say these things if he doesn't mean them? Therefore, says the Chafetz Chaim, we need to be prepared for the redemption by learning the relevant laws.

The Gemara cites the following parable to illustrate the above point. There was once a king who invited his servants to a meal but didn't specify when it would be. Those who were clever adorned themselves suitably for the occasion and waited by the door to the palace, since they reasoned, Is the king lacking anything? He has everything prepared, so we may need to enter suddenly. Therefore, we must be ready. The foolish ones went about their usual business, saying there is no meal without effort and that it takes time to make it. Suddenly the king appeared and invited his servants in. The clever ones entered, ready for the meal, and the king was happy to see them. Then the foolish ones entered, unprepared and in their regular clothes, much to the king's displeasure.

Let us finish with one final idea of the Chafetz Chaim.[35] He says that some people may ask, How can it be that Mashiach will come in our generation? We are so lacking in merits compared to previous generations. If they couldn't bring Mashiach, then how can we? The answer to them is that although we are weaker, Hashem places our deeds on top of the deeds of our fathers, so that we are standing on giants' shoulders, and now we can see even further, even though we ourselves are small. May we merit the redemption speedily.

Parashas Haazinu

Unquestioning

The Torah says, "The Rock, perfect is His work, for all His paths are justice; a God of faith without iniquity; righteous and fair is He" (*Devarim* 32:4). Why does the verse describe Hashem as being "without iniquity" when speaking about the fairness of His justice? Isn't this trait also expected from humans in judgment? Why then is it singled out here?

Rav Yitzchak Blazar[36] explains that while humans also attempt to do justice, nevertheless, they cannot understand the weight of the sin, nor can they fathom the true weight of their punishment. A judge will only estimate and try to guess correctly. The ways of Hashem, however, are different. The verse says, "The judgments of Hashem are true, altogether righteous" (*Tehillim* 19:10). The punishment is in exact response to the damage caused, no more and no less.

Rav Blazar then says that furthermore, when a human king punishes someone, for instance by imprisoning him, not only will he suffer but his family will also, even though they didn't sin. In contrast, Hashem takes everyone into consideration. A person has pain only if he is meant to have it. If the guilty one's family does not deserve the punishment's effects, then the punishment will not be meted out. This is the meaning of the words "without iniquity," that punishment is meted out with exactitude, taking everyone involved into account.

The Opening Line

Why did Moshe choose to open the song with this line, which speaks about Hashem's justice and accepting difficult events? Rav Yechiel Mordechai Gordon[37] explains that the entire song of Haazinu is said to allude to all that would befall the Jewish people in the end of days. *Chazal* say that Hashem showed Moshe all that would occur to the Jewish people until the revival of the dead. Moshe saw each generation and its leaders, the Torah scholars and their students. He then saw the flames and the destruction, how entire communities were wiped out. He subsequently opened his song with "The Rock, perfect is His work, for all His paths are justice" in order to strengthen the Jews in their faith even in the darkest of hours, the moments before dawn. However dark things may seem, there is a Divine plan in place.

The Me'am Loez cites the famous *gemara* (*Berachos* 7a), that when Moshe asked Hashem to "show me Your ways" (*Shemos* 33:13), he was really asking why the righteous suffer and the wicked prosper. Hashem answered that when an evil person prospers it is because he's the son of a good person, while a righteous person suffers because he's the son of a wicked person.

The Midrash says that when Moshe heard this explanation, he saw a vision. In it was a spring flowing in a mountain. A traveler came to rest by it, but in his haste in getting up he left his wallet. A second person came along, saw the wallet, took it and left. A third person came along and sat down for a while. Suddenly the first person came back and asked the third man where his wallet was, but of course he knew nothing of it. In his rage he killed the third man.

Moshe couldn't understand how the innocent third man got killed while the second man went unpunished. Hashem answered that Moshe didn't see the full picture. Hashem explained that the father of the first man had stolen the wallet of the second man, so the second man inherited the wallet of the first. In addition, the father of the third man had killed the father of the first, so by killing the third man he was avenging his father's death. Therefore, history had come full circle: the second man was reclaiming that which was his, while the first was avenging his father's death.

Let Me Know

A student of the Ramban[38] became very ill, and his teacher came to visit him as his end was drawing near. The Ramban told him, "In Heaven there is a great hall of justice where the Shechinah sits in judgment. I will give you an amulet which will give you access to all the chambers of the Heavenly Court. When you arrive in the hall of justice, I want you to ask a number of serious questions about judgments meted out to Yisrael, and you should come back to me in a dream and reveal the answers."

Indeed, one day as the Ramban was studying, his student appeared to him. "Know that your amulet did give me unrestricted access," he said. "However, as I was ready to present your questions to the main tribunal, I realized that they were not questions there, for that world is the world of truth, and every decree issued is just and fair."

Rav Levi Yitzchak of Berditchev[39] was once sitting as two chassidim bemoaned their respective lots. He asked them, "If you were masters of the world, what would you do differently?" One replied that he would make the lot of all men equal, eliminating the poverty problem. The second said that he would make peace and harmony and there would be no more war. Rav Levi Yitzchak replied, "If I were master of the world, I wouldn't change a thing. I have no doubt that all Hashem does is for man's benefit. It is our own shortcomings that make it difficult for us to see the justice of His ways."

The Chafetz Chaim[40] once asked a visitor how he was doing. The visitor answered, "It wouldn't hurt if things were a little bit better."

The Chafetz Chaim replied, "How can you be so sure it wouldn't hurt? Hashem has greater knowledge than you and seeks only your benefit. If He decided not to grant you more than what you have, it must be that He knows that giving you more would be bad for you."

What a Cruel Parent

On this theme the Chafetz Chaim asks, Why must a tzaddik scrape around for food to eat and clothes to wear? Surely the hand of Hashem is large enough to provide for everyone, so why is he subject to such treatment? He answered with a parable. There was once a wealthy man who had an only son who was sick. All the doctors tried in vain to cure him, until one doctor finally found a remedy that cured him. Afterwards, he warned the boy's father that his son should not eat any fatty meat whatsoever, as this would cause a reversal in his condition. The father personally attended to his son, keeping him away from the meat.

One day the father had to go to the next town on business, so he told his wife to follow the doctor's warning. At supper time the son smelled beef roasting, and, as fast as he could, he ran inside, grabbed a piece of meat and thrust it into his mouth. By the time his father returned the boy was rolling around in agony. The father ran to get the doctor, begged him to attend to his son, and promised that he would never leave his son, but would always attend to him himself.

The doctor came, managed to revive the son, and all was well. One day the father made a great feast for his family and friends. However, he forbade his son from coming anywhere near the gathering. All the guests were wondering how the father could be so cruel to his poor son, not letting him enjoy the fine meal. Only the father knew the real reason for his supposed cruelty.

Says the Chafetz Chaim, it is the same with the way that Hashem runs the world. Sometimes if a tzaddik is driven away from the pleasures of this world, it is for his own benefit. While we do not understand the reason why this happens, we trust that it is for the best.

Working It Out

P*arashas Vezos Haberachah* contains several verses which re-
fer to our Torah and its place at the forefront of our iden-
tity. In particular, there is the well-known verse "The
Torah that Moshe commanded us is the heritage of the congre-
gation of Yaakov" (*Devarim* 33:4). *Chazal* say this is the first
verse a child should be taught when he is old enough to speak.

This *parashah* forms our reading on Simchas Torah, so it is
appropriate to speak about some aspects related to Torah study.
Let us start with an incident related by Rav Yehudah Ze'ev
Segal.[41] Rav Meshulam Igra was a great rav in one of the towns of
Galicia. (He was also the illustrious teacher of the Ketzos
Hachoshen.) Once, two men who were passing through his
town came to him with a monetary case. It was a very complex
issue, and the Rav asked if they could return on the next day so
he could give the matter more thought. The men, however, were
in a rush, so they left without receiving a ruling and agreed to
bring the case to the rav of their city. When they presented their
case to their local rav, he didn't seem to have the same problem
as Rav Meshulam did. He heard the case, excused himself and
left the room, returning minutes later with a ruling which satis-
fied both parties.

Some time later, the men were back in Galicia, and they decided to visit Rav Meshulam and apologize for having left without receiving a ruling from him. While they were with him, they asked him what his ruling on the matter had been. As he related it to them, they smiled to each other knowingly, since their rav, an unknown by comparison, had given them the same ruling almost instantly. On hearing this, Rav Meshulam said, "Only a great scholar could have rendered this decision so quickly. Your rav must be a true *gadol*. I must pay him a visit."

Sure enough, Rav Meshulam set out to meet this rav. When they were alone, Rav Meshulam explained why he had come and expressed amazement that he could render this decision so quickly. The rav then explained, "The truth is that I didn't have a clue what the real ruling should be. The whole thing was beyond me. I was worried that if I didn't render a decision my reputation would be damaged. I excused myself and went into the next room to pray that Hashem should give me the ability to resolve the matter. Tearfully I beseeched Him for help. As soon as I finished praying, I had the idea to look in a certain *sefer*. I couldn't believe it when I opened the book to the exact page where this case and the author's ruling was found. I then went out and told the men 'my' ruling."

Rav Meshulam was unimpressed by this. "You found your answer by crying? We can also cry. The true way is through *ameilus baTorah* (toil and effort in Torah)."

Rav Segal added a significant point: Although the purpose of this story is to demonstrate the role and importance of toil in Torah, one shouldn't take lightly the role of prayer in successful study. Davening for success should go hand in hand with one's efforts, but not as a substitute for them, as with the unfortunate rav.

Rav Segal also related the following incidents. When Rav Shimon Shkop was a student in the yeshivah of the Netziv, he once found himself struggling to get to the depths of a difficult Rashbam located in *masseches Bava Basra*. It was late at night when he finally approached the Netziv for help. The Netziv told him, "My son, many times I visited the grave of Reb Chaim Volozhiner to tearfully pray that these words become revealed to me." This is unbelievable. People go to graves to pray for healing or some other pressing need. Yet for the Netziv, not understanding a comment of the Rashbam to its depths was something worth crying one's heart out over. His prayers were certainly preceded by intense effort and toil to understand the Torah's words. Only when he wasn't successful did he resort to praying at the grave of his teacher.

How Can You Eat?

The Netziv would always be the first in the *beis medrash* after breaking the fast on *motza'ei Yom Kippur*. One year someone else had the idea that he would precede the Netziv and get there first. Then he could say that he was as great as the Netziv. Once *Ne'ilah* was finished the man rushed home, grabbed a bite and ran back, only to find that the Netziv had beaten him to it. The man learned later that the Netziv kept some food in the building so that he wouldn't lose more time having to go elsewhere for it.

It is related that the Vilna Gaon once fasted for three days because he didn't understand a *mishnah* in *Challah*. To him, he just couldn't eat while he was faced with a difficulty; the food would have to wait. Ultimately it all depends on one's perspective and the importance he attaches to Torah.

Lehavdil, both the British Parliament and the Israeli Knesset continue into the early hours of the morning if there's a big debate; they don't just close up shop because it's time to go to bed. Has there ever been a businessman who has cut off a big meeting when he was on the verge of closing a lucrative deal, just because it was time to eat and take his afternoon nap? In other words, how much does our Torah matter to us?

The verse says, "He showed love to peoples; all its holy ones are in Your hands, and they were brought in at Your feet; He would bear Your utterances" (*Devarim* 33:3). The Gemara (*Bava Basra* 8a) says that this refers to "Torah scholars who move their feet from city to city and country to country to learn Torah."

Rav Yosef Zundel of Salant[42] observes that the Gemara doesn't mention that the verse is referring to Torah scholars who learn Torah. Rather, it refers to those who "move their feet" from place to place in order to learn. He says that this gives us a proof that the most important feature of one's learning is the effort he puts into it, and that is what Hashem wants from us. The reason is that through the effort one makes and the enthusiasm one shows, he reveals his love of acquiring wisdom and Hashem's Torah. One's effort is also a result of his fear of Heaven, as the more fear and awareness of the consequences of one's actions he possesses, the more he will desire Hashem's Torah.

This idea is logical from another point of view. People are born with varying capacities to use their gray matter. Is it fair that someone who is born a genius and can learn with relative ease in a short amount of time should receive the same reward as one of limited abilities who works himself day and night to accomplish what the gifted person achieved with ease? Rather, the starting point is from Hashem; the toil and effort is from us.

Humble Beginnings

Moshe was apparently not a naturally gifted and capable student of Torah. One day his father, Maimon, got fed up with this and kicked him out of his house. Moshe went out and sat alone and cried to Hashem. He went to learn and Hashem answered him. His mind was opened up and in time his greatness influenced the whole of the Torah world. Moshe the son of Maimon became known as the Rambam, whose works are among the most crucial and important in Jewish thought. He wasn't born a genius; rather, through toil and diligence he reached the heights of Torah learning.

Rav Pesach Krohn told the following story. There was once a rabbi who was walking in the zoo when he suddenly heard a ferocious roar coming from the lion's cage. He realized that had he been in the jungle when he heard this roar, he would have been frightened of the lion. In the zoo, however, he didn't even flinch, because he knew there was an iron cage separating him from the lion.

The rav made the following deduction. In the holy days of awe in Elul and Tishrei, we hear a "great roar," knowing what's at stake during these days. If, however, we are not frightened, perhaps it's because there is also an iron barrier between ourselves and Hashem. Our mission is to remove this barrier and realize the seriousness of the moment, as we say in the concluding prayer of the Hoshanah Rabbah service, "May it be Your will before You...and remove the iron partition separating us from You."

Driven Mad

I had a similar awakening recently when I took a driving test to convert my British driver's license into an Israeli one. Despite having driven for ten years, and despite the fact that the test lasts about four minutes, I found it a nerve-racking experience, as if one fails twice one has to undergo the full series of lessons at great expense.

It was an extremely tense morning for me; I feared failing the test the first time and then having to be under pressure to pass the second time. I drove cautiously, almost trembling at the decision of the all-powerful and mighty driving instructor. (Yes, I passed.)

What occurred to me was that this happened to also be the month of Elul, and shortly I would undergo an even bigger test in front of the King of kings, judging my performance over the entire year. Trying to internalize this lesson is no easy task, but ultimately the logic is correct, that if one trembles over a mere driving test, how much more so should one tremble over the Rosh Hashanah test.

Tape to Tape

In the Ten Commandments as they are related in *parashas Yisro*, the word *zachor* (remember) is used to introduce the portion of Shabbos, while when the commandments are again mentioned in *parashas Va'eschanan*, the word *shamor* (safeguard) is used. Which one was it then that was said? *Chazal* tell us that Hashem actually said the two words *shamor* and *zachor* at the same time, in one utterance, thus resolving the contradiction. The problem with this is that we have a principle that what the mouth cannot ordinarily speak, the ear cannot hear. What then was the purpose of this utterance if the ear cannot ordinarily understand it?

A certain *rosh yeshivah* explained that there are two ways of learning Torah. One is through regular absorption in the topic, while the other way is from mind to mind. This can be compared to copying a tape. Either you can put two machines next to each other and by playing one, the other will pick it up at regular speed, or you can use one machine and run it tape to tape, which takes only a few seconds. Similarly, the latter way of learning can be done more quickly, as it is from mind to mind.

The Ari Hakadosh used to sleep on Shabbos afternoon. Once his students entered the room where he was sleeping, because they wanted to hear him learning in his sleep, but the noise woke him up. The Ari then told them that he had just received two years' worth of *sod* (secrets of the Torah) in those few seconds.

How can it be that one absorbs all this Torah in just a few seconds? The answer is that the Ari was on the second level of learning. In other words, Torah was seeping into him directly from source to source. This is because there were fewer barriers between him and the higher spheres.

When one functions on the physical level, his earthly nature acts as a wall between him and the higher spheres. If he can release himself from this physicality he will be able to learn from source to source. At the giving of the Torah *bnei Yisrael* reached this level. Thus, although ordinarily they couldn't hear two words at the same time, according to *Chazal*, at that time they all reached the level of prophets. That transfer of knowledge was from mind to mind and wasn't through the regular hearing process. Therefore, they could hear both *shamor* and *zachor* simultaneously.

So too, we may not be quite on the same level as the Rambam, the Ari or the Netziv, but we are capable of reaching a certain level of toil and breaking those iron barriers. May we merit, as we say on this *yom tov*, that Hashem will "Bestow on us...the blessings of Your festivals...and give us our share in Your Torah."

Notes

Bereishis

1. *The Dubno Maggid and His Parables.*
2. *Peninim Mishulchan HaGra.*
3. *Michtav Me'Eliyahu*, vol. 1. *Kuntres Hachessed.*
4. *Peninim Mishulchan Gavoah.*
5. *Hadra shel Torah.*
6. Quoted by Rav Yissachar Frand.
7. Ibid.
8. *Peninim Mishulchan Gavoah.*
9. *Chafetz Chaim al HaTorah.*
10. Quoted by Rav Frand.
11. Ibid.
12. *The Parsha Anthology*, Rav Yissachar Dov Rubin.
13. *Inspiration and Insight*, ArtScroll Publishers.
14. Quoted by Rav Frand.
15. *Chafetz Chaim al HaTorah*
16. *Hadra shel Torah.*
17. Ibid.

18. *Oznaim LaTorah.*
19. *Peninim Mishulchan Gavoah.*
20. *Hadra shel Torah.*
21. Ibid.
22. *Chafetz Chaim al HaTorah.*
23. Ibid.
24. *Peninim Mishulchan Gavoah.*
25. *The Parsha Anthology*
26. *The Dubno Maggid and His Parables.*
27. *Mishnas Rebbi Aharon al HaTorah.*
28. *Chumash im Peirushei Rabbeinu Yehonasan.*
29. *Kol Eliyahu.*
30. *Ohr Yahal.*
31. Quoted by Rav Frand.
32. *Peninim Mishulchan HaGra.*
33. *Peninim Mishulchan Gavoah.*
34. Quoted by Rav Frand.
35. *Peninim Mishulchan Gavoah.*
36. *The Parsha Anthology.*
37. *Rebbi Akiva Eiger al HaTorah.*
38. *Kovetz Maamarim.*
39. *Hadra shel Torah.*
40. *Peninim Mishulchan Gavoah.*
41. *The Parsha Anthology.*
42. *Darchei Mussar.*
43. *Emes LeYaakov.*
44. *Perushei Maharal MiPrague.*
45. *Toras Chaim.*
46. *The Parsha Anthology.*
47. *Rav Frand.*

Shemos

1. *Torah Ladaas.*
2. Ibid.
3. *Emes LeYaakov.*
4. *Inspiration and Insight*, ArtScroll Publishers.
5. *The Parsha Anthology.*
6. *Lulei Torascha*, Rav Meir Tzvi Bergman.
7. *Daas Chochmah U'Mussar.*
8. Story from Rav Frand.
9. Ibid.
10. *Inspiration and Insight.*
11. *Peninim Mishulchan HaGra.*
12. *Hadra shel Torah.*
13. *The Dubno Maggid and His Parables.*
14. *Darchei Mussar.*
15. *Mishnas Rebbi Aharon al HaTorah.*
16. *Sichos Mussar.*
17. *Rabbi Yosef Chaim Sonnenfeld on the Parashah.*
18. Rav Frand.
19. *The Parsha Anthology.*
20. *Darchei Mussar.*
21. Rav Frand.
22. Story from Rav Frand.
23. Ibid.
24. Quoted by Rav Frand.
25. *Darchei Mussar.*
26. *Torah Ladaas.*
27. *Kol Eliyahu.*
28. *Daas Chochmah U'Mussar.*
29. *The Parsha Anthology.*
30. *Rabbi Yosef Chaim Sonnenfeld on the Parashah.*
31. *Sichos Mussar.*

32. *Taam Vedaas.*

33. *Oznaim LaTorah.*

34. *Toras HaChida.*

35. *Chumash Perushei Rabbeinu Yehonasan.*

36. *Torah Ladaas.*

37. *Toras Habayis,* chapter 7.

38. As cited by Rav Frand.

39. *Rabbi Yosef Chaim Sonnenfeld on the Parashah.*

40. As cited by Rav Frand.

41. *Torah Ladaas.*

Vayikra

1. *Hadra shel Torah.*

2. Ibid.

3. *Middos Ve'avodas Hashem.*

4. Cited in *Sifsei Chaim.*

5. *Rabbi Yosef Chaim Sonnenfeld on the Parashah.*

6. *Lulei Torascha.*

7. *The Parsha Anthology.*

8. *Parables from Otzar Hamashalim,* by Zeev Greenwald.

9. *The Dubno Maggid and His Parables.*

10. *The Parsha Anthology.*

11. *Rabbi Yosef Chaim Sonnenfeld on the Parashah.*

12. *The Parsha Anthology.*

13. *Otzar Hamashalim.*

14. *Inspiration and Insight.*

15. *Middos Ve'avodas Hashem.*

16. *Chafetz Chaim al HaTorah.*

17. *Middos Ve'avodas Hashem*

18. *Lulei Torascha.*

19. In his commentary on the Torah.

20. *Peninim Mishulchan Gavoah.*

21. Based on *Hadra shel Torah.*

22. *Darchei Mussar.*
23. *The Parsha Anthology.*
24. *Hadra shel Torah.*
25. Cited by Rav Frand.
26. *Darchei Mussar.*
27. *Inspiration and Insight.*
28. *Otzar Hamashalim.*
29. *Hadra shel Torah.*
30. *Otzar Hamashalim.*
31. *Sichos Rebbi Shimshon David Pinkus — Pesach.*
32. *The Parsha Anthology.*
33. *Darash Moshe.*
34. *The Parsha Anthology.*
35. *Darchei Mussar.*
36. *Darash Moshe.*
37. *Hadra shel Torah.*
38. *Otzar Hamashalim.*
39. *The Parsha Anthology.*
40. *Darchei Mussar.*
41. *Torah Ladaas.*
42. *Darash Moshe.*
43. *Mishnas Rebbi Aharon al HaTorah.*

Bemidbar

1. *Haemek Davar.*
2. *Sichos Mussar.*
3. *Darash Moshe.*
4. *Chafetz Chaim al HaTorah.*
5. *Daas Torah.*
6. *Daarchei Mussar.*
7. *Toras Moshe.*
8. Cited by Rav Frand.
9. *Darchei Mussar.*

10. *Talalei Oros.*

11. *Peninim Mishulchan HaGra.*

12. *Otzar Hamashalim.*

13. *Talalei Oros.*

14. Ibid.

15. Ibid.

16. *Chafetz Chaim al HaTorah.*

17. *Daas Torah.*

18. As cited by Rav Frand.

19. *Torah Ladaas.*

20. *Chafetz Chaim al HaTorah.*

21. *Peninim Mishulchan HaGra.*

22. *Talalei Oros.*

23. Ibid.

24. *Peninim Mishulchan Gavoah.*

25. *Lulei Torascha.*

26. *Chafetz Chaim al HaTorah.*

27. *Talalei Oros.*

28. Ibid.

29. *Otzar Hamashalim*

30. *Talalei Oros.*

31. Ibid.

Devarim

1. *Emes LeYaakov* to *parashas Vayeilech.*

2. *Lulei Torascha.*

3. *Rabbi Yosef Chaim Sonnenfeld on the Parashah.*

4. *Torah Ladaas.*

5. *Talalei Oros.*

6. *Peninim Mishulchan HaGra.*

7. *Peninim Mishulchan Gavoah.*

8. *Mishnas Rebbi Aharon al HaTorah.*

9. Cited in *Mishnas Rebbi Aharon al HaTorah.*

10. *Lulei Torascha.*

11. *Darchei Mussar.*

12. *Chafetz Chaim al HaTorah.*

13. Ibid.

14. *Peninim Mishulchan Gavoah.*

15. Cited by Rav Frand.

16. *Peninim Mishulchan Gavoah.*

17. Ibid.

18. *Otzar Hamashalim.*

19. *Peninim Mishulchan Gavoah.*

20. *Darash Moshe.*

21. *Peninim Mishulchan Gavoah.*

22. *Talalei Oros.*

23. *Darchei Mussar.*

24. Cited in *Darchei Mussar.*

25. *Talalei Oros.*

26. Ibid.

27. Rav Frand.

28. Ibid.

29. *Otzar Hamashalim.*

30. *Talalei Oros.*

31. Ibid.

32. *Rabbi Yosef Chaim Sonnenfeld on the Parashah.*

33. *Peninim Mishulchan Gavoah.*

34. Ibid.

35. *Chafetz Chaim al HaTorah.*

36. Cited in *Sichos Mussar.*

37. *Peninim Mishulchan Gavoah.*

38. *Talalei Oros.*

39. Ibid.

40. *Chafetz Chaim al HaTorah.*

41. *Inspiration and Insight.*

42. *Peninim Mishulchan Gavoah.*